CALL OF THE GREAT SPIRIT

Dahti,

Happy Birthday!

I miss the days when we lived closer to each other and could visit more often.
Hope you enjoy the read, it is a good one going into a summer of moosehide tanning, as it will spark every tidbit of traditional knowledge you have already.

Love you lots! ♡ Noah
(+ London)

CALL OF THE GREAT SPIRIT

The Shamanic Life and Teachings
of Medicine Grizzly Bear

BOBBY LAKE-THOM

Traditional Native Healer and Spiritual Teacher

Bear & Company
Rochester, Vermont

Dedication

This book is dedicated to my children, Frank Kanawha-dedali, Chay-gam-em, Moon-Raven, and Wind-Wolf. It is also dedicated to my brothers Ron Lake and Mike Thom; to my nephews and nieces; to Dad Charlie and Cora; to some special former college students (who have now gone on to become professionals in their fields) by the names of David Shaw, Art Martinez, Deanie Ron Davis, David Tripp, Loren Bommelyn, Michael Hazel, and Ken Jernberg; and to a whole number of Native American students across the country—I am proud of you all! And to the many Indian students who have gone into the fields of natural resources and health sciences: May you never forget the cultural, spiritual, and traditional-religious Native perspective of your heritage and culture as you attempt to study, preserve, and protect the environment, sustainable resources, and ecosystems of this sacred Mother Earth. Remember, our traditional Indian way is "holistic" in approach and method!

I extend special appreciation to Assistant Professor Tami Haaland at Montana State University–Billings for her editing; to my longtime colleagues in the profession, including Jack Norton, Sr., Jim Swan, Mike Brown, Tom Pinkston, John Veltri, Jerry Roybal, and Bob Ulibarri; and to all my former patients and the people who have participated with me in the past decades in sweat lodge rituals and Earth-healing ceremonies. Please remember to pray for the Earth and do Earth-healing ceremonies across the World, at least on Earth Day. If we don't pray for it, we are going to lose it.

With ancient prayers and a sincere heart I give special honor, recognition, and appreciation to the following Native Elders and medicine people who taught me so much, and who helped advance my spiritual growth, development, and understanding.

Beeman Logan (Seneca medicine man)
Mad Bear Anderson (Tuscarora medicine man)
Rolling Thunder (Cherokee medicine man)
Calvin Rube (Yurok Indian doctor and mystic)
Charles Red Hawk Thom (Karuk medicine man and mystic)
Dewey George (Yurok holy man)
Bonita Masten (Yurok medicine woman)
Georgina Matildin (Hupa medicine woman)
Florence Shaunessey (Yurok Elder)
Thomas Banyaca and Dan Katchavanaga (Hopi mystics)
Florence Jones (Wintun Indian doctor)
Rudolph Socktish (Hupa holy man)
John Fire Lame Deer and Martin High Bear (Lakota medicine men)
Mamie Kapris (Yurok Elder)

Bear & Company
One Park Street
Rochester, Vermont 05767
www.InnerTraditions.com

Library of Congress Cataloging-in-Publication Data

Lake-Thom, Bobby.
  Call of the Great Spirit : the shamanic life and teachings of Medicine Grizzly Bear / Bobby Lake-Thom.
    p. cm.
  ISBN 1-879181-66-5
  1. Lake-Thom, Bobby. 2. Shamans—California—Biography. 3. Karok Indians—Biography. 4. Shamanism—United States. 5. Indians of North America—Medicine. 6. Indians of North America—Religion. I. Title.
  BF1598.L35 A3 2001
  299'.7'092—dc21

                        2001005515

Printed and bound in Canada

10 9 8 7 6 5 4 3 2

Text design and layout by Priscilla Baker
This book was typeset in Berkeley, with Papyrus and Stone sans used as display typefaces

Contents

Preface

The information you will read here will probably be considered fiction by most people because they have very little knowledge and experience with the world of spirituality, psychic phenomena, and Nature. But to me, it has all been real. What might be considered "supernatural" to one person or group of people may, indeed, be very natural for someone else. So in this respect, perhaps what follows is more of an autobiography than fiction.

As you read, you will find yourself entering into a new and strange world, a world that has existed for thousands of years, despite any influences or changes by modern, scientific thinking and behavior. If you find some things unbelievable because the cultural context in which they occur is different from your own, don't feel embarrassed. There are also not that many Native American people today who are aware of these realities because they too have become assimilated into the artificial world of Western society. They have lost contact with the mystical and magical side of Nature and the Earth, their traditional-culture ways, and their indigenous forms of knowledge and philosophy.

Unfortunately, most people, Indians or otherwise, have become removed from the spiritual side of their own heritage, culture, environment, and ancient systems of knowledge. It is not their fault. They were forcibly removed from it, and Western society even passed laws to keep them from having the opportunity to learn and practice it. So now when it does come up to haunt them, they don't know how to respond to it except with fear, denial, or some form of defensiveness. Some of the more educated Native people try to cover it up with verbal reactions rather than truly reflect upon it. They try to rationalize that such knowledge and realities are simply a form of New Age hype, Indian romanticism, or shamanic hucksterism. But sooner or later some form of spirituality and supernaturalism will come back into our lives and we will be forced to either deal with it, or try to hide from it. I know because I was one of these kinds of people myself. And we all have phantoms in our lives to deal with, sooner or later.

It really doesn't make any difference what your race, nationality, culture, or religion is. We are all part of this Earth, and the Earth is both physical and spiritual. It is full of spirits, powers, and forces. Not all of them are good. And they can take many different forms, whether in our mind or manifested in the physical environment. They can appear in dreams and visions, or be seen in a psychic way. They can help us or harm us, or even leave us alone. They don't affect everybody and they don't affect us all the time. But when they do affect us, for whatever reason, what can we do? Who can we talk to for help when we become scared or worried, and feel stress? How do you tell your parents, mate, family, friends, colleagues, peers, that you are being tormented by a ghost? How do you tell your priests, preachers, ministers, or even therapists or physicians that a strange force, being, entity, or creature from Nature has been stalking you, tormenting you, and making you sick? How do you tell people that you have had encounters with ghosts, spirits, forces, and strange entities; or that you had a vision, premonition, or spiritual encounter that was real, whether it had a positive or negative effect upon your life? Who will believe you in Western society? It is like trying to tell someone that you were abducted by alien beings and experimented upon, or like trying to tell a friend or professional that a family member has molested you. They just don't want to hear it, they just refuse to believe it, because they aren't educated enough to handle such beliefs, possibilities, or realities. And yet such things do happen, don't they?

I don't know if there really is a God in the sense that Christianity has tried to impress upon us. Some anthropologists have claimed that primitive cultures and indigenous people didn't believe in a God, per se, that they worshipped a variety of gods and deities. And yet most tribal Elders and medicine men and women from different tribes that I talked to in my search for the truth all seem to have a special version of the word

God—the concept of a Supreme Being, Infinite Ruler, or Great Spirit—in addition to the other spirits they historically identified, related to, and perhaps worshipped. And these godlike spirits, or deities, had their ranking order within the spiritual system of the Universe. But I have come to learn the hard way, through disease, accidents, dying, death, doctoring, questing, and perhaps destiny, that there is, indeed, a Great Spirit, that can manifest Itself in whatever form It wants, be it a higher or lower form of spirit, multiple spirits, or Supreme Spirit. And I also know that if this Great Spirit can talk to Moses through a burning bush, to Job through a whirlwind, to Noah through a cloud, or to Mohammed in the form of a Hawk, and to Buddha as a Deer, or to Ezekiel via a giant wheel in the sky, then It can also communicate to our Native American people or anybody else, for that matter, through an Eagle, through Lightning and Thunder, a Bear, a fish, a bug, a mountain spirit, an ancestral ghost, a vision, or perhaps even a UFO. As a consequence, I too, like my ancestors, am lost for words to describe It, other than calling It the Great Spirit. To some people this term might seem a little too much like a Hollywood stereotype, even blasphemous. However, I can think of no other way to describe the strongest and most creative force in the world, the highest form of infinite intelligence, the greatest multifaceted spirit that permeates all living things, from the microcosm to the macrocosm. Maybe it is just a matter of semantics and cultural perceptions, or just plain ignorance. Define It how you will, in whatever way or term you feel comfortable, but if you don't learn anything else from this book and the teachings here, I hope you will be sensitized enough to at least come to the realization that there is a supreme or ultimate reality that we, as spiritual beings, can turn to when all else fails us in life. This TRUTH can only be discovered in a natural and spiritual way, or what you might call a psychic and supernatural way; it cannot be discovered by any artificial, scientific, or rational means. And, this Great Spirit has the power, wisdom, ability, and energy to create or destroy, to terminate or heal.

One time, during the many years of my spiritual and shamanic trainings, I had to fast, hike, pray, and quest up in our sacred High Country, the wilderness, for thirty days and nights. It was during that time that I made the ultimate connection with the Great Creator, the true Great Spirit that flows through all living things in Nature and in our Universe. And I knew while standing upon the ancient and holy mountaintop that there was, indeed, a Great Spirit. In Yurok Indian language, this experience, connection, and realization is called *mer-werk-ser-gerth!* Every culture and religion, whether primitive or so-called civilized, has the teachings, knowledge, and original instructions for you, as a human being, to discover the truth and make your own connection with the Great Spirit. It is never easy, and it requires suffering and sacrifice, and it requires a cleansing of your own mind, body, and soul . . . but if you are willing to purge yourself of all sins, violations, phantoms, and Karmic debt, so to speak, then you just might qualify to make that discovery and connection.

Hopefully, what you learn here will help you with that process and spiritual path.

Disclaimer: The names of certain people and places have been changed to protect their identities, so any similarity to people in the community is simply a coincidence. Parts of the information and stories in this book might appear to be sexist or offensive to some contemporary readers but in no way should be considered reflective of the author's insensitivity; hopefully I too have changed from twenty years' past experience. So please keep an open mind and realize that things are portrayed here in a realistic, endogenous, Native tribal-cultural context; therefore, certain beliefs, practices, and perspectives might be different from yours. I am providing certain concepts and forms of knowledge and personal experiences in this book that did not appear in my earlier books, *Native Healer* (HarperCollins, 1993) or *Spirits of the Earth* (Plume/Penguin, 1998).

Death and Dying

The Call to Shamanism

(Fall Quarter, 1969)

"I need your help, René. There's no one else I think I can trust." I gathered up my medicine bundle.

"No," he said, pacing back and forth. "I can't let you do this. I can't be a part of this. You've gone crazy, man. You can't just go out in the city, do some kind of weird Indian ceremony, and commit suicide!"

"Yeah, you're right, René. I am crazy. But this pain is driving me crazy, and I can't take any more of it. What else am I supposed to do, brother? I have a young, beautiful wife, a loving and devoted wife who looks like a model, and I can't provide for her anymore. Hell man, I've turned into an invalid. I'm in so much pain all the time that I can't even function. I'm impotent. Can you understand that, bro? I'm not even a real man anymore! Lilly has to get me up two hours early before she goes to work, pump me up with painkillers, help me get into a hot bathtub, and nurse me until I can finally get the stiffness out of my joints. I can barely walk to my college classes, I can't concentrate and listen to the lectures, and I can't work anymore. Shit man, I'm in so much pain that I can't even get turned on when I see Lilly undress. She's so loving and caring that she tries to use sex to help me forget about the pain, but her sensuous body doesn't do anything for me, and I know the rejection hurts her feelings. She really loves me. She waits on me hand and foot, she tolerates my

1

temper, frustrations, and complaints. But it just isn't fair to her, or me. She deserves better."

I loved Lilly more than anything in the whole world, even more than my own life. She was all I had, except for some of my inherited Native regalia and artifacts that I cherished and kept secret. I was twenty-six years old when I married her. I guess I had waited a long time for the right woman, a special woman, to bring meaning into my life. She was the only woman who ever made me nervous whenever I was around her. She would make me shake all over as if an electromagnetic force were passing through both of us. And God, was she beautiful: tall and lean, but filled out just right. Her movements were graceful, like a Deer's. Her long, black, wavy hair bounced when she laughed, in perfect rhythm with her walk. Her large, almond-shaped eyes were always full of light, love, and a certain mysterious twinkle. She was then, and still is, a radiant soul on this Earth. The first time I saw her I spilled coffee all over myself, stuttered, and just couldn't seem to look her in the eyes. I knew at that moment that I had known her before. I knew that whatever had been missing out of my life all the past years had suddenly, and mysteriously, come back, perhaps from a former lifetime. There was something special and completely unique, a certain form of naturalness that existed between Lilly and me that doesn't occur with most people in this world. We were drawn together, in the right place, at the right time in our lives, and in the right way. It was synchronistic, as Carl Jung would call it. We were just like two Salmon who were called by destiny, to reconnect with spirit. They do this by some strange force in Nature. By instinct, they are guided to leave the giant Ocean at the right time, find the right opening at the right river, and then go all the way up the creeks and streams until they find the right mate. Their destiny has already been mapped out by a supreme spiritual master plan, a natural life plan that will require constant struggle for survival, against fear, against overwhelming odds and obstacles, and against the inevitable threat of dying. The life plan for the Salmon also includes new challenges, new experiences, new tests, and temptations for selecting the wrong mates. However, if luck is with them, and if they have the right kind of power needed to succeed, then they will, indeed, find the perfect mate and fulfill their destiny, and the species will survive.

It is by Universal design that they are drawn to each other by some unknown guiding force. They do the same ancient dance their species has been doing for thousands of years, amongst a large crowd of their peers and relations, but as if nothing or nobody else even existed. They flirt with each other, then they dance, and as they come closer to the sacred nest on ancient ground, they share their spirit-force with each other, then bond, spawn, and die. That is their destiny, that is their predicament, but it is also the secret source of their power.

That is how it was with Lilly. We were like two Salmon in this life. Although I had been dating a lot of different women when I first met her, nobody else mattered. The first time I met her I knew she was the right mate, and she knew I was the one for her. The first time we had sex was different from anything I had ever experienced with other women. Sex with Lilly was sacred. She was a virgin, so pure, so full of untapped energy and power. She didn't drink or take drugs. She came from a traditional, middle-class Hispanic family with high values and old morals. She was the first from either side of the family to make it to college, where I met her. There was a freshness and naturalness about her that can only be found in mountain streams, the kind of regenerating streams where Salmon go to find their source of power. At that time, and at that moment, when we first made love, I, like my brother the Salmon, had finally found my soul mate and natural spirit. I had discovered power that in turn would now give meaning and purpose to my life. During the act of intercourse I had received a cleansing, a healing, and a rebirth. Prior to that time I had just been swimming around in the waters of life as if it had no meaning, no direction, no purpose. It was through Lilly and her pure spirit and love that I truly thought that I had found reason for living. As a result, the thought of losing her because I was becoming incapable of taking care of her needs was just too much for me to cope with while I was in so much pain. I was slowly dying but I didn't want her to suffer needlessly and die along with me. It just wouldn't be fair. She was too beautiful and too special; and like Salmon, whose species was already on the verge of extinction, she deserved the right to move up the stream without drowning beside me.

I had come to the conclusion that there was no other choice. I couldn't take the physical and psychological pain any longer. And I couldn't stand seeing the effect it was having upon Lilly. I was afraid that if I didn't end my life soon, it would destroy the only thing that I loved more than life itself, which was her. I had made up my mind that there really wasn't any other way. I had tried everything else that Western medicine could offer and nothing worked. I now had no choice but to fulfill my destiny.

"Come on René, I haven't got all night to do this. I want to get up on Mt. Diablo just at sunset so I can try to do this thing right, okay?"

Good ole René. We had been buddies for quite some time but more like brothers, or perhaps even like Heckle and Jeckle, the two cartoon Crows. We had met each other at Chabot Community College in Hayward, California. We were two lost souls trying to find our way in an environment where neither of us felt comfortable. He was a Chicano, and I was a half-breed Indian. Both of us were returning Vietnam vets. Both of us were low-income, older than the average college student, and felt completely out of water. Man, we had been out of school so long and were so stupid that we had to get tutoring, go through counseling, beg for financial aid, and struggle like hell against ourselves to try and adapt. We were like two greasers from the hood trying to be accepted in White yuppyville, and we were constantly reminded that we were out of place. So it was only natural that we became partners for progress. In time we started up our own ethnic-minority clubs and vets' clubs, and we carved out our own niche on campus. Eventually we became quite popular, shared a bachelor pad that was corrupt to the max, and spent more time partying than we did studying. We drank together, fought together, smoked together, got jailed together, and we even shared our women, secrets, dreams, aspirations, fears, failures, sicknesses, and successes with each other. So it was only proper that we both fell in love with women who were friends, got married, served as best men at each other's weddings, and probably looked forward to the day, way off in the future, when we would probably share old age and death with each other. The only thing I didn't like about René was the fact that he teased me that he looked more like an Indian than I did.

"Hey René, hand me the crutches, will you, and let's get going," I shouted to him from the front room. "I think I'm about drunk enough to do this, so let's go."

It suddenly became quiet as he helped me down the steps from the apartment toward the car. He had tried to argue with me for over an hour, using all the logic he could muster up as to why I shouldn't commit suicide. But what else was I to do? I had chronic osteoarthritis that had started in my feet and, as months went by, moved into my hands, wrists, elbows, neck, and eventually my spinal column. I tried everything and every kind of doctor I could find. I was taking more than a bottle of aspirin a day, tried staying drunk, got cortisone shots, and was even put on a drug called phenylbutazone. The damn cortisone started eating up my body, and then I found out later that the phenyl was beginning to destroy my white corpuscles and cause leukemialike symptoms. I was on all kinds of painkillers and nothing worked except some strong marijuana whenever I could afford to get it.

Eventually I was referred to a doctor at St. Mary's Hospital in San Francisco who was trying new experiments on patients. His approach was to surgically clean the bone joints, removing calcium deposits and thus hindering the deterioration of the bones. I went there with some last ray of hope, having already been told numerous times that there was no cure for arthritis. But when I was waiting in line for my appointment, I could see all these sorry souls all butchered up, crying in anguish, waiting for more torture: people in wheelchairs, people on crutches, people all twisted up in severe pain, desperate for help. I looked at all those people, the majority of whom were probably made worse by the new experiment, and I freaked out.

That was the straw that broke the camel's back. So there was no sense in arguing with René anymore about choices and alternatives. There weren't any. The Indian side of me said I had to approach death like a warrior: be brave, develop a strategic plan, perform an ancient ceremony, sing my death song, and prepare for a journey into the spirit world. I had no choice left. I had already fought death and dying with everything I could use, with every ounce of my willpower, with every form of medicine that I could find in Western society. Now it was just a matter of choice: either wait and let disease and death slowly devour me, or greet death with open arms and get it over with. Besides, given the kind of condition I was in, I couldn't run from it.

Mt. Diablo seemed an appropriate place for an urbanized Indian to do a ceremony. It got its name from the Spaniards, who got it from the local Oholne Indians. I believe, however, that something must have gotten lost in the translation. To call it "devil mountain" and consider it an evil place is really a matter of perspective, and perhaps ethnocentrism. From what I understood about it from my association with the local Indian people, it was historically considered a sacred place, used for vision seeking and ceremony. It was both feared and respected by the indigenous people, and perhaps by the Westerners out of superstition, not because it was notoriously guarded by Rattlesnakes, but because it was a place of power and mystery. Civilization had grown all around it, and although Mt. Diablo too had become urbanized, I felt a primal and symbolic connection with it that went beyond the physical, modern world. The closer we got to it, the more it seemed like the most appropriate place to go and die in privacy.

"Damn, Bobby," René said, "I can't go through with this. How am I going to face Lilly when she finds out I helped you kill yourself?"

"Oh shut up and keep driving," I said. "Nobody has to know anything."

"But what about the suicide note you left behind?" He paused and looked at me sternly. "You did leave her a letter of explanation, didn't you? Come on Bobby, you did, didn't you?"

"No, René," I said angrily, "I didn't have the heart to do it. And besides, I had to leave her something to make sure she's provided for until she can finally get on with her life. The insurance company won't pay for suicides you know; but poisonous Snakebites are a different story."

"What in the hell are you talking about man, poisonous Snakes?" I could see the hair begin to stand up on the back of his neck as he tried to dismiss the thought. Traffic was heavy as usual, especially the main streets leading through residential areas and the old main highway out of Hayward to the Sunol and Mt. Diablo area. And the smog was just as thick as usual with the Wind blowing it all down from the Bay Area. I never did like being in the city. I really missed the trees, mountains, streams, fish, animals, and birds—the peace and quiet of Nature. I wondered how it would be on the other side. I wondered if there really was a heaven or hell. As an Indian, would I go to some kind of Indian-camp–type world, or what they call in the movies the happy hunting ground? I was a half-breed and was raised mainly as such. Would I end up with all the White people in some kind of White heaven? Man, to me that would really be hell. Or would the spirit world be devoid of races, nationalities, and cultures, just full of ghosts? I was starting to get a little scared even though I had died three times before in my life.

"Shit, Bobby, why me? Why did you pick me to help you? Why didn't you get one of the Indian guys like Jerry the Apache, or Robby the Navajo, or your friend Richard Oaks, the Mohawk from back East? Or how about one of those counselors down at the Indian Center like Archie Fire Lame Deer, who hangs around in Oakland or San Jose?" He kept grinding his teeth and squirming around. "Hell, man, I'm just a Chicano and a Catholic on top of it. I don't know anything about Indian rituals and death ceremonies. This kind of stuff is against my belief. Not only that, but what about the cops and the law? Besides, suicide is against God's law."

I looked at him sadly and said, "Because you are like my brother, René. You're the only one I can trust. You're a warrior. You've dealt with dying and death before, so you have the experience and skill to handle it. Look at what you went through in Vietnam, bro!"

"Yeah, Vato, but that was different. There we didn't have a choice. We had to fight, kill, and face death all the time. We didn't like it but at least we had some training to prepare for it. Sure, I lost a lot of good partners over there and had a lot of close calls myself, but it's different than watching some crazy dude you love just go up on the side of a mountain, do some kind of weird aboriginal ceremony, and kill himself. Now that's really savage, more savage than war! Are you going to use a flint knife or something? How are you planning on doing it?" He was just about crying. "You're not going to use a pistol and blow your brains out are you? Somebody might hear the shot."

"No," I said. "I'm not that dumb. Like I said, it's got to be done in a way that Lilly can collect insurance, understand? So the time is right. She's over at her mother's house, we're going into a full moon, and everyone will just think I OD'd, had an accident, or something. No big mess, no fuss, no big deal. All I do is take all these damn pills with me, the fifth of Old Crow, some of my regalia here, and sing. It's simple, like having a going away party, right?"

Damn, it seemed like it was taking forever to get there. The Sun was getting low in the sky, leaving a strange, burnt orange color that appeared to be reflecting off the smog, creating a sick and dismal scene across the city. It was the same color and feeling I saw once in a dream I had about René. "Like I said, René, you're a warrior, you dealt with dying and the shadow of death coming after you."

He turned and looked at me as if puzzled. "What are you talking about?"

I laughed at him and pointed. "Look up at that strange-colored sky. See the Sun dogs? Doesn't it bring back some memory? Like the time you were sitting in the foxhole over there in the jungle all by yourself and all hell had broke loose around you. The Sun was going down, the smell of chemicals and smog was all around you, and you felt numb."

We finally went through the suburb housing section and were beginning to get into the countryside. Mt. Diablo was just up ahead, looking silent and foreboding.

"It was sort of like this, René, remember? About the same time in the evening, in the middle of nowhere, with dead trees all around you, dry grass, the stench of something dead in the breeze, and a feeling of uncanny silence. You were scared and all alone because you knew, at that time, that Death was stalking you. Just like it's stalking me. You had been fighting for days and weeks and months for your life. You were beyond exhaustion. So you just reached a point of frustration beyond fear, and unconsciously prepared for death. In fact, you even made a death wish. You were tired, lonely, fed up, drugged up, and just flat didn't give a damn anymore. As you sat in the hole painting your face black, a small Snake crawled up into your lap. Just when you thought you were all alone in this world, a cute little Snake came to keep you company. And you talked to it. You said, 'Damn, I wish you were poisonous and you would just bite me and end it all.' But it never did. You fell asleep with that Snake in your lap all night until daybreak. Then you heard the scream of a Hawk, looked up, and stood up to see who was coming from the voices you heard talking in the distance. The Snake slowly crawled out of the hole and started heading toward the bush. One of the soldiers started cussing after almost stepping on it, and he warned the other guy to steer clear. He told him that it was the deadliest Snake in the country; its venomous bite is lethal and there is no known antidote for it. Then all of a sudden the Hawk swooped down, grabbed the Snake, and headed into the sky. Remember, René? The two soldiers had come to take you home." I then noticed that tears were running down his face, sweat started beading up on his forehead, and his hands were shaking on the car's steering wheel. "How in the hell did you know about that, Bob? I never told you anything about that experience. I know we've shared a lot of secrets with each other, but I never told you anything about that, even when we got drunk and stoned together."

He just kept looking at me for the longest time, deep into my eyes, searching. "Shit," he hollered, "you're always doing that to people. How in the hell do you know these things? You're definitely weird, man!"

I just laughed and started gathering my gear. "Well, like I said, René, you are the only one qualified to help me. You've been here before. That's why I can trust and depend upon you. Now help me out of the car and up the hill, but be sure to take the crutches back with you when you leave. And besides bro, the way I figure it, you must have a way with Snakes, otherwise you'd be dead by now, and I just don't want whoever it is that's helping me to get bitten by Rattlesnakes and die before I do."

We both laughed. I prayed and threw some tobacco into the grass, toward the little mountain, and for the Snake people, and asked for permission and protection for us to pass through safely. We could hear them all around us in the dry grass and rocks, we could feel them all around us in every direction, and we occasionally saw some of them slither out of our way as we hobbled up the side of the hill. It was late fall and most of the trees were becoming barren. The Sun was going down in the distant Ocean on the other side of the city while a salty breeze from the west began pushing the rotten smell and cloud of smog toward the east, clearing the sky for the Moon to rise. I found a spot with a view of both directions that I felt comfortable with and flopped down on the ground with my gear. I was shaking all over but René was calm as an oak tree. There wasn't much left to be said, so he bent down and gave me a long, hard hug. As he left I heard the scream of a Redtail Hawk, and then I saw it swoop down and follow him down the hill. Intuitively I knew that the dream I'd had about him years before had some kind of meaning and purpose, and even at this precarious moment in my life I could not help but feel that the profound symbolism going on all around me, the same natural symbols I'd seen in the dream about him, also meant something. But it was only fleeting, now gone on the wings of a bird, behind the shadow of a man whom I had come to know and love as a brother. The whole scene gradually faded out of sight as I turned my mind, heart, and soul to the task at hand: to face and do battle with the spirit of Death.

Well, there wasn't much left to do except get out my medicine bag and prepare for ceremony. I really didn't know what I was doing because I hadn't been raised completely the traditional Indian way. I spent half my life on the East Coast with my mother's people, who are Seneca-

Cherokee, and the other half of my life in California. I knew my real dad lived somewhere on the mighty Klamath River and high mountain areas but I didn't have a lot of time to connect with him and learn from him. I was a product of war: soldier meets young woman on the East Coast, soldier goes to war, woman has baby and marries soldier, marriage gets off to a bad start and things become dysfunctional and abusive. My step-father was allegedly half Seneca Indian from Tonawanda, with relatives around Buffalo, Salamanca, and Jamestown. But the Indian people I knew when I was growing up were mainly Catholic and alcoholic, living a life in poverty and just barely surviving against the forces of acculturation and assimilation. Whatever traditional ceremonies and forms of knowledge were available remained fairly well hidden and underground.

The same can basically be said about the California tribes. In the early 1950s the U.S. government decided to dissolve the smaller tribes and reservations, so they passed a law to "terminate" certain Indian tribes and no longer recognize them as Indians. The government no longer had to honor treaties or provide services. Forced education by the earlier missionaries and follow-up by the boarding schools set up by the Bureau of Indian Affairs (BIA) did a good job of whitewashing the indigenous people and culture. There weren't too many left up in "Indian Country" who could still speak the indigenous languages and carry on the ancient ceremonies and traditions, and they too were struggling in poverty. So a considerable number of Indian people ended up in the large cities like I did, partly because of the notorious BIA relocation program that coerced Indian people off the reservation to specific large urban areas on the pretense of getting an education, a trade, and jobs. Los Angeles, San Francisco/Oakland, New York City, Buffalo, Minneapolis, Seattle, Portland, and Phoenix became islands of Native transients who found themselves like fish out of water; they either had to adapt to mainstream society, die from alcohol and poverty, or hitchhike home. A lot of them died in Indian bars, jail, and slum alleys, and some were run over on main highways, their bodies scattered like dead Deer. Nobody seemed to care. After all, as one redneck truck driver once told us in a bar, "They were only Indians. Why shouldn't they die like the other animals? There is no use for any of them, Indian or animal. They're all just in the way of progress."

So despite the constant discrimination and urbanized pecking-order struggle against other racial groups, a certain degree of Indian conscious-ness and culture was maintained and perpetuated, although it was mostly intertribal and intercultural, and all mixed up. And for me, like many others, it was the only tie I had to the past, to some form of my heritage and culture, to some degree of Native pride. Although I was a half-breed, I was raised knowing I was Indian and I had always identified myself as Indian, even when I met other Indian people who first said they were Italian, Polish, Spanish, or something. At least I had some artifacts from the family and bits and pieces of ceremonial medicine and power ob-jects. At least I had graduated from high school and could read. And from a few books I had read for anthropology classes, I knew how to prepare for a death ceremony.

I began to shake all over as the Sun was going down, and I felt a cold chill run through my body. I pulled out the old pipe, a Bearclaw neck-lace, some Eagle and Raven feathers, an angelica root, some cedar, Bull Durham pipe tobacco, and a beat-up abalone shell. I offered it all to the Great Creator, the four sacred powers and directions of the Universe, and the Mother Earth.

I took some of the black soot off the end of the burnt root and made symbolic streaks of paint across my face. Black represented the last power of creation, the direction of west, the water, and death. Then I took a little of the red paint left, spit into the powder, and put it on in a ritualis-tic way. Red represents the second power of creation, the east, the Sun and fire, protection and rebirth. I then gathered a little dry grass and made a tiny sacred fire in the abalone shell, four tiny sticks for the four sacred directions, and sprinkled on dry cedar and tobacco. I prayed the best I knew how, circled myself four times with smudge, set the shell at the base of my feet while I was facing east, and started to load the pipe. I didn't know exactly what kind of prayer to make, so I just tried to talk from the heart with tears pouring down my face. Flashes of Lilly kept coming across my mind, thoughts about children I could have had but would never get to see, and bits and pieces of my life. I could hear a Coyote crying his ancient song from the east, a Great Horned Owl flew into a nearby oak from the west, and the Rattlesnakes were starting to gather around me.

"Oh Great Creator, the four powers of the Universe, the Mother Earth, my relations in Nature, and my ancestor spirits. I come before you in a sick, sad, and humble manner. I ask for your forgiveness for what I am about to do. Although I have died three times before in my life, I am still scared. I know that it is just a passing from one world into another world, and perhaps a better world. But I don't know if I am doing the right thing here. I don't know if I am violating any kind of spiritual law, cultural law, or Whiteman's law. I just don't really care anymore. I have nothing, I am a nobody, and I can't take the pain, suffering, stress, and slow death any longer. So I give my soul to the Great Creator and my body to the Mother Earth."

I started to put my artifacts and medicine away and thought I heard footsteps. It was dark now, the Sun had set, the Moon was rising but not yet visible. I pulled out the fifth of Old Crow and dumped all the drugs and pain pills out in front of me. Then I started to wash them down my throat by handfuls. I was getting drunker and dizzier but I still had enough coordination and consciousness left to remember to pack up all the empty drug bottles and throw them down a big hole in the rocks, and then cover the hole up with old wood and dead leaves. I staggered back to my power spot, my ceremonial seat, and tried to sing what I thought an Indian death song might sound like, like the kind you see in the movies. I kept taking more pills and drinking more whisky as I heard the footsteps coming closer. More Owls were coming in from all over the place, hooting and screeching. Rattlesnakes shook tails in alarm from my periodic moving around but I hadn't gotten bitten yet, and even if I did, I probably wouldn't have felt it.

I looked over toward the clump of trees and saw the shadow of what appeared to be an old man sneaking around. A little light was beginning to shine through from the rising Moon. At first I was scared but then I got angry. "Hey you over there," I hollered. "Get the hell out of here. Leave me alone, you damn parasite." When I started hollering he stood still but then he began to creep closer. *Damn,* I thought to myself, *I can't even die in privacy without some old wino coming around to rip me off.*

I was getting real weak but kept taking the last of the drugs and large gulps of whisky. Things were getting blurry all around me and starting to swirl. All I could see was the vague formation of an old man coming closer and I kept cussing him out, hoping to drive him off. Just before I lost consciousness I saw him up close. He was the same old grandfather spirit I had seen when I first died after getting lost in the Allegheny Mountains, when I was only about four years old. He was the same old grandfather ghost I had seen when I drowned in a river near the Cherokee reservation in North Carolina when I was about nine years old. And he was the same grandfather spirit I had seen when I was mashed between a telephone pole and a car, killed in a teenage accident when I was sixteen and living in Chesapeake Beach, Maryland. Was he here now for the last time?

Following an Eagle in Blind Faith

I woke up with an extremely bright light shining in my face and eyes and thought I was in the spirit world, but the brilliant light was suddenly interrupted and intermittently blocked by the shadow of an animal. It had a large furry head, big yellow eyes, and very foul breath. A damn Coyote was standing on my chest licking my face! I jumped up in shock, scared half to death, and fell to my knees face-to-face with the wild animal. We both stood there shaking, two feet from each other, staring each other in the eyes. I could feel a calmness come over me, as if a force or warm energy were moving directly from the Coyote into my own body, and a new source of strange-feeling strength. Then he flashed his teeth in a threatening manner, tilted his head, and yelled out a series of four cries to the Universe. It scared me so badly that I fell on my back. By the time I could get back up and start to run, he had already left; I could see his tail and hind legs heading downhill through the tall grass and brush.

At this point I noticed I had vomit all over me, in my hair, on my neck, chest, crotch, even on my arms and down my legs. But worse yet, I also had shit all over the back of my pants, all the way down my legs, and into my boots. Damn, it stunk worse than the city smog or the Coyote's breath. I was still kind of weak and dazzled, trying to gather my composure and get a sense of where I was, what was going on, and what to do next. Then I felt the swooping noise, *whoosh-whoosh*, of a large bird passing over my head from behind.

A huge Raven flew over me and landed in a nearby tree, and he started squawking and clicking his beak as if laughing at me. He was so funny that I started laughing. We both kept laughing while I tried to peel the nasty, spoiled clothes off my body and started looking around for a stream to wash up in. Then it suddenly dawned on me, at daybreak, that I wasn't dead; or was I, and was this the spirit world?

I don't know how long I stood there naked thinking and trying to figure out if I had died and gone to the spirit world, or if I was alive by some miracle, and still in the physical world. The Raven was real, so I figured the Coyote also had to be real, just as real as the Rattlesnakes and Owls the night before. But what about the old Indian ghost? Was that real, too? It had to be and I was sure he must have had something to do with all this, but what? I also began to notice that I wasn't in much pain and for the first time in months I could actually move about without feeling cemented in my joints and spine. I smelled water down below the grove of trees and headed toward a ravine in search of a creek. It wasn't very big, but wide enough and deep enough for me to bathe and wash the clothes and boots. The purity, strength, coolness, and movement of the water felt so wonderful that I started crying again, and kept thanking it over and over for its natural gift and cleansing. After a considerable time of soaking and getting chilled, and after washing out the clothes, I started back up the hill toward the rock outcrop where my medicine bag and power objects were still lying.

Just then I heard the scream of an Eagle and looked up toward the sky. As it circled lower I could tell it was really a Golden Eagle and not a Buzzard (which would have seemed more appropriate under the circumstances), and as it came down lower it dropped a feather for me. In my head I could hear it talking like an old man: "Remember the dreams we shared with you last night. Take this feather and head north to the mountains, way up in the mountains, above a big river, and there you will find a medicine man to help you, near your ancestral grounds and on a reservation."

If it hadn't been for the Eagle feather connecting me with reality, I really would have thought I had gone crazy. It was obviously time to show my gratitude, so I got out my pipe, loaded it, and prayed with all my heart and soul. I tried to recap in my mind all that I had experienced in such a short period of time, and during the meditation and reflection, I realized that there had been a few times in the earlier years of my life when I had heard other creatures in Nature talking to me. But I still thought it was just my imagination gone wild, or a hallucination and backlash from the drugs. I was sitting there for quite some time, just smoking, enjoying the flavor and power of the tobacco, and trying to figure things out, when down the hill I heard René hollering for me. I stood up as he came running toward me with tears in his eyes, arms outstretched, and we gave each other a big bear hug. We laughed, cried, and danced in joy until I thought my penis would fall off. As I finally pulled away from his clutches he started laughing again and said, "Damn, Bobby, I didn't even realize you were all naked. And man, I don't understand why all the women are so crazy about you and always after you. There ain't much of a sacred root hanging down there."

"Yeah, stud," I snapped back sheepishly, "at least it works and I'm still alive, and hopefully it came back to life, too." René went back down to the car where he had stashed some old gym clothes and a set of janitor's coveralls. He was still laughing at me while he brought the clothes over. He shook his head and talked to himself while I dressed. "Need any help walking down?" he asked. He reached for my wet clothes and medicine bag.

"No, *hermano,* I think I want to try and make it on my own," I said, grinning in pride.

We got into the car and headed toward the city, toward my apartment, and it seemed like an eternity before I would get to see Lilly again. I was deep in joyful thought when suddenly I exclaimed, "Oh shit, René, what am I going to tell Lilly? She doesn't know anything about this, does she? Damn, she must have been worried sick all night; damn, I hope she doesn't have the cops out looking for me!"

"Hey, relax, *compadre,*" he said, laughing. "I already took care of that just to be on the safe side. I called her last night and told her you went out to get drunk with a few of the Indian buddies and probably wouldn't be home until late the next day. But she didn't like that either, so I'm on her hit list for sure now. Besides, by the time we get there she'll be at work and you can call her, okay?"

We pulled up to the apartment complex and got out of the car. René turned and said, "You want some help getting up the stairs? And what about the clothes? I can pack them up, too."

"No, that's okay, *hermano*, just throw the clothes into the Dumpster over there for me, will you? I think it's a symbolic custom in Indian culture when somebody dies that you don't keep the clothes."

"Well, what now?" he said. "Do you want to talk about it? What the hell happened anyway? You took enough drugs and booze to kill an Elk."

I just stared at him and then laughed. "Yeah, I guess you're right, René. I don't really know what happened. It was like being on a bad drunk and having a bunch of weird dreams. But these dreams are different. They're very lucid, I guess more like a vision or something. All I know now is that I've got to find out who I really am, travel up north in the mountains, and talk to some old medicine man about the strange dreams I had about Salmon spawning in the creek, a Bear trying to devour me, a weird, face-to-face encounter with a Coyote, a talking Eagle, and maybe try to find out who my real father is."

"Damn, Bobby, don't you ever learn? You mean you want to find a *brujo*? What the hell for, man? They're bad news and nothing but trouble," he said seriously.

"No, René," I tried to explain, "not that kind of medicine man. Not a sorcerer, but more like a healer, or what your people call a *quendeto* involved in *curandismo*. You know, like the dudes we studied about in the anthro class?"

He just shook his head and replied, "I still think you're nuts, man. You'd better chill out for a few days, get some sleep, and get the rest of those drugs out of you before someone commits you to Napa, man. I'll catch you later. I've got to go to work, okay?"

"Yeah," I said. "And René, thanks with all my heart and soul for helping me. I knew you wouldn't let me down. You're a true brother and friend, a real special person, but let's keep this a secret, too, okay?"

I was anxious to see Lilly now. I didn't know what I would say to her and was thinking it would be best just to never mention what happened. René's car pulled out toward the street, and then I heard him stop for a moment and holler back, "Hey, Bobby, maybe now you should let your hair grow long, wear some beads, and quit wearing those black leather coats that make you look like a gangster. Besides, I'm getting tired of always picking you up from jail and the hospital, and getting you out of fights all the time. Go back to the blanket, man, because there ain't no way I can handle any more of this death wish bullshit. Don't you think you've punished yourself enough already? See ya later, skin!"

I never did tell Lilly what happened to me. I felt so good, so different, and so much alive that I felt it was best just to leave it alone. I was still in some pain, and a little stiff, but nothing like I had been. For the first time in a long time I felt really horny. Lilly was my pristine mountain stream, my source of power and regeneration. The next few days were spent entirely with her, in constant play, lovemaking, and exchanges of affection until I was recharged from my exhaustion.

Gradually I got back into my classes and began to catch up at school. I also made plans to head up north a few weeks later, to find a medicine man and get doctored. I didn't see much of René after that, just occasionally at school.

I did some preliminary scouting prior to the planned trip, and as I headed out I asked some of the people at the San Francisco Indian Center if they knew about a reservation up north. I was told that the only reservation left in California was near a place called Eureka, inland by the Trinity River, and it was called Hoopa. So I got a map, got out and prayed with tobacco by throwing it to the Wind and the north direction, and looked for an Eagle. I didn't see anything that even resembled an Eagle until I started crossing over the Russian River. At first it was sitting in a dead tree on the other side of the bridge, on Highway 101. Then it screamed and flew alongside me as I headed north. I really don't think it was the same Eagle, but I did periodically see Eagles along the way, even up into Hoopa.

It was about an eight-hour drive up the famous Redwood Highway. It is one of the most beautiful trips in America, through San Francisco, over the bay, out through the countryside past Santa Rosa, then up into Ukiah where small wooded mountains begin to lead into the thick, mysterious, and magical giant Redwood trees. Some of them are so large that a car can drive through a tunnel cut in the trunk. The air is always fresh and crisp, with a hint of salt in the fog and dampness that permeate the Redwoods. Eventually the highway leads out of the darkness and into more countryside, and then into Eureka, an old-looking city full of foul-smelling logging mills, and then through Eureka into Arcata with the bay and swamps on one side and skirts of partially logged Redwood forests on the other side. Eureka had a lot of Seagulls flying around it in the fog and hardly any trees along the streets, and it felt cold and damp. Outside the city and along the swamps and farmland could be found a number of White Egrets, different kinds of Ducks, Blue Herons, several species of Hawks, and a lot of Ravens and Crows—but no Eagles.

The Arcata area was rich with fowl, and it had a certain beauty of its own when compared to Eureka. For one thing, it looked clean and spacious. The houses in Eureka were mostly old, two-story Victorians, and the outlying farmhouses and barns I saw heading toward Arcata were very old looking. I don't know why, but even to this day Eureka seems dismal and spooky to me despite the lush countryside surrounding it. It has always had a cold, damp, foggy, lonely, and eerie feeling about it.

From there I had to turn on Highway 299 and go over an old and windy highway that was packed with logging trucks and tourists, over small grass-covered mountains, and down into a place called Willow Creek. The reservation was somewhere near Willow Creek so I stopped and asked directions, and then I studied for quite some time a large, wooden carving of Bigfoot.

I had heard stories and old legends about him as a child but I wondered if he was truly real. Could there actually be such creatures in Nature living in the woods and mountains, hiding from civilization? If so, what purpose did they serve? I wondered what I would do if I ever saw one.

From Willow Creek I was guided to turn left at the main point of the small town onto a very small, narrow, and windy road known as Highway 96. It was dangerous, in very poor shape, with high cliffs on one side and deep, jagged cliffs on the other side that seemed to be falling into the Trinity River. Several times I had to stop and let a pickup truck, car, or logging truck squeeze by because the road was caved in. A couple of times I even had to get out of the car and move rocks just to get through. Every once in a while I would see a mangled car down at the bottom of the river, some of which were still lodged in trees and boulders. I couldn't help but wonder just how many Indian people had died on this old road every year, and how in the hell their bodies could even be removed from such rugged terrain. I learned later that many of them were never found and that is why flower-covered crosses dotted the side of the road.

Off in the distance I could see a beautiful valley, with an emerald green river running through it, surrounded by small mountains. The oaks and maples were turning fall colors, causing a certain mystical aura to radiate from the valley. I could see a few Indian people camped down by the river, some in boats and others gathering Salmon out of long gill nets.

I finally pulled into the main part of the Hoopa reservation. There wasn't much to it, just a small store and gas station, a few BIA-type houses scattered here and there, a few clusters of decrepit mobile home and trailer parks, a run-down bar, and an old lumber mill with huge cone-shaped, rusted wood burners. It was evident that the mill had not been used for quite some time because weeds and patches of blackberry bushes were taking it over. On the left side was another store, a small post office, a very small sheriff's substation building, and off in the distance the standard green BIA buildings. The valley was rich with fruit trees scattered here and there, on small farms, along the highway, and up and down dirt roads that left the highway and went into patches of oak tree forests, farmland, and the river. It was warm here and the air smelled very fresh, with a fall crispness and the periodic fragrance of fruit, smoked fish, and cattle dung.

I needed gasoline and pulled up to the pumps at the old station. A few Indian guys were coming out laughing with bags of groceries and a couple cases of beer. Some of them were dark in skin color and others were half-breeds, with strong Indian features, but fairly light. The Hupa historically are a short, stocky people, darker in complexion than their neighbors the Yurok and Karuk, and they have a tendency to become obese with age. They are also well known for being happy people, friendly, and hospitable to strangers, and for being kind, generous, and especially gracious during ceremonies, cultural events, and holiday gatherings. So I didn't feel threatened asking questions of the locals, even though there were a number of them drunk and staggering around outside the store, or sitting on the ground drinking. I had been to other Indian reservations across the country where the locals didn't like strangers and were prone to fight, especially if they were drinking, and it didn't matter if you were Indian or not, half or full. But these guys were an all right bunch.

"Hey, cousin," I said to the younger guys sitting on the log parking marker. I reached out and offered cigarettes, which is an intertribal tobacco custom, to the older guys who were staggering around and trying to out-sing one another. "Hey, I need some help on directions. Do any of you know a man named Charlie Thom, or do you have a medicine man around here?"

There were about five or six of them, mixed in age from early twenties to gray-haired men. They were dressed in jeans, cowboy boots, and T-shirts or no shirt at all. They stopped singing and talking and began to gather around me. One of the older men took a couple of cigarettes and said, "Charlie Thom, a medicine man? You've got to be joking!" And they all laughed. "He ain't no medicine man. He's a Coyote," the older guy said. "But he's also a damn good singer and gambler, and he's hell with the women."

"No, I mean, I wasn't asking if Charlie Thom was a medicine man. I was just asking if you knew who he was and where he lived around here," I said quickly.

"Yeah, I know him," said one of the younger guys. "He lives up on the other end of the reservation, back that way from where you came in. Go over the bridge, turn right on the dirt road. When you come to a fork, turn left and keep going until you come to this house at the end of the road. You'll probably see his brown-colored Chevy pickup, a few chain saws, and a stack of firewood. I was supposed to go help him today but I got sidetracked here with my uncles."

They offered me a beer and started laughing and joking around with one another, telling a few stories about Charlie. I wasn't about to tell them that I thought he was my real father, or that I was a lost bastard coming back in search of identity. Besides, some of the things they were saying about him were a little embarrassing. One of the older guys who had been singing most of the Indian songs looked at me soberly, and after staring for quite some time, he said, "Yeah, we have a medicine man here. Not too many of them left anymore. His name is Rudolph and he lives over there on the other side of the river in a small white house. He doesn't speak English all that good, so speak slow and give him time to answer, if he will even talk to you."

I thanked them all and went inside the store and paid for the gas, picked up a couple cans of coffee to use as a gift for the medicine man, a pack of pipe tobacco, a pack of aspirins, and some corn chips and a Pepsi for myself. My bones and joints had started aching more since I left Hayward and I didn't know if it was because of the anxiety or the long hard trip and driving, or if the damn disease was just coming back.

I was nervous as hell going down the road toward Charlie's house. All kinds of strange thoughts went through my head. Was he really my father like Mom had told me? I tried to see him once or twice before when I was younger but he wouldn't have anything to do with me. How in the hell was I going to approach him and try to talk to him, to get to meet him, and try to start up a relationship? What if he denied everything and was embarrassed because I'm half White?

I was shaking all over by the time I found the house at the end of the road but there was no truck or chain saws, only a fresh pile of cut and split oak and madrone wood. A very large and very dark-skinned Indian woman came out. She was about five feet three and must have weighed about 240 pounds. She had a reddish tint to her hair and looked quite mean. I sat in the car for a long time before building up the courage to get out and ask questions, but I guess I just made myself look even more suspicious. She walked over to the car with an ax and hollered, "What the hell is your problem?"

"I'm looking for Charlie Thom," I said, half scared. "Does he live here?"

"Who wants to know?" she asked curtly. "Are you the young guy that was supposed to come over and split up our firewood, because if you are, you're late!"

"No," I said in a half-nervous laugh. "I just wanted to see Charlie on a visit."

"Well, he ain't here. I'm his wife, Velma. He went up the river toward Happy Camp to cut firewood and hunt for Deer, and I don't think he'll be back for a few days."

I wasn't about to get out and try to strike up a friendly conversation with this woman, and I was getting more aches and pains, so I just said thanks, and went back up the road to look for the medicine man.

I got lost at first. All the dirt roads looked the same, and there were a lot of small white houses. Finally I asked some kids on the road who pointed me to the right house. When I pulled up in the driveway I saw an elderly man sitting on the porch steps working with some feathers and what appeared to be ceremonial regalia. I looked up toward the sky as I got out of the car, and I could see a Golden Eagle circling over the house. The elderly Indian man and I both looked curiously at each other but then turned our heads when we heard the scream of an Osprey. It was swooping along the river and disappeared out of sight. Then suddenly I saw it dive into the water, reappear carrying a large fish, and fly north. I had an intuitive feeling that the birds were a sign, an omen of some kind, and that seeing them in action was not just a coincidence.

I reached over to the backseat of the car and picked up the coffee and tobacco and walked over to the Elder. He had a very strong presence of peace and spirituality about him, a tremendous amount of light, love, and beauty shining through his eyes, but physically he could pass for any old Indian anywhere. I don't know what I really expected a medicine man to look like—long hair in braids, holding a staff with a stuffed Eagle head on it, and a bunch of animal teeth hanging from his neck and ears, I guess. But Rudolph was just a short, medium-sized, plain-looking, and humble man with an old pair of pants, a country-style flannel shirt, and cropped hair.

As I walked up to him I said, "Are you a medicine man?" I felt nervous while trying to hand him the coffee and tobacco. I had some carryover of Indian custom and values as a child growing up, even if I had become assimilated and urbanized. And I had read in college books during my search for Indian identity and Nativism that a person always approaches the Elders, and especially medicine men and women, with a gift of respect when asking for help or just visiting.

He stood up while placing the feathers and regalia down on the porch, and with a swoop of his hand, he pointed for me to sit down. He accepted the gifts with a smile and said, "Not too many of the younger people seem to do this anymore. Thank you for showing respect. Well, I guess my people call me that, but I just consider myself a servant of the Great Creator, the Earth, our ancestors, and the spirits," he said quietly in a form of broken English.

I then proceeded to introduce myself and ask for his help. I told him that all of this was new to me, that I didn't really know how a person goes about getting a healing from a medicine man, or if a medicine man would even do a ceremony on someone not from his tribe. He went back to working on the regalia while listening intently, and then there was a long period of silence. I was getting nervous so I lit up a cigarette and asked him if he wanted one. "No thanks," he said, "I never use them." Then he started talking in such a low voice that I had to strain to listen. "I think what you are looking for is an Indian doctor. I am not that kind of medicine man. I am a ceremonial leader and religious leader. I make medicine for conducting our sacred dances and rituals. But there is a Yurok man who lives up past Weitchpec. His mother, Nancy, was a well-known doctor. I heard he doctors sometimes but we rarely see him except during times of our ceremonies; he comes down and shares his family regalia with us. We don't have any Indian doctors in our Hupa tribe anymore, at least none that I know of."

It was starting to get late and sunset comes early during the fall. I really wanted to stay and visit with the Elder much longer. I felt better just being near him, but I knew I had to move on before it got dark. He gave me directions and warned me to be very careful, that the road was dangerously narrow, caved-in in certain places, and often blocked with rock slides, thus making it difficult to pass. He told me to pass through the reservation valley heading north and stay on the winding, narrow road that followed along the river until I came to a large bridge with a store on the left. He said it was an old village site known as Weitchpec but had now turned into a tourist trap for fishing. He directed me to pass Pearson's store on the left, go over the large bridge, and then turn sharply to the left. I was to then follow this other very narrow road shaded by oak trees, pass a garbage dump on the left, and then look for a mailbox on the right, directly in a sharp bend, that read WAHSEK. Evidently another marker to look for was a small, rustic wood house just a little way up the dirt driveway, with a car-engine hoist in the yard.

He said the man who lived there was a mechanic, but I had to pass this house and go all the way up the side of a mountain until I came to an old fallen-down barn and an old two-story farmhouse. He also said that at one time the farm was the prettiest piece of property along that side of the river but it was becoming overgrown with blackberry bushes. He advised me to use the blackberry bushes as a marker because the neighboring farms and driveways didn't have the same problem; in other words, it would be obvious in comparison if I just happened to go up the wrong road.

I left with a sad feeling but I knew that someday I would probably return and visit with this special man. As I headed through the valley I couldn't help but laugh at René's departing comment about letting my hair grow long, like some of our urban brothers were starting to do. So far most of the Indian people I had seen on the reservation had short hair, and they were the real Indians, less acculturated, living closer to their heritage, culture, and land, fishing the old way.

The elderly Hupa religious leader was sure right about the road being dangerous. There were places in the bend that were caved in with the sides running down steep cliffs toward the river. I saw wrecked cars, pickups, and even a couple of large trucks. And I remembered his warning about watching out for falling rocks, some of which were really boulders. I had to stop a few times and load the trunk with rocks for extra traction because he also told me I might not be able to make it up the steep mountain road leading to the Indian doctor's house.

It seemed like it took forever just to cover about fifteen miles, but eventually I came up to Pearson's store on the left and a very large bridge covering a deep gorge in the bend of the river. It had to be a much larger and stronger bridge than any of the others I had crossed over so far because at Weitchpec, the mighty Klamath and Trinity Rivers converge into each other.

I began to go even slower just to be on the safe side but couldn't help noticing that there were some small groups of Indian people hanging around outside the store. Most of them had long hair, old jeans, hiking boots, and hunting knives strapped on their belts. A couple of them were fighting with a White man and obviously drunk, while some of the others were hollering around. I didn't think it would be a good place to stop and check on directions, so I just kept driving ahead until I crossed over the bridge, made the sharp left turn, and proceeded down a country road partially covered by oak trees, Douglas fir, and madrone. The cracking sound of acorns being smashed by the tires was almost hypnotic. A few people were down on the riverbank fishing and I couldn't help but think how long it had been since I had taken some time out in my own life—time out from the cement, glass, steel, traffic, people, noise pollution, smog, constant rushing to classes, and worrying about getting to work on time.

A large fish jumped up through the riffle, turned sideways, and flashed radiant colors of silver, red, and a tinge of green. Such colors could only be created by rays of the Sun that were shining down on a pristine river, as if in an ancient agreement that all things in life need light and energy in order to become harmonious and beautiful. Within an instant the large fish fell back into the mist rising from currents of water that came crashing over large boulders. But then it tried again with all its strength to jump against what seemed insurmountable odds. Its body twisted and jerked from the stress and pain but once again rays of sunlight shot into it, creating radiant streaks of color that appeared to flash. The force of the river against this Salmon was incredible. I couldn't take the suspense any longer and stopped the car right in the middle of the road. Beads of sweat were running down my face and I was filled with a rush of excitement. This was better than watching a San Francisco 49ers sudden death playoff. Could the fish really do it? Did it have another chance, or was it over just as soon as it had started? The river looked too big, too strong, too powerful. And yet, the fish never gave up. As if driven by some unknown source of strength and magic, it surfaced again, probably this time with all its might, probably far beyond its innate strengths and limitations, until it had overcome tremendous obstacles in its path and reached its destination.

I felt a sense of awe and inspiration in what I had just experienced with the Salmon, and a feeling that such an accomplishment could only be achieved by an ancient ceremony. I caught myself cheering for it while my heart was beating so fast that I could hardly catch my breath. I was glad that I had taken the time to watch it try one more time, to watch it attempt suicide, and I felt honored to see its silver-tipped tail fin slowly dance off and disappear into calmer waters.

3

Symbolic and Spiritual Synchronicity

I heard the squawking of a large Raven as I started the car back up and saw him fly over me and then turn right up ahead, past what appeared to be a bend in the road. I started looking for mailboxes and dirt driveways. Was it just a coincidence that the mailbox the Raven was sitting on read WAHSEK? The road leading up the mountain first went through a small forest, past the rustic house with a car hoist in the yard, and then gradually came out into a clearing where the farm fields were covered with blackberry bushes. I never saw such a weird sight in my life. They covered everything in sight, as far as a person could look in every direction. It looked spooky the way this foreigner had taken over so much of the beautiful countryside and obliterated the natural vegetation. It seemed symbolic of what had historically happened to our Native people.

The dirt driveway leading up the mountain was rough, full of holes, washouts, and rocks. I had a difficult time trying to get up the hill, and I could feel the front end, oil pan, and muffler system taking a beating underneath the vehicle. A Chicken Hawk swooped down toward me, as if attacking, and then continued to circle while I struggled with the rough spots of the road. I thought that was a strange sign but kept gunning the gas pedal. Eventually the road started leveling off toward an old fallen-down barn. About a hundred yards away stood an old two-story farmhouse, with a very steep tin roof, and a few junk cars scattered about on both sides of the driveway. The cars appeared to reflect symbols and pages of history, with some from the 1920s, 1930s, 1940s, and 1950s.

The Hawk was circling over the house, and then it flew toward me and circled, and then it flew back toward the house, and I could see it circling in the sky with another bird that appeared to be much larger. The whole place looked old and like something out of the past. The house had to be at least a hundred years old, and even the few fruit trees and walnut trees scattered around the place looked decrepit.

The yard around the house was barren. A woodshed with a few stacks of firewood stood on the right, with a small coop attached to it, and chickens were running around wildly all over the yard. A pack of hogs were grunting and digging up the ground wherever they felt like it; and behind them in a withered garden a billy goat was chasing after a few does. I saw an old, beat-up, white GMC pickup truck with a cattle rack on it parked on the other side of the woodshed, so I thought I would park there. A couple of scruffy sheepdogs came running and barking from the porch while I tried to negotiate a parking spot without hitting any of the bent and twisted fruit trees, scattered blocks of wood, or rusted farm equipment.

As I got out of the car I could not help but notice that a number of Eagles were circling directly above me, and much to my surprise, there were about seven more sitting in old trees and upon fence posts quite some distance from the house, on the edge of the forest that surrounded the farm. An older Indian man who had obviously been cutting kindling wood by the shed, but who had been obscured from sight when I first pulled up to the house, was standing about twenty feet away. He still had the ax in his hand but was pointing to the different Eagles as if counting, and I could hear him speak loudly in his Native language. Then he started singing as the Eagles got lower. Suddenly the Chicken Hawk screamed and began diving at the Eagles. We both stood watching in bewilderment, periodically glancing at each other. Even the dogs who I thought were going to attack me when I got out of the car had stopped and were looking toward the sky.

I didn't think the Hawk stood a chance against four Eagles, but they kept dancing around one aother in combat, periodically diving with out-stretched claws, missing one aother by only inches. The Sun was beginning to set, and the air started feeling chilly. A sudden and strange-feeling Wind was now blowing in from the east, and the older Indian man turned and started walking toward the house. Then there was dead silence. The Wind seemed to stop the moment he went through the door. The Eagles and Hawk left. The chickens settled down and were moving toward the coop, and the hogs had now all gathered around an improvised trough made from a junked hot water heater.

I reached back into the car and gathered up the wool Indian blanket, can of pipe tobacco, and can of coffee, and I double-checked my wallet to make sure I still had a hundred-dollar bill hidden on the side. I intended to use these gifts as a donation in exchange for getting doctored. I left my sleeping bag and groceries in the backseat, not knowing whether I would be accepted or not, and not knowing where I would be spending the night.

The dogs seemed less intimidating now, although they were carefully watching me. I walked up to the front door and knocked. I could smell smoke and food being cooked. It was coming from the kitchen and an old-fashioned woodstove. A loud voice hollered out *"Oat-la-ma,"* which I figured meant "Come in." It was a very poor-looking house, to say the least. The front door was open, and directly in front of me, a little to the right, between the front room and the kitchen, was another door. I assumed it led upstairs to an attic or storage area.

The walls, floors, and ceiling were boarded with plain plywood. No wallpaper, only a few family pictures scattered here and there, half hanging on nails and mostly crooked. An iron woodstove sat to the left of the doorway and behind it a ragged, old blue chair. There was a door that I assumed led into a bedroom, and a long, large old couch that was torn, tattered, and partially covered with an army blanket. Toward the back of the front room on the left was another closed door, and to the right was a window, an old wooden table with Indian baskets and a kerosene lamp sitting on it, and a couple of wooden chairs and an old kitchen table.

The kitchen table was covered with a worn-out tablecloth, and upon it sat an ashtray, a few packs of cigarettes, a can of pipe tobacco, some coffee cups, farmers' and outdoor magazines, and another large kerosene lamp.

To my right was an open area leading into the kitchen that was partially blocked by a heavy, handmade picnic table. It was covered with a clean tablecloth, salt and pepper shakers beaded in Indian design, a sugar bowl, and some more magazines and newspapers. To the far right behind the end and sides of the kitchen table were windows half covered with dirty-colored shades. I remember thinking how strange the house looked with no curtains on any of the windows, just those dirty shades. The rest of the kitchen was small and cluttered with a large wood cooking stove from the 1920s that had a wood box full of kindling next to it and was surrounded by a few cabinets and homemade shelves. There was an old porcelain sink in the rear of the kitchen, with iron skillets, pots, and pans dangling down within short reach, although the height of the ceiling was above average. Dishes, plates, bowls, cups, and glasses were mix-matched and stacked haphazardly wherever space could be found. A few large bags of dog food, flour, rice, beans, and dried acorns took up the remaining wall space between old-fashioned glass cabinets. There were no appliances in the kitchen: no refrigerator, no toaster, no radio, no washing machine. Evidently the house was not hooked up for electricity. Despite all the disorganization and poverty, the floors looked swept clean and everything else looked fairly neat.

A very short, dark-skinned Indian woman was busy at the woodstove cooking bread in the oven. She was about as wide as she was tall, dressed in an old dress, covered by a large apron, with her hair braided in coils and tucked on the top of her head. She never turned to greet me. The front room was getting dark, but smelled warm and friendly from a fire that had just been started in the stove, and directly behind it the Indian man I had seen outside was now sitting in the blue, worn-out chair. He stared at me so intently that I started getting very nervous.

He seemed somewhat obscure, almost as if he were hiding behind the small woodstove and protected by a shadow that was now taking over the room, replacing the light from the setting sun. The small window next to him didn't provide much light anyway because it was half blocked by a dirty window shade, dust, soot stains, and cobwebs. All I could see at first was the form of a medium-sized man peering behind two very strange eyes, eyes that did not look human. His eyes reflected a strange light and wildness beyond dilation, in the same way that animal or bird eyes look when a flash of light hits them in the darkness.

I felt a wave of unseen force, a kind of power surge through me, that was different from energy that is electrical in nature. I had been electrocuted when I was a teenager so I had some basis for a comparison to the feeling. This was different. It was beyond a physical type of shock, and it made me shake all over, almost into convulsions.

I finally got hold of my composure and stopped crying and shaking. The uncontrollable crying came with the sudden surge of power that initially went through me when we first made eye-to-eye contact. I reached down and picked up the gifts, staggered over to the couch, and asked if I could smoke. He was still staring at me but not quite as piercingly, and the light in his eyes now changed to a feeling of warmth and acceptance. Although there was a profound presence about him, something extremely spiritual and uncanny, it radiated pure love.

It was a feeling of love beyond the kind I had felt with Lilly, and it was different from the kind of love a child feels from and toward his parents. It had to be some sort of spiritual love that I had never experienced before. I was lost for words to explain it.

I told him my name and who I was. I told him that I was part Seneca, part Cherokee, part White, and that I thought I was also part Karuk but at this time I had no way to prove it until I could talk with the man who I thought was my real father. I then asked him if he was a medicine man, if he was the kind that does healing, what the local people call an Indian doctor. I also apologized and told him that I did not know how to approach a medicine man for a healing and ceremony according to his tribal protocol, and as a consequence I didn't have the slightest idea what

"Indian doctoring" would involve. I offered him the tobacco, coffee, an Indian wool blanket, and a hundred-dollar bill.

He said humbly, "I knew you were coming. I already saw you and know you. But I don't know if I really want to get into this because you're going to be a lot of trouble and a tough job to handle."

"What do you mean?" I said defensively. "I came a long ways just to find you, and I came with a good heart and good intentions."

"No, it's not that," he said curtly. "It's just you. You're complicated, not like the average person who might come and ask for help and a healing." He paused and closed his eyes as if searching for the right words, then continued. "Remember what happened to you along the way? Remember the different birds you saw, the salmon down at the river, and the battle you saw happening right over my house? Do you remember how you even got here as a result of trying to commit suicide?"

How in the hell could he possibly know all that? I thought to myself. There was no way. Nobody could be that psychic. After all, we had never met before, and he lived more than three hundred miles away from me, isolated in the mountains, in an entirely different world and way of life. He must have been reading my mind because he interrupted my bewildered thoughts and said, "Nothing can hide from the spirits. Nothing is hidden from the Great Spirit. All of Nature is witness to our deeds and actions. The Great Creator has many workers who report everything. Nobody can hide from the Sun, the Moon, the Wind, or any part of Creation. And the Great Creator, the Great Spirit, is in every part of Creation, both seen and unseen."

I started to get scared and began shaking again. Coincidentally the pains started getting worse and I asked if I could have a glass of water to take a handful of aspirin. (I had refused to take any stronger drugs since the suicide attempt.) About that time the elderly woman in the kitchen hollered for us to come in and eat. He responded that he had to get out and feed the hogs and chickens first, so to save time I volunteered to help with the feeding. We went outside with all the leftover buckets of food that had been combined with dry animal feed and a large coffee can of cracked corn.

On the way back he stopped and looked around. By now it was dark, slightly after sunset, and it was difficult to see. An Owl was hooting in the barn and I felt a strange cold chill go through my body. Somehow I got the impression that he had felt the Owl before he heard it, or that perhaps he was in telepathic communication with spirits and the Great Creator. "Do you hear that?" he turned and said coldly. "Do you know what that means?"

"Not really," I said sheepishly. "Is it some kind of sign or omen?"

"You bet," he answered. "And a real bad one at that."

He told me to go into the house because he wanted to stay outside for a few moments and pray. He said he wanted to check things out, so to speak, and that upon his return he would let me know if he would doctor me. I went into the front room, lit up a cigarette, and pondered my predicament. It was obvious that I was becoming a real pain in the ass for him and I seriously thought about just leaving. All of this was too far out of the real world, beyond Disneyland. It was just too weird for me. Birds, animals, and fish as signs and omens, talking creatures, spirits, mind reading, bogeyman bullshit, God stuff, and all the rest of the psychic or supernatural crap associated with it.

I had to admit that I would probably be much better off if I just gave in and went to a shrink. A psychiatrist would logically be more qualified to help, especially with the effects of drugs that were still probably screwing with my mind. How else could a person explain all these crazy events?

I was helping to light the kerosene lamps when he came in and started washing his hands. On the way over to the table to sit down he said, "Oh, by the way, this is Gina. She is a Hupa woman from a well-known medicine family. I am Wahsek, a Yurok Indian, the grandson of Lucky from Wahsek, and the son of Nancy and Charlie Wahsek. I am one of the few from the original lineage of the ancient and secret House of Talth. And I am a psychiatrist so you came to the right place."

Man, this guy nailed me again. "How in the hell did you know I was thinking I would be better off if I went to a psychiatrist?" I asked. "And what about my request for help? Are you willing to do a healing ceremony on me?"

"Well, it's like this," he said, looking at Gina and laughing. "I guess I'm psychic, whatever that means!" We couldn't stop laughing. I honestly didn't know if he was joking or serious, but I did know one thing for sure: this dude was definitely telepathic, with spiritual powers, abilities, and knowledge far beyond the normal. Perhaps even far beyond highly educated human comprehension.

We had acorn soup, smoked Salmon, Deer meat, biscuits, and wild mint tea for dinner. Damn, I don't ever remember eating anything that tasted so good, so natural, and so powerful. Gina kept looking at me while I was eating and I thought she was waiting for a compliment. "Man, this is great," I said. "It really is the best meal I've ever had. It's been a long time since I had venison." But that didn't seem to pacify her because she kept looking at me all over. I got the feeling she was studying something, maybe reading my aura. Then she snapped, "It's not Deer meat, just local beef. We don't eat Deer meat and Salmon together at the same meal. It's against Indian custom!" I felt chastised.

Wahsek broke the silence. "I've decided to doctor you so we'll get started a couple of hours after dinner, okay? Mr. Hoo-hoo outside wasn't after you, although that is normally the case when he comes stalking as the Death Giver. He's a bad omen but sometimes can also be a tough challenger. It depends on how he comes, who sent him, or how he acts. In this situation he was reporting a death that was about to happen."

We heard the Rooster crow three times. Wahsek and Gina looked toward each other gravely, then toward the barn that was in a southern direction, and I thought I heard them saying a little prayer under their breath, although it was in the Native language. I got real nervous and shook with a cold chill going up my spine. "So you know what that means, huh, when a Rooster crows at night when it's not supposed to?"

"Well yeah, I think so," I responded. "I guess it's foolish to be superstitious but yeah, I've heard since I was a child that it's a bad omen when the Rooster crows after sunset. It usually means someone is going to die, right?"

"You're right, and it's not superstitious. It's just a different system of knowledge, an ancient form of creative intelligence, a form of spiritual education, you might say. So believing in such things doesn't make it any better or any worse, it just makes you more intelligent."

"What do you mean?" I asked. "I never thought old wives' tales, superstitious beliefs, or supernatural acts were a form of higher intelligence. In fact, Western society has spent a great deal of time, effort, and money to make most of us believe superstitious people are ignorant, uneducated, crude, and low class."

He looked at me and busted out laughing. "Then I guess you're a real fool after all, huh? With all your Western education, military training, and college you still believe in and react to what you call superstitious things!"

"Okay," I said, "so you're right and I'm wrong. Maybe you can really talk to birds, animals, and spirits; maybe you do hear what they have to say for some strange reason. So what did the Owl tell you?"

"Remember when you were going to stop at Pearson's store, down below, next to the bridge, to get a soda pop and ask for directions? But you got an eerie feeling when you saw a few long-haired Indian people drunk and fighting with a White man? Well, one of the Indian guys, Jimmy Johnson, who has a reputation for getting drunk and causing trouble, got killed just a little while ago, around the same time the Owl came in hooting. A representative of his family will be coming up to see me tomorrow to ask for spiritual help, just wait and see." He grinned and looked at me for a response, and then continued, "Then we'll also see how your highly educated, Western-oriented, intelligent mind tries to rationalize it all, huh?" On this note we all started laughing again. "And don't you even dare ask me how I knew what you were going to do at Pearson's and what you saw take place!"

He finished his meal, got up, and went to the bathroom, and I volunteered to help clean up the mess. Gina acted a little more friendly but still kept her distance from me, being cautious to not even bump into me while we were moving around in a crowded kitchen. I thought her behavior a little unusual but I told myself that different people have different customs.

She took off her apron and hung it on the door next to the stove, and then turned down the glow of the kerosene lamp and waddled like a duck over to the small table in the front room. "Can I have one of your cigarettes?" she asked. "It's now time to smoke and relax while he gets prepared for doctoring, but first he wants to explain to you what he actually does; in other words, how the ceremony is conducted, understand?"

I nodded to her, handed her a cigarette, and got the whiff of what I thought was an herb being burned on the stove. I was familiar with the smells of tobacco, cedar, and sage, but I had never smelled this kind of herb before. I didn't want to be rude but I couldn't help asking Wahsek what kind of medicine it was, because my nose and eyes were becoming irritated from the strong, menthol type of odor.

He didn't say anything in response but kept burning more of the leaves and praying, until it got pretty smoky. Then he turned and opened the front door and stood to the side as if addressing somebody, probably a ghost or a spirit, and he appeared to be ushering it out with a warning. At least I assumed it was a warning by the way he abruptly closed the door in a gesture that connoted, "You had better leave, because we don't want you here, and don't let the door hit you in the ass on the way out!" Gina interpreted his language and actions for me, and to my surprise, my assumptions were pretty close to what he was, indeed, doing and saying. She also told me that the herb was called pepperwood, and the leaves were from a local tree that was noted for its religious significance and power. It allegedly had the power to fight evil spirits and ghosts, ward off bad forces, and protect people from supernatural harm. The herb looked like bay leaves.

Wahsek then proceeded to explain how he doctored. "I don't charge for doctoring and healing. I don't have the right or authority to sell the Great Creator's gift and powers for a profit. I am therefore not like the White man's doctors, although my training and schooling was just as difficult, if not more, and just as expensive, and probably even longer. But according to Indian custom and law the patient is supposed to offer something as a sign of respect, a gift or donation, of comparable worth.

This is what we call the Law of Reciprocity."

He paused for a while to let the concept sink in, and then he continued, "You just don't take something for nothing. You just don't take things for granted. Even when gathering plants, foods, or herbs, we always make a prayer, ask permission, offer tobacco, and give thanks. That way the circle is completed with respect. What goes around comes around in the great circle of life. The circle is holy. It has no beginning, it has no end, it is infinite. And we are all part of the circle, we are all part of the great web of life, we are connected in one way or another. Thus we must learn to be accountable for our actions. That is the law."

His eyes kind of drifted off into space, and then he returned to the elaboration. "So in some tribes the patient might have to make arrangements to go through the medicine man's family member first, or an apprentice, to be screened. We used to do that here too but I don't have a family or apprentice. As an example, with the Plains Indians a patient might have to offer a loaded pipe, tobacco in red cloth, a horse, money, and make a large pot of stew.

"It all depends upon what kind of medicine man the patient is seeing for what kind of sickness or problem. A Bear medicine man, who has his primary power from the Bear, specializes in broken bones, torn ligaments, arthritis, wounds, and diseases. A Rattlesnake medicine man specializes in Snakebites, bug bites, and skin problems. An Elk medicine man has the gift and knowledge to specialize in emotions, family problems, love matters, women's illnesses, and so forth. Different medicine men might specialize in witchcraft and handle psychological problems involving ghosts, bad spirits, and evil forces. Their main power might be the Owl, Blue Jay, Spiders, Snakes, Water Dog (salamander), or Skunk, for example. And they might even doctor."

Gina spoke up. "Yes, but Wahsek can handle all those things. At one time we also had Indian doctors who specialized in different illnesses, but that changed over the years as we started becoming extinct. We had women doctors who specialized in childbirth and women's illnesses, and child doctors who handled only children, and in fact, most of the best

Indian doctors were women. Weitchpec Susie who lived down the road there specialized in gunshots and wounds and was good with herbs. She got her powers from the Frog and Moon."

Then Wahsek interrupted, "Well, I guess I'm more simple here. Normally I'd rather doctor the patient with his or her family because what affects the patient also affects the entire family, and vice versa. Understand? It is like the circle concept, a more holistic approach. But then again, because of changes in society, as in your case here, we can't always include the family, so we just try to do the best we can. Therefore there are certain rules, or what we call customs. The patient must be clean before, during, and after doctoring; and so must the doctor. This means no drugs, no alcohol, no sex, and I can't do ceremony with women on the moontime, meaning their monthly period. But this also includes women who are bleeding from childbirth. The patient is expected to stay clean about three to four days before being doctored, while he is being doctored, and after being doctored."

He looked at me sternly and explained further, "When you leave here you can't eat in any restaurants and take any chances of eating food cooked or shared by a woman on her menses, and you can't eat or sleep with your wife, or any other woman for that matter, who might be on her moontime. In the olden days everyone knew about these laws so special arrangements were made, but nowadays I have to be real careful because I could get hurt and the power could backfire on me; and the patient could get hurt with all the hard work in doctoring becoming undone."

I was very curious about his philosophy, especially about the ideas of sex, menses, and food as contaminants. I just didn't understand because it was totally foreign to my value system. I tried to ask him for clarification but he said that we didn't have time, and he promised to explain things later.

Then he continued. "Healing is a very complicated affair. Each case is different, people are different, circumstances are different, and it is all spiritual. In the majority of cases people become sick because they are ignorant, they have violated spiritual laws: the Great Creator's Laws, the Laws of Nature, Indian custom and laws. It doesn't make any difference what race, nationality, culture, color, religion, or beliefs you have, either. Believing in something helps the healing process but it really doesn't cause the illness, accident, sickness, or disease—or even death. Being ignorant of the laws and not believing in the laws cause these things to happen."

His eyes turned toward the sky as if acknowledging the Great Creator, who I assumed was listening in to the teaching. "So part of the healing ceremony will require finding out what laws you have violated, trying to find out the cause or causes of your illness. Then you will have to *pegusoy*, which means you will have to confess for your violations or sins. We will plead for your forgiveness, you will be required to promise that you will never commit the violation again, and then we will blow it away. In the same way that the Great Creator sends in the spirits of the Wind or the water to purify the Earth, we try to cleanse your mind, soul, and body."

I listened intently to his instructions and explanation but I was still a little confused. "You mean like going to a priest in the Catholic Church, we confess for our sins?" I was thinking to myself that acculturation had also influenced our Native religions and that these people weren't really as traditional as I had originally thought.

Once again the man read my mind. "No," he said curtly. "The Whiteman didn't change our religion. He might have influenced and changed some tribes and some Indians, but not us. We are following the same way of our ancestors, and they used what you call confession for thousands of years, long before the Whiteman came to our land!"

He shook his head as if he were a little disgusted with me, paused, and then continued. "So when we get ready, I will sit down, light my pipe, make an offering to the Great Creator and the good spirits, use the spirits and my mind to look into you, meaning make a diagnosis, then we will talk about things for a while. Afterward, I will sing and dance and use my hands on you to pull out the sickness, bad powers, pain, or whatever is causing you to be sick, and I will throw it to the Sun to be burned up, into the water to be taken away, or deep into the Earth where it can't return. I will also use the power in my hands to transmit healing into your body, to charge you with spirituality, and for rejuvenation. And if needed, I might make some herbs for you to drink or bathe in. So the ceremony could go several hours, it could last all night, or it might continue for a day or two with several breaks in between while we all rest up. Now I'm assuming you are clean, right?"

"Yes," I said. "I haven't had any alcohol since, well, you know, since I tried to kill myself, and I haven't taken any kind of drugs except aspirin." I started to laugh, embarrassed. "And I haven't had any sex for about a week because I wore my wife and myself out, I think. And I know she wasn't on her period when I left."

About that time the dogs began barking outside, and then we heard a Coyote howling. Gina looked at me sternly and said, "Yeah, macho man, and that's a lot of your problem. You're hell for women, a womanizer, and payback time will be a bitch, Coyote!"

They both started laughing to the point of almost rolling on the floor, until it suddenly got dead silent. I could feel the pains coming on stronger, the aching was becoming unbearable, my body was beginning to feel very stiff, with cold chills, and I was beginning to go into a severe state of anxiety because intuitively I felt that the disease had come back, even worse than before, and that Death was stalking me again. I started crying.

The Exorcism

Wahsek told me to strip down to my underwear and sit on the couch. Gina put the other kerosene lamps out, so it was getting pretty dark in the house, with only one very dim lamp and periodic spurts of light coming from the old woodstove. She started to pray in Indian language and pulled a root or bark and a small, tubular wooden pipe out of an old animal-hide bag. She then lit the end of the root and burned it like incense, making an offering to the Great Creator, and a number of different directions I wasn't familiar with. I had déjà vu upon smelling the incense. I knew that I had smelled it someplace before, perhaps in a dream, but I just couldn't remember where.

After the root-burning invocation, Gina proceeded to load up her pipe with tobacco from a can of Sir Walter Raleigh. Wahsek opened the woodstove and put a piece of firewood in it, and then he took a small shovel and raked out a few hot coals. He then offered his hand up to the sky, made a circle over his head to represent the Circle of Creation, and placed a handful of the pepperwood leaves on the coals. It got pretty smoky and spooky looking in the room. Upon making medicine with the leaves, he proceeded to take off his shirt, boots, and socks. He then went into the kitchen, stayed for a while running the water, and came back with a small bowl and a chair, which he placed directly in front of me. He was bare-chested and barefoot with pants rolled up, and much to my surprise he didn't wear any kind of special regalia or go through any kind of ritualistic formalities.

There were no fancy headdresses, no Eagle wing fans, no animal teeth claws or necklaces, no painting up of colors on himself or the patient, no big hides to lay the patient on, no animal or bird skulls for an altar, nothing. It was much different from what I had expected after reading books about Indian culture and seeing a few films in a college course. There was no flimflam or the mumbo jumbo that has so often been portrayed in Hollywood movies. This guy was so simple and so humble that he didn't even fit the stereotype of an Indian, much less a medicine man.

I had learned a little lesson not to stereotype from my earlier encounter with the Hupa ceremonial leader, so I wasn't too shocked when I first met Wahsek with his short, almost styled hair. He wore an old sweatshirt with no logos or symbols, a pair of logging boots, and Oshkosh-type pants, the kind that utility men, mechanics, farmers, or loggers wear. I had judged his age at about late forties to early fifties because of the way he was built and how youthful he looked. I found out later that he was turning sixty, and Gina was a few years older. As he sat before me he reminded me of a Sicilian-Italian or Hispanic professional boxer, about five feet ten, approximately 180 pounds, and still well muscled, with an olive complexion. His hair was thick black on top, short on the sides, and combed straight back, with a slight tinge of silver beginning to show. He had thick eyebrows, high cheekbones, a strong jaw, and few wrinkles, except around the eyes and forehead.

Physically he looked strong and tough, and he reminded me of the older, full-blooded Italian tough guys I had grown up with on the East Coast. But he could also pass for some of the older, full-blooded Indian tough guys I had grown up with who were high-steel workers. In other words, his skin was not as dark as a full-blooded Hupa's or Pomo's, and his features were not Asiatic, but seemed more Mediterranean. Coincidentally, as I told René a few days later, he had the same East Coast hairstyle I had been wearing for years, the type of style other people labeled as the "greasers" and "gangsters" look, but not the Elvis Presley look. And as long as I knew him, up to his death more than a decade later, he never changed.

Although a lot of other Indian people young and old all across the country started growing their hair long, he kept his short and neat, and greased back. I remember a number of years later when I came to see him, I had started letting my hair grow long. He asked me if I needed money to see a barber. I defensively told him no, and said that Indians with short hair were considered apples and assimilators. I asked him why he didn't change with the times. He told me, "I never lost the blanket, so I don't need to go back and find it. I don't have an identity crisis. The Great Creator and the spirits know who I am, and personally, I'd rather remain obscure to the public. I enjoy and need my privacy. I don't need people telling me what they think I should be or what I should look like just to fit their own insecurities or stereotypes. And by the way, how in the hell can an acorn become an apple?" It took me a long time to figure out that philosophical question.

Wahsek pulled out his pipe, loaded it with tobacco from a little leather pouch, and it was so strong smelling that it reminded me of cigar smoke. It gave me a bad headache. I found out later that it was wild, local, indigenous tobacco, the kind that the spirits preferred over commercial tobacco because it had integrity and power in it.

His pipe was also tubular and appeared to have a small stone bowl on the end of it. It is the custom and habit of most medicine men to share their "peace pipe" in prayer with the patient and company, so I found it strange that Wahsek did not offer to share his pipe with me to smoke. He then proceeded to talk in his language in what appeared to be a conversation with the Great Creator and spirits. I could feel an eerie heaviness coming over me, as if I had been drugged, to the point that his speech seemed garbled. He said, "As I told you earlier, sometimes a person can become sick and in pain because he has violated the Creator's Laws or Natural Laws of the Universe, so what do you know about the Bear?"

"I don't understand," I remarked slowly, trying to think. "I don't know what all this would have to do with a Bear."

"The spirit of the Bear is very angry with you. Evidently you have abused and violated it, so it has been stalking you, tormenting you, clawing and gnawing you apart in an effort to get your attention."

All of a sudden we heard the dogs begin to bark wildly. Then came the loud, wild growling of a large animal just beyond the front door. At first I was scared, but then I figured it had to be the medicine man using ventriloquism. "What I am talking about is this," he continued to say firmly. "Is it true or not true that you have a Bear hide, Bear claws, Bear teeth, and related power objects?"

The growling got louder and closer while the dogs barked and growled back more viciously, and all this was going on while the medicine man was still talking. Was he really using ventriloquism to make the ceremony seem more dramatic, or was there actually a large animal out there? It couldn't be a Bear, I tried to rationalize, because this was all just too coincidental, unless of course he had a pet Bear trained to be part of the act. "Have you ever eaten any Bear meat?" he asked loudly. "If so, would you please tell the Creator and spirits here when you did it. You owe them a very sincere apology, otherwise I don't think I am going to be able to help you get rid of this disease. You see, it's like this. If you ate Bear meat that was not hunted with the proper ceremony, or if you ate Bear meat that was cooked and handled by women on their moontime, and shared with people while having sex, then you have violated the Natural Law. The Bear has power, more power than most animals, and there are spiritual laws involving the use of such power. And that Bear can be very mean when he wants to be. If you violate him he is going to let you know it, sooner or later."

I sensed a degree of anxiety in the tone of his voice and felt that he knew I was having apprehensions about his diagnosis. He was not only probing me for answers but also appeared to be a little pushy in getting a response. Maybe it was all the growling around outside that was making him appear so impatient, or maybe it was just my own ignorance. I didn't mean to be uncooperative. I just couldn't get a grasp on all this. "Yeah, I guess," I finally said. "I know I ate Bear meat as a child growing up. My mother's brothers and grandfather hunted Bear. We were poor, living in the mountains, and had no work. I don't know if my mother, aunts, cousins, or other women were on their menses or not. They could have been. As for sex, well, I know they were screwing all the time. It seems to run in the family, especially during long winter days. All of us kids could hear it going on."

Wahsek listened intently. The growling and barking outside stopped for a while. Gina looked at me and shook her head in disgust. "Okay," he said, satisfied. "Now it's time to *pegasoy*. I'll help guide you through this, so repeat after me. Great Creator, the good spirits, my ancestors, and the Bear people. I want to confess for my violations against you and ask that you forgive me. I admit that there have been many times in my life when I ate your body and took your power in a bad way. I apologize if my relatives did not offer you payment and take your life with ceremony. I apologize if the women in our family cooked and shared you while they were on their menses, or just after childbirth, or while people were having sex."

After hesitating for a moment, he continued, "I am sorry we insulted you, many different Bears, and I ask that you remove those violations off my life. I ask that you remove all the torment, pain, sickness, or disease you are giving me, and I promise to never do that again. I also ask that you not let my children (if you do have children now, or when you have children in the future) inherit those violations, punishment, and sickness."

I had difficulty remembering the long speech but I did the best I could to get rid of the transgression. Although I didn't understand all this, and I had difficulty believing in it, I was willing to do anything at this point to get well. Wahsek and Gina both talked in their Native language for a while, and then they simultaneously said, "Please forgive him for these violations and sins against the Bear and the Creator's Laws, and remove all torment, pain, and sickness from his life." They then blew over me three times while Wahsek dipped his fingers into the bowl and sprinkled water on me in a blessing. The ritualistic act was similar to what I had seen priests do with holy water while praying and blessing people.

They both proceeded to light their pipes, blow smoke to the heavens,

and pray some more in their language. With their eyes closed and squint-
ing intently, they appeared to be running a scan on me, looking me up
and down, all over, and peering deep into my soul. They seemed to be
searching for something, or trying to see something that was not apparent to the naked eye. I couldn't help but feel very uncomfortable and
wonder if they, indeed, had some form of psychic, mental X-ray type of
ability.

The intense silence was suddenly shattered by the howl and yelping
of a Coyote. The dogs took off barking in pursuit, and it was apparent
they were chasing the Coyote because their barking got fainter. Wahsek
remarked, "It appears that we are not finished with the Bear. He is very
angry with you. Is it true or not true that you had a habit of trying to be
a macho man, a great lover, act like a Coyote, and impress the women
with your Indian stuff?"

"What do you mean?" I asked defensively. "What Indian stuff?"

"Don't act stupid. You know exactly what I'm talking about!" he
snapped back. "The way I see it you are a womanizer. You're addicted to
sex. You will do anything to lure women into your bed. It's like a game,
some sort of sick power trip with you, probably as a result of the way
you were raised and even abused. But the fact of the matter is this. You
and your partners had bachelor pads down in the city. Sure, you were
proud of being Indian but you didn't know what being a real Indian is.
You had an identity crisis and a critical lack of cultural upbringing. All
you urban Indians are the same, but then again, it's really not your fault,
just simply your predicament and demise. So you guys liked to booze it
up, party a lot, be popular with the women, set traps for group hunt, and
lure the women into your clutches. Big game hunters, right? Whoever
scored the most became the hero. The rest of the guys, and even women,
looked up to you. But the whole time you were playing with power and
when you violated the laws, power started playing back and getting
rough."

He fondled his pipe while thinking and looked up at me. "For example, you had the large Bearskin rug on your bed, the necklaces dan-

gling down over the bedposts and walls, Eagle feathers and herbal medicine laid out on the nightstand, and you even used your sacred pipe to smoke marijuana. Instead of using your sacred objects and inheritance for spirituality and doctor tools, you used them for aphrodisiacs. You used sacred power to lure, entice, trap, and seduce women for sex. Many of them were even on their menses at the time. You not only hurt these innocent women but you also hurt yourself with your own stupidity. Therefore you harmed, insulted, and tormented the Bear almost beyond forgiveness. You abused a very special, sacred, and powerful gift from the Great Creator, Nature, and your ancestors. That's what you did, isn't it? That's why that Bear is so mad at you. That's why you're being punished with an incurable disease, pain, and suffering. You can't eat and abuse your own power, especially the higher powers, and if you do, the circle will come back on you. The spiritual law and the physical law are the same. There is no difference. It's like the law of physics: for every action there is a reaction."

I was starting to shake all over and cry. A feeling of remorse enveloped me that was beyond shame, guilt, and embarrassment. The truth hit like a force beyond comprehension and for some strange reason everything he said made sense to me.

Suddenly all hell broke loose. A series of large growls started outside the front door. Something huge was slamming up against it, clawing, pushing, and pounding violently. Terrified, we all turned our attention to the door, wondering if it would hold whatever was out there trying to force its way in.

The door was ripped off its hinges and slammed up against the wall. A large Black Bear came slowly walking in. His big, white teeth were flashing with foam, slobber was running down his jaws, and he was shaking his head back and forth in anger. There wasn't the slightest doubt in my mind that this awesome beast was real, and that he was coming after me. He didn't stare at anyone else, only me, and I felt a hot burst of shit splatter into my shorts as I shook in fear, desperately looking for a place to run and hide.

The Bear stood up and started growling at me with outstretched claws.

Wahsek made a sudden dive for an old .30-.30 Winchester rifle that was lying up against the wall near his chair. He almost hit the hot woodstove. Luckily he missed it because there would have been one hell of a fire in the old house, with our only way out blocked by a large, fierce animal. The Bear started to walk toward me when all of a sudden Gina jumped up from her chair and whacked it in the penis with her cane.

She hollered and cussed at it, said something in her Native language, and then she whacked it again as it stood in shock, not knowing how to react to her. It groaned in pain so loudly that my own scrotum started hurting. The Bear doubled up and fell backward, crying like an over-sized baby, and then before she could swing at it again, it rolled over onto all four legs and ran like a maniac into the darkness. The sound of crashing brush, logs breaking, rocks cracking, and leaves snapping followed the continuous crying and moaning until it was finally out of hearing range, and probably well over the ridge.

"See, you men are all alike. You all got a weak spot even though you think you're so damn big and bad," she said. "Now can we get on with the doctoring? I've had enough entertainment for one night. I'm ready to go to bed."

On that note, Wahsek got up off the floor and put the rifle back in the corner, reached for his chair, and tried to compose himself. Gina hollered across the room before he started lighting his pipe, "Hey, I think you better let him go to the bathroom and wipe the shit off himself before you start singing and dancing." They both busted up laughing while I ran to the bathroom. They didn't have any hot water in the pipes, probably because of no electricity, but the cold water felt clean and refreshing.

I had to leave my underwear in the tub to soak and used an old, woolen-type feed sack to cover with while I came out and grabbed my pants off the couch. They were still laughing as I sat back down and prepared for the rest of the healing ceremony. My hands were shaking as I tried to light a cigarette and calm down.

They started singing. Gina pounded her cane in perfect rhythm on the hard wooden floor, while Wahsek periodically reached down into the bowl, washed his hands, then made a series of stroking motions upon my head, back, arms, legs, and feet. His hands felt like two hot, burning coals each time he touched my body. Sometimes he would pull on a particular spot where I was experiencing severe pain, clasp his hands together as if pulling something out, bend down and make a sucking noise, and then raise back up and throw it toward the sky, blowing it away.

At other times he danced with his arms and hands outstretched toward the sky, whistled like a Flickerbird, and reached down and grabbed more water from the bowl. In a massaging motion, he laid his extremely hot hands upon different joints in my neck, spine, knees, ankles, elbows, and wrists. I could feel a tremendous amount of heat, and a form of electricity being transmitted into the injured areas. There was a sharp, agonizing pain every time he pulled something out, and a very hot, penetrating current every time he reapplied his hands to the main joints. Much to my surprise, he even bent down and started sucking on my chest, in the solar plexus area, and upon my back, up and down the spine. At first I didn't know how to react but it happened so fast that all I could do was squirm, laugh from embarrassment, and hope like hell that this guy wasn't trying to molest me. I wasn't familiar with men putting their hands on me, much less trying to suck on my body, and I cringed.*

Immediately after sucking out the pain and swelling, he would turn and spit into the wood heater. The burning mucus smelled like rotten eggs as it hissed and cracked in the fire, leaving behind a very foul and poisonous odor that made me want to puke. It was obvious that he was using his mouth and his powers to suck the psychic poisoning and negative energies, the sickness, out of my body. I guess it must have tasted as

---

*Certain shamans, those who suck negative energies from their patients, are called "sucking doctors." They get their power from the Hummingbird or the King Snake or another animal that sustains itself by sucking. In the same way that a Hummingbird sucks the nectar out of a flower or a King Snake sucks nourishment from its prey, sucking doctors use their mouths to suck out the pain, sickness, fever, disease, or spiritual intrusion that they find in their patients' bodies. In recent generations, some sucking doctors use a tubular shaped pipe to suck through. Theirs is a very ancient form of healing and is used in addition to pulling negative energy out with the hands and throwing it away, as well as "laying on of hands," which transmits healing power and positive energy to the patient.

bad as it smelled because eventually it got the best of Wahsek, too. On the fourth sucking application he got up and ran past the woodstove, through the broken doorway, and onto the porch. He was out there quite a while before returning to the kitchen, where I could hear him washing his mouth out and gargling with cold water.

The singing and dancing got faster and more intense. The constant banging of their canes upon the wooden floor became hypnotic. Tables and glasses rattled while the flickering light from bouncing kerosene lamps flashed across a dark, very smoky, and eerie room. The place seemed old-fashioned, almost primitive. I started getting dizzy and began to hallucinate. The small room began to feel crowded. I thought I could see birds flying around, animals dancing with Wahsek and Gina, ghosts flying in and out of the walls, a procession of Indian people dressed in different kinds of regalia walking in through the doorway, and a mountain lion purring next to me on the long couch. It kept sitting there waving its tail and looking at me affectionately as if it wanted me to pet it.

A Time for Healing

I don't know how long they sang, danced, and doctored because I finally passed out from the swirling motion of everything in the weird room closing in on me. When I woke up the next day Wahsek was busy repairing the front door. Gina was cleaning up the kitchen, and I smelled herbs being boiled. I could see chickens scratching around in the dirt outside the front door and the dogs sleeping in the warm sunlight on the porch, and I could hear the hogs rubbing up against the side of the house trying to scratch off their fleas. I tried to get up and move the blankets off that somebody had laid on me when I was asleep, but I couldn't move. I was paralyzed and in excruciating pain. "What in the hell have you people done to me!" I screamed. I was scared to death.

Maybe René was right, I thought to myself. *Maybe this guy is a* brujo, *a sorcerer, instead of a healer, and he's witched me up beyond repair.* Damn, I was so naive—no, just plain stupid! I was so filled with rage that I wanted to get up and kill somebody, but I couldn't move. Here I was way up in the middle of nowhere, hidden in some mountain farm, totally isolated, with no way to call for help or protection, staying with a bunch of crazy Indian people who could do anything they wanted to me and probably get away with it.

Christ, for all I knew they could kill me and take my money and car, and feed my body to their wild animals as part of some kind of primitive or satanic ritual or something. Down in the city we read in the newspapers all the time about people disappearing after attending religious cult meetings. *Oh man,* I kept thinking, *me and my weird ideas!*

"Hey macho man," I heard Gina holler sarcastically, "don't you urban Indians live by the motto 'no pain, no gain'?"

Damn, I thought to myself, *she doesn't talk much but when she does, she always has something smart to say.* "How about this as an answer to your predicament: if you're going to play, you have to pay, right?" She laughed. "And don't sit there making excuses for yourself while you insult us; we might be pagans but we're not savages. We might not be perfect but we ain't weirdos, or devils either. So watch your thoughts around here. We put our lives on the line for you last night, or did you forget. We're not the ones who got you into this mess. You've got nobody to blame but yourself."

She brought over a cup of hot herbs and a cigarette for me at the end of the verbal reprimand. I really felt like an asshole. No wonder Wahsek initially said that he didn't want to try and doctor me. I really wasn't worth it with all my arrogance, ignorance, and scapegoating.

Wahsek came in and sat down in his chair. Although it wasn't much to look at, it always had the aura of a throne. "Things got pretty exciting around here last night, huh?" he inquired. "I told you I was a psychiatrist, among other things, but I guess you could say I'm also similar to a dentist."

I was puzzled by the comparison and asked, "What do you mean? Do you also doctor people who have toothaches?"

"On a few occasions I've done that, yes. I didn't do the drilling and filling kind of work, only the emotional and spiritual part. But let me explain. Have you ever had an abscessed tooth that was driving you crazy with pain? Well, what did you do? You tried taking all kinds of aspirin, painkillers, even got drunk hoping to get rid of it, right? Finally you had no other recourse but to call up the dentist and make an emergency appointment."

He paused a minute to scratch fleabites on his leg, which were probably from the hogs, and then he kept talking. "He tells you that the tooth is decayed, dying, and beyond repair, and the only way to stop the pain is to pull it out, and throw it away. With this approach the pus and poison can finally get out, otherwise an infection could start spreading throughout the rest of your body. That sounds logical, and it gives you some hope for relief, so you let the dentist do his job, pull out the tooth, and you figure that's the end of the problem. But much to your amazement, the pain and swelling start getting worse after the anesthetic has worn off. Man you're pissed! You call up the dentist and cuss him out because you're now in worse pain than before. Looking for someone to blame, you start thinking that the dentist must have done something wrong to make the sickness and pain worse, otherwise you would be feeling much better."

Shaking his finger in a gesture of scolding, he proceeded to elaborate. "But in reality, he didn't cause your problem in the first place. Finally he gets you calmed down, tells you to take some aspirin, to cleanse your mouth with warm salt water, and give the operation some time to be purified and healed. So the first day after being doctored you feel worse than before, but with each passing day as the healing progresses, you notice real improvement. Well, that's the way it is here. I'm sorry that I forgot to warn you but we didn't have much time for a more complete orientation to the ceremony. But be patient, cooperate with me, and if all goes well, you should begin to feel less pain and more improvement in your health."

I understood now and nodded agreeably. "Is that what you did on me last night, an exorcism?"

"I guess you could call it that, but there's a lot more to it," he said seriously.

My mind was now filling with all kinds of questions but I guess he knew the pain was becoming unbearable and said, "We can talk about this later. Right now Gina has your herbs made up so I want you to drink four full cups today, and bathe in the tub back there, as hot as you can stand it, and soak. Try to relax and let the herbs do their job. They're special spirits and have power. They're the real doctors."

I had noticed that Gina was busy carrying buckets of hot water back and forth from the kitchen while we were talking, and despite her old age and obesity, she seemed to handle it with ease. I also felt that there was a ray of kindness in her after all, even if she did seem unfriendly and sarcastic most of the time.

It was all I could do to get into the large, old-style tub full of herbal tea. It had a mentholated, medicinal fragrance, and it felt very soothing. The cups of tea tasted like mint but were bitter. I wasn't in there more than fifteen minutes before I had to jump out and vomit, then rotate back and forth on the toilet from puking to shitting. Then back into the tub to soak some more. By the time I came out, dried off, and dressed, I felt drugged and dizzy. I staggered out of the bathroom, over to the couch, flopped down, and slept. I think I slept most of the day.

The noise of people walking around, moving chairs, and talking woke me up. Some Indian people had come to visit Wahsek about the death of a family member. It concerned the person who Wahsek said had been killed last night when the Owl was hooting. I couldn't help but wonder how he knew these things, and how he could be so accurate with his predictions. I felt it was none of my business and a private matter, and went outside to smoke and look around. It was sunny and cool, typical for a late fall day, with the smell of broken pumpkins, freshly picked apples, and smoked fish in the air. The fragrance of green oak wood, cedar, and fir drifted in the cool breeze as I got closer to the woodshed.

I watched that Hawk circling around again, and not knowing what else to do, and feeling a little bored, I thought I would try splitting some wood and kindling for the house. I didn't realize until I had piled up a fairly good stack of firewood that I had been doing all this without experiencing any pain. The Indian family was beginning to leave while I took a break and smoked a cigarette. They appeared sad and sullen, and as a consequence didn't bother to wave or look my way. The Hawk followed them down the road and out of sight, as if escorting them back.

Gina came out and hollered for me to come and get a cup of coffee. Wahsek scolded and said, "I'd rather not have you drink too much of that poison because I'm trying to use my herbs on you. I appreciate your help with the chores but you need time to rest and recuperate, okay?" He paused, looking sternly at me. "By the way, how do you feel?"

"I'm still sore and experiencing some pain, but nothing like it felt when I first woke up," I responded. "Should I leave the herbs in the tub, or do you want me to clean them out when I finish washing my underwear?"

He looked toward Gina and grinned. "She'll take care of it. She's like a nurse around here, among other things. She's a good woman, not too many Indian women around like her anymore. The younger ones all want to act like liberated White women. They don't know their roles and responsibilities, and could care less about it. Gina might be mean sometimes, but she's a traditional Indian woman with good upbringing and good values. She knows how to take care of the men, even if she has to whack them in the groin to get them to behave, right?" They both started laughing.

"Damn right," she growled back. "A woman who can control the jewels, rules. Even a Bear learned that lesson the hard way!"

We all started laughing again. "Speaking of Bears," I said curiously, "what has he got to do with my sickness and disease?"

The conversation suddenly moved into a state of seriousness. Wahsek walked over to his chair and motioned for me to follow. I sat down on the couch across from him and prepared to listen intently. "I couldn't help but notice when you first got here that you were watching the Hawk and Eagles, in the same way that I was studying their behavior. Did you understand what you were seeing? Did you think that such a display of natural signs and omens was a coincidence, or did you sense something supernatural about it all?"

"Well," I answered, "I felt that it had to mean something special but I didn't know what. It all goes back to when I tried to commit suicide." I started to cry, then proceeded to tell him everything that I had experienced, up to the part about a talking bird, other birds that had appeared during the death ceremony, the encounter with Rattlesnakes, the grandfather ghost, the dreams I'd had while thinking I was dead, the Coyote licking my face, and following an Eagle in blind faith to his house.

I went on to explain, "So in my own naive way, I thought that all the Eagles lined up in the trees, on fence posts, and flying around in the sky were a good omen, although I really don't know what signs and omens mean, and I felt at the time that it was a sign of confirmation. In other words, I thought that they were all the different Eagles who had been guiding me along the trip, and now it was their way of saying, this is the right place. But I got confused by the Hawk. I didn't understand what kind of sign he represented, and I didn't know why he was trying to fight the Eagles."

Wahsek got a wry grin on his face and responded, "The Great Spirit moves in mysterious, mystical, and mythic ways. He communicates to us through Nature by using a system of symbols. His language is telepathic, or what you might call psychic or spiritual, but it is also physical, although it appears to be supernatural because the Earth, the World, our Universe, as we know it, is both spiritual and physical. That is the ultimate truth and reality within realities. It is beyond most human realization, and there can be many realities even with differences of perception. That's why it's important to understand the symbolism. Otherwise to the common person it has no purpose or meaning. You had to become aware of this reality, to experience some of it, in order to start thinking about it. And you have to start thinking about it before you can begin to learn about it, and eventually comprehend it."

He paused for a few moments while I drank another cup of herbs Gina brought to me. "This is really difficult to explain," he continued, "but let me go on. So there were a number of significant things going on in your life all at the same time, including the sickness, disease, chronic pain, suffering, dying, death experience, symbolism, and supernatural activity. You were being tested. You were being taught lessons. You were being observed, studied, guided, disciplined, and cultivated by spirits and power itself. You were being guided by destiny, not fate, in the same way that the Salmon showed you." He paused again as if waiting for his point to get across.

"Strange things, mystical things, spiritual things, and encounters with the supernatural have been stalking you all your life as they do most shamans. Power itself has been stalking you. For example, the White doctors told you that you had an incurable disease, right? They called it chronic osteoarthritis. They also told you that they didn't know what caused it, and further, they had no way to stop it or cure it. They also said that they thought it could be inherited or possibly caused by stress, whatever that means. What do they call it, psychosomatic? When you were first being diagnosed, you told them that you felt constant pain eating away at your bones and joints. You saw the truth. You had an awareness of the reality of the situation better than they did with all of their scientific thinking and tools."

He stopped for a moment to look out the window toward the Sun, and then continued. "Their X-ray machines used for diagnosis proved the fact that something, indeed, was eating away at your bones and joints, that something was attacking your life and trying to devour it, but the thing that was actually doing it could not be identified by physical means. Why? Because it was spiritual in basis. Most sicknesses and disease are spiritual in basis even if manifested physically. But you knew what it was, you knew intuitively. You just didn't have the right system of knowledge, the right kind of education, the right kind of language to identify, describe, and deal with it in a conscious way."

At this point in the conversation I began to notice a change in his appearance and behavior. His eyes were becoming strange and animal-like. I couldn't actually see the pupils of his eyes because of the tremendous light being reflected. He looked possessed. The tone of his voice had been changing, and I got the impression that an entity was talking through him—that he was no longer the human being I had come to know as Wahsek, the same person who had been laughing with me earlier. He appeared to be doing what modern White people call channeling.

In a louder and more authoritative manner, he continued, "So the White doctors were close when speculating that stress could possibly be the cause of the disease. But they never told you what was causing the stress or what to do to stop the stress, right?"

He went on talking as if there were an audience listening. "We might say that your sickness and disease was caused by stress, not the kind of mental stress created by worrying about bills, trying to go to school and work full-time, taking on a new marriage, or by fear, shame, and guilt. Sure, that kind of stress can also cause sickness and disease. It can manifest into ulcers, high blood pressure, strokes, heart attacks, arthritis, cancer, all kinds of illness, or even drive a person crazy. The stress I am referring to is different. It is caused by phantoms, things that you can sense and feel but can't see. For example, remember when you and your Chicano friend had a bachelor pad together?"

"Yes," I said agreeably, "you brought that to my attention last night. You scolded me for violating the spiritual laws. You said I had been abusing and contaminating the regalia, which were power objects. You also said that my lack of ethics, morals, and spirituality, or the misuse of spirituality, was making me sick. That I had to atone for my transgressions, including the abuse of women, and for being verbally abused and molested by my aunts. You said that I had violated the laws and as a result I was being punished for my sins, right? I didn't understand all of it, though—the part about sex being dirty and menstruating women, and how it all relates to power."

I waited for a moment for my point to get across to him, and then continued, "But you were definitely right about the Bear being mad at me, and I still don't know how you could be so psychic to describe all the negative things I did wrong in such detail. So if I had any doubts, the incident with the Bear last night, as a sign or omen, definitely couldn't be ignored!"

"Well, this is the kind of truth that I have been trying to teach you," Wahsek replied. "I guess you could say it can only be known in a ah, ah—what is the word this White doctor who came to get a healing once told me—metaphysical sense? Truth exists in reality. It can only be known by discovery and experience. You can't try to rationalize about it. It has to be experienced in order to be confirmed, individually or collectively. Understand? So the truth of the matter in this case is, yes, you did have a disease and sickness caused by stress, there was something eating you alive, and Death was stalking you. In fact, it put you in a constant state of fear because you didn't know how to deal with it. Remember? You tried to tell your Chicano friend about the nightmares, about the feeling of an unknown presence in your bedroom, but at first he didn't believe it. He thought you were crazy, so you weren't about to tell anyone else. Then eventually he too began to hear it walking around, to feel it, and it scared the hell out of him."

He stopped talking for a moment as if waiting for a response, and then said, "It often got so bad that you both didn't want to come home at night. Your cultural power objects were knocked on the floor, the Bear-skin rug pulled off the bed, lamps moved, doors mysteriously opened and closed. You both thought it was a ghost or an evil spirit. But the activity didn't stop there, did it? The spirit of the Bear kept stalking you even when you got married and moved to a different apartment. It was relentless in its pursuit, and it began clawing and chewing on you, eating away at your bones and joints, penetrating your life force to the point that the pressure upon your mind-brain complex began to fight back. The negative energy had now been converted to a physical intruder, an innate alarm system went off, the body sent out scouts and warriors, but the human spirit was weakening. This entity that had invaded the organism was just too powerful. It was new and different. The mind and body became confused, and it didn't know how to deal with it. In a state of desperation the brain sent out a system of chemical warfare to destroy the invader, but the toxins released by the body now began to erode the same system it was sent to defend. The organism began to deteriorate physically from degeneration of the spirit."

I was speechless. I knew this guy only had an eighth-grade education, so his description of my problem and disease was incredible. He never ceased to impress me with his unique intelligence and knowledge. He was something far beyond the average human. He was more impressive than any philosopher or professor I had in college. What he said, and how he explained it, made sense—a lot more sense than any explanation the White physicians had given me.

"But like I said before," he asserted, "there is a reality beyond the physical as we know it, beyond the rational. That part of us that civilization and education in Western society has tried to suppress and eliminate is the spiritual side. And to some it will seem supernatural, but it hasn't been lost. It has only been hidden. It's still there, even in the brain and body, even in the mind but in the deeper levels of the mind, and it is out there, all around us in the physical world. And that is what saved you. Somewhere in your state of desperation, an ancient alarm system went off. Archaic symbols hidden in the subconscious mind began to surface and communicate. A signal from your tiny spirit to the Great Spirit went out into the Universe like an ancient song. The cry for help was so powerful that it broke through the physical doorway into the world of the spiritual unknown. That's how powerful the right kind of prayer can be, that's how strong the spiritual force can be, even more powerful than an unseen, phantom Bear suddenly becoming a physical reality to the point of breaking down a thick old door. So you see, this kind of knowledge is esoteric, it is primitive, ancient, secretive, and it has its own universal language. That language is based on natural symbols. To discover this secret and learn the truth, a person has to learn the language of Nature."

My mind was burning from the impact of his statements. A million questions began to whirl in my head. It was as if an old treasure trunk had suddenly been opened up, and I wanted to find out just what the treasures were and how valuable they were. I grasped at one of them, the concept of the symbol that he kept referring to. "So all this time the spirits, Nature, and the Great Spirit had been communicating to me but I just couldn't see it, hear it, or understand it, right?"

"Right." He nodded.

"So all the different birds, animals, and natural creatures that I have seen in dreams or come into contact with in a strange way while I was growing up were also part of this spiritual system of communication?" I paused. "The signs, or what some people call omens, had a definite purpose and meaning? They weren't just coincidental?" I said, all excited. "I thought so!"

"I told you before," he stated. "You already knew this. You knew it intuitively, in a spiritual way that had been suppressed. That is why you were so intrigued by the Eagles and Hawk fighting. But even when you had doubts in the past, and on the way up here, the Great Spirit and Nature would throw you another test, a wake-up call, or a reality check you might say. Different kinds of birds appeared, animals, a Salmon, and so forth."

"Is that why you decided to doctor me, because you saw all the Eagles and it was a good sign?" I asked confidently.

"No," he replied. "The Hawk you saw was my patroller and protector. He told me you were coming and that there would be problems. The Eagles were a good sign for you, and are usually a good power and omen, but in this situation they were symbolic challengers. I was being shown that I was going to be challenged by a lot of different spiritual problems related to one case, and that things would be complicated. So in some ways I knew that there would be more than just one cause to your sickness, and that helping you would become a longtime, spiritually complicated relationship."

It was getting late so I thought I would ask only a few more questions. "Can I ask another question? Is that how you're so psychic? In other words, do you use symbols and signs for diagnosis and curing of sickness and disease?"

He nodded and explained, "Yes, that's one of the ancient tools of the medicine man, but in addition, I can see and feel the pain, sickness, intruder, or cause of the problem."

I was getting more excited and asked, "You mean, see in a clairvoyant way, and feel like an empath? An empath is somebody who has the ability to sense, feel, and experience things beyond normal senses, in a psychic way—for example, the pain or sickness others might have or be experiencing."

"I don't really understand those words but it's like having a built-in X-ray machine in my brain or mind. I can see things in the human body, I can hear things, I can feel the patient's pain. I usually see and feel the sickness before the patient comes for a healing, or I experience all this in a dream. It's like this. Suppose a Snake is making you sick, causing ulcers and skin problems. You, as the patient, don't know what's causing the sickness, or maybe intuitively you might know when you tell the

Indian doctor, 'I feel like my stomach is all twisted up with Snakes.'"

Wahsek paused to scratch his head. "So by using a ceremony, the Indian doctor will smoke, talk to the Great Creator and the spirits, and then turn on his own innate mental power, and see what the problem is. Maybe you really do have a Snake, in symbolic and spirit form, in your body. The only way to cure you is to find out how it got there and take it out. Maybe it got into your body by biting you. Its spirit can enter you that way. Perhaps an *umaa,* or what you call a sorcerer, sent it against you; or maybe you killed a Snake without just cause and it wanted revenge. In this way it spiritually enters your body and begins to take control, to possess you. The only way to get rid of it completely is to capture it and take it out, destroy it so it can't return. Whiteman's medicine, drugs, or surgery can't get rid of it because it is spiritual in basis. It therefore takes a spiritual ceremony and spiritual tools and power to take it out. So that's an example of exorcism."

He reached over for a few feathers on the mantle and pointed authoritatively at me. "These things often put up a fight. They too have power, so I use another kind of power to take them out, like the power of a Hawk or Eagle. But once the intruder is removed it sometimes leaves behind a poison, and therefore I will try to suck the poison out with my mouth, or use herbs to purge it out, or sometimes use both methods. I guess you might say it's similar to following the laws of Nature. Everything in Nature is eaten by something else."

Almost laughing, he continued, "By the way, there's a difference between possession and repossession. Possession is when a ghost, bad spirit, or evil entity has entered your body and begins to take over your mind, and depending upon how much power it has, it will sometimes try to devour the soul. Thus in your case it really wasn't a situation of possession, at least not in a negative way, because good spirits, entities, ghosts, or certain natural powers can do this, too. The Bear was attacking you in response to the violations you had committed. It was stalking you and tormenting you because you had tormented it, and it was calling this problem to your attention. However, in your particular case there is more involved here with the Bear. That's why I said you were complicated. Your case is an example of repossession," he said, laughing. (This was a new concept, or reality, to me!)

"What do you mean, there's more involved with the Bear?" I asked.

"You're not ready for that kind of explanation and special knowledge right now, so for your own sake, let's just focus on the healing process and get you well," he said firmly. "It's getting late and I still have to go down to Hoopa and pray on a house. Would you be willing to help me pick the medicine I need, the bear grass and cedar, and drive me over and back?"

"Sure," I said. "I would feel honored!"

Wahsek told Gina that he was going to do spiritual work involving a death over at Hoopa and that he would be back in a couple of hours. He brought the keys and a couple of feed sack bags over to the truck. I had a little trouble getting it started but eventually we got down the hill and onto the curvy road. Then we had to turn up a long dirt road and go past a couple of farmhouses, one of which he said belonged to the Jones family, where we would be going. The dirt road began to turn into an old logging road, which eventually led into brushy terrain with a few cedar and fir trees scattered around. We got out and he proceeded to walk up to some stalks of isolated grass patches. I saw him bend over and pray, sprinkle tobacco as an offering, and then gather what he needed. Afterward he went up to a cedar tree and did the same thing.

On the way down the hill he began to talk in his Native language and wrap the bear grass into a circle, and then he did the same with the cedar, making wreaths similar to what people put on the doors during the Christmas holidays. He was not talkative, except for periodic mumbling and singing, which I assumed were prayers to the Great Creator and his spirits. He did, however, tell me that the wreaths were used as a symbol and source of power to keep the deceased person, the ghost, or any other ghosts or bad spirits from entering the family's house; otherwise without this part of the protection ceremony, the ghosts or bad spirits might try to come back and take the life of another family member. He said, "Nothing can break the power of the circle. It's holy. It has no beginning and it has no end."

Although I did not assist him in the ceremony I did get to observe his actions. For example, he greeted the family members at the front door, went inside, and smoked his sacred pipe and prayed with them. He smudged up the house with the Grizzly Bear root (angelica root), and then I saw one of the women sweeping the house with a handmade broom from Douglas fir boughs. The circular wreaths were hung on the front and back doors of the house. I didn't hear him singing as he usually does when doing spiritual work but I did hear a lot of crying and mourning inside. A Hawk circled the house the whole time he was there and at one point it screamed, made a fast dive toward the backyard, and then emerged with a large Snake in its talons. It left when we left, just slightly after sunset.

He was solemn on the way back and didn't talk much. Upon our return to his house he said, "I'm going to go in and wash up in pepperwood leaves tea to cleanse and protect myself because I don't have a sweat lodge here to use. Then afterward we'll eat and get started on the healing ceremony for you, okay?"

I was starved but the only thing they would let me eat was acorn soup. Gina said, "This is our traditional food. It's sacred, but it is also medicine. Wahsek doesn't want you eating anything else for a while except these acorns. I guess even the White people discovered that the acorns have power. This one White woman told me she did research on it and found out the acorns are high in potassium, magnesium, zinc, and other vitamins and minerals. But most of all, it has the strength of the oak tree and it will help build strength in your body and spirit."

We sat down to the table with kerosene lamps providing ample light and the wood heater in the front room cracking from a new fire. The kitchen was a little scattered with cracked acorn shells, an old hand-cranked type of meat grinder covered with acorn flour, a few piles of herbs, and a variety of pots and pans indicating a freshly cooked dinner. The coffee smelled great, somewhat stronger from being cooked on an old woodstove, but I knew Wahsek wouldn't let me have any while I was being doctored.

The acorn soup was prepared like mush, or cream of wheat, and much to my surprise it didn't have a bitter taste. Acorns are naturally saturated with tannic acid, and as a result they must be dried for about a year, then hulled and dried, and then ground up into a flour and leached with water. Prior to European contact and up to about the 1930s, the process was all done by hand. Acorns were stored and dried in large beautiful baskets, then hulled and sorted with a large, round, flat basket, and the acorns were converted into flour by being pounded with a stone pestle and mortar. Another specially designed basket, loosely woven so that water could seep out, was used for the leaching process. Sometimes the acorn flour was actually leached out in the creek by making a stone and sand leacher.

Acorns leached in the hot sunlight had a tendency to be sweeter than acorns prepared in the house and leached with cheesecloth. At any rate, the acorns were to the California Indians what corn was to the Iroquois, Cherokee, or Navajo. It was their traditional food and provided a yearly staple resource, the kind of food that can save people during famine and natural catastrophes.

I told Gina the acorns were delicious. It was the first time I had tasted any since I was a teenager. The compliment made her smile with pride. Wahsek interrupted and teased, "Yeah, if she could make love as good as she cooks, I'd never get any doctoring or spiritual work done!"

Gina reached for her cane in a threatening but teasing gesture. She retorted, "And if that thing of yours was long like an Elk's instead of small like a Mountain Lion's, then maybe I would be a little slimmer and happier around here."

Wahsek got a grin on his face and then snapped back, "Just like you women. You all think that bigger is better. A bigger boat, a bigger diamond, a bigger house, even a bigger wanger, huh? And sooner or later you all finally learn that quality is better than quantity. Now just think Gina, if I had that kind of power you would be waiting in line for your turn, having to compete with all those other cows in the herd. Now how would you like that?"

Gina got embarrassed and teased back, directing it to me this time. "Well, at least yours is not as bad as the Bear power, a big and stout manlike creature who in comparison has an unusually small wanger, and I should know that for a fact, huh?" They both looked at me and laughed so hard they started choking on their food. Was this an exhibition of their psychic powers or just a good guess? I wondered. And what does having a certain kind of animal power or ally have to do with a man's virility?

I was about to ask but then decided not to make myself a further target of ridicule. I was done with the acorn soup and homemade piece of acorn bread, so I decided to sit and wait for them to finish their meal while I drank herbal tea. I thought about how they joked around so much about sex. I figured it was a subtle form of teaching, that there were lessons or some form of knowledge to be learned because as wise people they really didn't waste words. Maybe it was all just a form of psychological release as a result of living such an isolated and religiously strict life. My pondering stopped when Gina motioned for me to help clean up the kitchen while Wahsek went outside to pray in preparation for the healing ceremony.

After lighting his pipe and making an invocation he turned to Gina and said, "We have to *pegasoy* over him for violations against the Bear and get all that cleared up. The spirits are telling me that he will also need to confess for violating Deer and Elk meat, and other four-legged wild animals such as Raccoon, Rabbit, and Squirrel." At that point he turned to me and said, "You heard what I told Gina right?" There was a pause while he waited for a response. "So I am going to ask you, on behalf of the Great Creator and the spirits, is it true or not true that you have eaten those kind of four-legged wild animals that were cooked and shared with women on their moontime?"

I thought for a long time about all the different species of animals I could have eaten while living with different relatives and responded,

"Yes, I believe that could be true, although I don't know if the women were on their menses when they cooked and shared the food. But to be on the safe side I will confess and admit to that and ask the Great Creator, spirits, and the animals that were violated to forgive me, and I promise to be more careful in the future."

"*Skuyent,*" he said loudly, which means "very good." They both asked for my forgiveness and blew wind on me three times, as if trying to blow feathers out of my hair with their mouths. He explained, "This is the way it is in healing. The world is governed by a set of physical and spiritual laws. It is against the Great Creator's Laws, the Natural Laws, and the laws of the animals and other creatures to be violated. An example of violating them is to hunt them without ceremony, without making payment in exchange for taking their life, to kill them without just cause and waste their life and power. It is also against the laws for a menstruating woman to cook, share, or eat any kind of four-legged wild animal, and even certain birds, fish, or reptiles. I don't care if you are a Cheyenne from Montana and live on Buffalo, the laws still apply. It doesn't matter what race, color, religion, or culture a person comes from; ignorance is no excuse for violating the law. The laws might be considered old-fashioned, archaic, dogmatic, or even ridiculous by modern people, but that viewpoint doesn't change anything. This is Indian Country they are all in, and the laws are strong and operating in full force here. So it doesn't make any difference what people believe or practice in Europe or Los Angeles; if they violate the law they will, indeed, become sick sooner or later from it. Understand?"

"Yeah, sure, I'm willing to learn and have a code of spiritual laws and ethics to live by if it will help keep me in balance and healthy," I said. "I don't care what other people may think or say, I've learned the hard way, so from here on out I'm going to be more careful, but without getting paranoid about it, okay"?

"Good, then you're learning to be accountable for your own actions but also for the actions of others, because sometimes, innocent bystanders can get hurt. All I can say at this point is be careful how you hunt, what you hunt, and who you share your food with. If not, that Deer's spirit will be following you home to see how you handle his body and power. That's why we consider our relations in Nature as sacred, they are special, they are not just a food resource but also a source of medicine. But like any other kind of medicine, if it's not handled in the right and proper way it can turn into a poison."

He paused and looked at me firmly, and then continued, "I'm not saying that every person on the face of the Earth will be punished instantly if they violate the Natural Laws, but I am saying that sooner or later, sometimes decades later, someone will have to pay for the transgression, whether it be the violator or his or her family, the offspring, or all of them. So learn the laws and try to abide by the laws and your life will be healthier and happier."

I took time to let it all sink into my heart and mind and then asked, "What about the Ten Commandments? Do they apply also?"

He looked at me curiously and then turned to Gina, who recited the Ten Commandments to him and then turned to me. "He doesn't know what you are talking about. He hasn't read the Bible and he wasn't raised in Christian beliefs or religion," she said as if apologizing. "But to answer your question as his interpreter, I would have to say yes, we have similar laws—assuming those Ten Commandments are also God's laws, and they seem like they are but we have more than just ten for a person to follow and use as a spiritual code to live by."

Wahsek interrupted. "We don't want to tell you too much at this point in your development and transformation; otherwise it will overwhelm you. So now I would like to get on with the doctoring. The spirits are anxious to sing and dance."

Gina interrupted with a reminder. "Don't forget, he also needs to confess for trying to commit suicide. It's against the Great Creator's Law to kill ourselves because we are all put on this Earth for a reason. We don't have the spiritual right or authority to terminate ourselves or the lives of other people."

I began to pray and cry in response while they pleaded on my behalf, and then they finished by blowing over me. I was now hoping that the methods they used in doctoring would also serve to blow away the shame and guilt I felt in my mind, heart, and soul. I also wanted to talk to them about this philosophical concept, and their ideas about mercy killing and abortion, but it was obvious we didn't have time for such questions during a ceremony.

Once again Wahsek sang, danced, and used the water and his hands to work on me. Sometimes he appeared to be pulling out negative energy, and at other times I could feel his hands becoming hotter, as if transmitting healing power and positive energy into my head, back, spine, and major bone joints. He did not use his mouth or a pipe to suck anything out this time, however. He mainly used his hands, occasionally massaging certain damaged and swollen areas of my body. I could feel a strange heaviness in the room, which in turn made me feel as if I had been drugged. Although Wahsek and Gina were singing and dancing very fast, in perfect rhythm, they gradually appeared to be doctoring in slow motion.

The old farmhouse was filled with the presence of many ghosts, spirits, and entities who appeared to be singing and dancing. I could swear that I actually saw them, although it was periodically vague in my mind. Was it just a figment of my imagination? Eventually I passed out from the hypnotic singing, dancing, cane pounding, the warmth of the room, and the light flickering from a distant kerosene lamp. I guess it was all just too spooky for me. I must have gone into a very deep sleep because the next morning I didn't remember having any dreams to share.

Wahsek liked to use dreams that he might have had after the healing ceremony, and any dreams that the patient might have had, as part of his shamanic diagnosis and psychotherapy. While eating breakfast he told me of one dream involving a Grizzly Bear, and he asked me if I had ever had any dreams about the Grizzly Bear. It was at that point that I told him about certain dreams I'd had as a child, then about the car accident I'd gotten killed in when I was a teenager living on the East Coast, and the dream I'd had about a Grizzly Bear chasing me after I awakened from a coma. I was hoping for an interpretation from him but it never came.

When I tried to probe him, he became defensive. "One of these days, in the future, you will know why you had those dreams. Besides that, everything else seems to be cleared up, and after your bath in herbs you can be discharged from doctoring here. I want you to spend the next few days at home drinking some herbs I've made up for you, and you will be required to abstain from sex and food cooked by unclean people, okay?"

I felt a certain lump of sadness suddenly hit my throat because I didn't expect the healing ceremony and process to end so abruptly. "So does that mean we're finished?" I asked sheepishly.

He sensed my sadness and confusion and responded more affectionately. "Yeah, that's about it. The spirits don't seem to be reporting anything else in through dreams, signs, omens, or telepathic communication. You don't have any more swelling or pain, right?"

"No," I said, "I feel better than I have in months. I feel great. Do you think it will last?"

"That's all up to you and how you conduct your life from here on out," he said as if trying to reassure me, "and I don't think it will be necessary to engage in any more philosophical questions and discussions. You can always come back for a visit if you want to and we can just talk, okay?" That offer made me feel relaxed and confident that I hadn't done anything wrong, and it also made me realize that Wahsek did have a farm and life of his own to manage. After breakfast, and after bathing in herbs, I gathered my stuff and prepared to leave.

I wanted to give them both a big hug to show my appreciation and affection but I sensed that was not their way. I started to leave through the front door, took one good look around to seal the impression in my memory, and thanked them both for all the help and hospitality they'd given me. A large Pileated Woodpecker landed on the apple tree and started banging away. Wahsek walked with me outside and pointed to it. "See that? He's the doctor reporting in, and hear the Flickerbird whistle? The spirits are reporting in that someone else will be coming to get doctored in a couple of days, so I better get back to my ranch chores, huh? Take care and come back and visit us again."

I reached over to Gina and gave her my last pack of cigarettes and a twenty-dollar bill. "Here," I said, "thanks for all your help, and I don't think you're really as mean as you would like people to believe."

She took the gift and donation and replied humbly, "Take care, Neekwich. I know we will see you again."

As I got into the car I couldn't help but stop and ask, "What does Neekwich mean? Did she call me a witch of some sort?"

Wahsek laughed and hollered back, "She knows things too you know. She's a seer. It means Grizzly Bear. That's you, right?"

I hadn't the slightest idea what they were talking about, so I just laughed, thinking they were teasing me again, not realizing at the time just how much truth I had learned from this short visit—and that Wahsek was right about my having unfinished business with the Bear spirit.

Flowing with the Current of Time

I had plenty to think about on the long drive back to the city. When I left, the Chicken Hawk escorted me down the hill. Then I didn't see much of anything except Ravens coming in occasionally, and at several points they actually flew right alongside me, guiding or following the car. I did see a couple of Buzzards but I didn't know what that meant as a sign. I was sure, though, that they must have some purpose or meaning. I tried to telepathically and verbally communicate with them but I didn't receive any response, at least none that I was cognizant of. I did, however, become aware that the Buzzards seemed to appear whenever there were problems in the road, such as construction going on, a pedestrian walking, cattle in the way, or tourists going real slow in their trailers.

It didn't take long to slide back into the physical reality of city life, marriage, school, and work. I stayed "clean" as instructed for the required four days. I didn't eat in restaurants on the way down, or while at home. As a substitute I just bought fruit that I figured was safe and made sure to wash everything off with water. I also drank the herb teas that Wahsek had given me.

Lilly was really happy to see me and couldn't believe how much I had changed. It was as if I had gone through a complete metamorphosis. She said I looked stronger, healthier, happier, and that I had a strange light about me. I could feel us becoming closer as the weeks and months went by. I started to become more active in Indian activities, along with trying to finish college and work part-time. I now started to flow with the current of life, rather than fight against it.

Indian consciousness was really waking up in the San Francisco Bay Area, California in general, and different parts of the nation. I became a student leader attending local, state, and national meetings on issues involving Indian education, culture, religion, rights, and the environment. I could feel my pride and identity taking shape. Some of the meetings became very emotional, the concerns and issues really touching hearts and nerves, and as a result I saw the movement waking up a lot of full-bloods, mixed breeds, and wanna-bes.

It was during this time that I got an opportunity to meet a variety of leaders. Some were tribal leaders involved in politics on reservation problems, others were medicine men and women, and still others were considered radicals and militants.

During this time, for example, Richard Oaks, who was probably responsible for waking up the First Nations people with the symbolic takeover of Alcatraz, got killed. Lehman Brightman, a tall, lean, well-muscled Lakota Indian who was known for wearing a large black hat, had formed an organization called United Native Americans, and he was stirring up Indian people and communities about their civil rights. We became close friends over the years and I'll still never forget just how many times he put his life on the line, cussing and fistfighting prejudiced Whites, and often sellout Indians, in order to help our tribal people return to Nativism.

Groups like the Native American Student Alliance, the Tribal Chairman's Association, and the National Congress of American Indians were all holding conferences and meetings. This period also witnessed the birth of the Indian Historical Society with the First Convocation of Native American Scholars. Indian leaders were finally starting to emerge all across the country, who in turn became role models for many of us to emulate. California tribes had their fair share of problems as a result of termination, which was a law that the United States government used to remove California tribes from former treaty obligations. It was a forced policy of acculturation. Termination took away our land, our rights, our religion, our ceremonial grounds, language, culture—everything. We were no longer federally "recognized" as Karuk, Yurok, Pomo, Hupa, and so forth—hence no longer eligible for sovereign status and federal support and benefits. Rather, we were forced to become citizens of the United States. A number of us "educated Indian college students" found ourselves going back to the *rancherias* to help with local issues, although in reality we were going back to find our roots and learn about our heritage, culture, religion, and rights. (California Indian land bases were too small in acreage to be considered reservations; instead they were called *rancherias,* a name borrowed from the Spanish.) I frequently found myself going over to Pit River to help on land restoration, up to Nisqually to work on fishing rights, and back to the coast to defend Indian burial grounds and hunting and fishing rights, and to protest discrimination. Finally, in 1980 we proved termination illegal and won our federal recognition back, but we never regained our land and all the rest.

So the Indian movement, even the more radical activities that eventually got the movement national attention, became a spiritual awakening and rebirth for many of us. It was also during this time that I got to meet Elders from different reservations, who in turn became my teachers, and different medicine men who took a special interest in me and started teaching me spiritual practices. I didn't feel pulled to the Plains Indian religion as did most of my peers, although I did participate in their pipe ceremonies, sweat lodge rituals, peyote ceremonies, and all-night-long healing ceremonies. I knew I had my own river in life to follow.

I felt pulled to the Iroquois side of me and the California side of me, and it wasn't long before I started to learn from Mad Bear Anderson, Rolling Thunder, Beeman Logan, and John Fire Lame Deer, and spent some quality time with Thomas Banyaca, Grandpa David Monongye, and the high Hopi spiritual leader, Dan Katchavanaga. I also finally got the opportunity to connect with a full-blooded Indian cultural-spiritual leader who I thought was my real father, the person I had been secretly looking for all these years: Charles Robert Thom. I met him at one of the conferences where he was doing a demonstration on Indian songs, Coyote stories, and ceremonial dances.

I felt him before I saw him. He was standing in a crowd surrounded by a group of admirers and talking. I kept looking at him from a distance and he kept staring back. I got nervous all over and began to feel a force pulling in my solar plexus—almost the same feeling I had when I first met Lilly, but this feeling was different. I finally got the courage to go over and talk to him, to introduce myself, and he seemed nervous and embarrassed. I asked him if he could stay and visit with me for the night, after the conference, and he agreed. This is one of the stories he told:

How Coyote Painted the Birds

A long, long time ago, Coyote was living upriver, up the mighty Klamath River, by Katimeen. One day he got up after sleeping all night and felt ashamed of himself. He woke up just before daylight, when it was still dark, and he started to rub his eyes. His eyelids were stuck and irritated from the campfire smoke in his den. He had used the wrong kind of wood, a pitch-type wood instead of manzanita. He said to himself, "Damn, I shouldn't have slept all night. I missed out on a good hunting trip. I am starved." Then he noticed something in the way, and looked down. "Hey, what's this?" he said, looking at his penis. It was sticking straight out and bouncing around. "Gosh darn it, I must have been dreaming about women all night," he scolded himself, "but that's okay. I don't have to follow the hunting laws. I got my own kind of power."

He was walking kind of funny down the trail, you know, like this. He was wobbling because the hard-on made him sway from side to side. It wouldn't go away. It wouldn't go soft. It just stayed big and hard.

Now off in the distance he saw something. It looked like a couple of women. One was standing up, reaching out to gather moss from the tree limbs. From the shape of the silhouette he could tell that the woman was young, well built, firm, and beautiful. The other woman appeared to be bent over gathering roots or herbs. The closer he got the more excited he became thinking that he had so much power that he would jump both of them.

Being who he was, he didn't care who the women belonged to, whether they were married or not, young or old. And being horny all the time, he lacked self-control. He was still rubbing his eyes, hoping to see better, when he decided to take off running and make a jump into one of them. He missed the first one, who was bent over, and got stuck in the one standing up, a little bent over in posture.

"Good choice," he said to himself. "This one is really firm and tight." He tried to withdraw a couple hours later after rubbing himself raw, but it wouldn't come out. He grabbed the woman and pulled every which way but still couldn't break loose. By then the Sun had come up and he noticed that he was stuck in a tree stump. He started howling in pain, scared half to death. Pretty soon all the different animal people and birds came around to find out who was making so much noise. Coyote pleaded with them to help but they just laughed at him. Besides, nobody trusted him enough to help anyway, and they left. But Coyote, he is very smart. He figured out a plan.

Now back in those days the birds were all white and they really didn't like it. So Coyote, well, he made up different-colored paints from the moss, dried clay, and plants that were close to the old stump. He hollered at the birds to return and help him. At first nobody came. Then he saw Woodpecker over on the other stump, hammering away for worms. He said, "Hey Mr. Woodpecker, I can make you the most beautiful bird in the world if you will help me."

The Woodpecker stopped and listened. "Yeah, that would be good," he said to Coyote. "I want the best colors so I can be the most powerful."

Coyote reached down with the end of his tail and stuck it in the red paint, and he gave Woodpecker a beautiful red head. Then he dipped his paws into the black and colored the Woodpecker some more. This made Woodpecker so proud that he started pecking like crazy, to show off, and it attracted the other birds.

In a little while more and more came. They got their different colors and immediately went to work, trying to set Coyote free. Eagle, Fish Hawk, Redtail, and some of the larger birds of prey couldn't do much with the shape of their beaks, so Coyote didn't give them the brightest colors. After some time he started running out of paint but he was also getting loose. About that time Raven and Crow came by. They saw how the other birds looked, so beautiful and colorful. They said, "Hey, Coyote, we want beautiful colors, too." But it was too late. Coyote fell down upon the ground and was free.

"Why should I help you?" he growled. "You never did nothing for me!"

"Because we always help you and your cousin, the Wolf, in hunting," they said. "We are the ones who show you where the game is when you're tired and having bad luck." Knowing that was true but not having any paint left, Coyote agreed. He reached down and got the last remaining color and painted them both black, and then he laughed and ran down into the creek to wash off. This is why you sometimes see the Crows or Ravens hollering at Coyote in a field or down by the creek. They are mad at what he did.

The stories Charlie Thom told started to push buttons in the deeper levels of my subconscious mind. Ancient symbols and visions emerged so fast that I got dizzy. But I really felt an awakening and calling inside when he sang certain songs that intuitively sounded familiar. I knew I had heard these songs before and I couldn't hold back the emotions. I felt a primal calling to return home.

Lilly was just as impressed and pleased as I was to meet him. I never told her that I believed he was my real father. I was too embarrassed about possibly being a bastard child. I also didn't think it would be right to tell anyone until I had proof, or at least permission from the man.

We had a good visit at dinner and told a lot of jokes. I was full of questions about him, me, my mother, my life, and the bitterness and resentment I had been carrying all these years. I didn't want to overwhelm him, so when Lilly wasn't in the room I just asked him about myself and if I could be his son—a product of his encounter with my mother during the war. His response was defensive and evasive. "It could be a possibility," he said, "because I know I have children all over the country, probably even overseas. But let's give it time for me to think about it, then when I make my decision we can go from there." It was a long number of years before a decision was made, so in the meantime I didn't tell anyone. I just kept the secret to myself, hoping, waiting, knowing that someday the truth would come out one way or the other and then I would have to deal with it.

I finally graduated from Hayward State College and started looking around for a job. Some of the Indian students I had met told me they were trying to get Native American programs started at Humboldt State College, up near Eureka, California. This was during the emergence of ethnic studies programs and the beginning of other ethnic-minority programs, such as the Educational Opportunity Program, Special Services, Talent Search, Upward Bound, and Affirmative Action, all of which were in the embryonic stages of development, with the Blacks politically taking the lead and the Chicanos and Indians coming in on the apron strings. An administrative position in minority affairs became available at Humboldt State University. I applied for it and the local Indian students and other minority groups supported me. I was hired to start up and manage programs in ethnic studies and Native American studies, an Indian teacher education program, and a Native American natural resources project. Lilly and I moved north into the heart of the ancient Redwoods. I found us an apartment thirty miles north of Eureka in a little fishing town called Trinidad.

Little did I realize at the time that it was a power center, a doorway into the spirit world and other dimensions, and another new path into the unknown for me. Now, after all these years, I was beginning to realize that destiny had been guiding me all this time to this sacred place, and from that point on my life changed drastically.

Lilly was pregnant, and after a number of months in Trinidad she decided it would be safer to go back home to Hayward to have the baby. We didn't know too many people in our fairly new area. At least this way she would have her mother, aunts, and sisters for support down there. We had a boy and named him Frank Kanawha, the first name after his grandfather on Lilly's side, and the Indian name from a dream I had. It meant Great Water, and it was partially in honor of the oldest river in the United States where some of my mother's ancestors originally lived. I was proud and happy but also concerned because the child had been born with a crooked foot.

It didn't take long, however, to get caught up in work. I had ideas about developing new programs to address the specific needs of our Indian people, the ethnic-minority groups, and nontraditional students. The best way to approach it was through a cooperative effort by volunteer professors on campus and participants from the groups in need.

I wrote grants, secured funding, and planned and developed new programs in student services and in academic departments, and then I was assigned the responsibility to coordinate and manage the diverse programs. I got Charlie a job as a cultural specialist because of his unique knowledge, but it also gave me an opportunity to spend time with him. More Indian and ethnic-minority people got hired on campus, more Indian and ethnic-minority students began attending and graduating from college, and after a while the programs began to function efficiently with a minimum of supervision, so I began to turn my free time toward teaching. Eventually I was teaching full-time as the classes became popular, and within a number of years I became the coordinator of the Native American/ethnic studies department, with a combined teaching and administrative assignment.

In the meantime, I was swept up in the current of Indian affairs. There was always something going on, something new to learn, and a new problem that had to be dealt with in the local community and on the nearby reservation. The cultural activities and events were going strong. It seemed like the Indian people all over were waking up and wanting to learn more about their heritage, culture, and religion in order to preserve and perpetuate them. I became deeply engrossed in cultural activities, met new Elders, and became more involved in pursuing my own spirituality.

Beeman Logan, the Seneca chief and medicine man, had been coming out to northwestern California a lot to doctor local people over at the Hoopa Reservation. Some of the other medicine men came with him, and as a consequence we were often involved in ceremonies. My dreams increased—dreams about spirits, certain places in Nature, certain people, and dreams about animals, birds, fish, plants, trees, mountains, waterfalls, and a mermaid from Trinidad. I felt they were teaching and guiding me, but sometimes the dreams were scary and confusing so that I felt tormented. In some dreams I turned into a Bear, or was swimming with Sharks, or sleeping with Wolves, or flying with Ravens and Eagles. I shared the dreams with Beeman, and he told me that I was destined to become a medicine man.

Beeman's assessment was confirmed when I went to the other medicine men in private and asked for an interpretation of the same dreams. They all said that if I lived a proper life, followed the shamanic training, and passed my tests, I could become a medicine man like them; but I would have different powers and use a different approach in doctoring, an approach that would vary from patient to patient and case to case, and would draw upon all the knowledge and methods I had learned from my mentors.

Although Beeman was willing to put me into a secret apprenticeship, he said I would eventually have many teachers, because of the special kinds of dreams I had been given. He also said I was being tested, guided, and cultivated by the ancestor spirits, powers from Nature, and the Great Creator. Thus it was from him that I first learned how to conduct and use the sacred sweat lodge ceremony for developing my own psychic gifts and for helping others in need. I also got to spend time with Rolling Thunder whenever he came through the area; I frequently went over and stayed with him.* Because a number of the spiritual mentors lived so far away, I had to be guided by long-distance telephone conversations. I guess you could call it a form of distance learning, but in a cultural and shamanistic context.

A new mystical experience, a new dream, a new encounter with spirits, or a new sickness, accident, or injury usually served as the catalyst for contacting Beeman, Rolling Thunder, John Fire Lame Deer, Mad Bear Anderson, and eventually, Wahsek on occasion. Something strange was always

---

*Rolling Thunder (John Pope) was a famous medicine man—the Billy Jack movies were based on him, as well as some Grateful Dead songs and a Bob Dylan tribute. For more information on Rolling Thunder, see Doug Boyd's book *Rolling Thunder* published by Dell in 1976.

happening to me, especially during sacred sweat lodge ceremonies, at local rituals and dances, or whenever I was around the older medicine men.

Over the years they all contributed to my growth, development, success in completing my apprenticeship, and my official ordainment by the Elders as a bona fide shaman—or what the local Indian people called an Indian doctor. All in all it took about fifteen years, with the major portion of my training under Wahsek and Charlie Red Hawk Thom. However, this was supplemented with support and guidance by Native spiritual leaders from other tribes, such as Flora Jones who was Wintun, Chief Harry Watts who was Seneca, Rudolph Socktish who was Hupa, Gina the Hupa medicine woman, Wahsek's sister Bunny who was a medicine woman, and Dewey George who was a Yurok holy man. I also came into contact with a few disguised sorcerers who periodically tried to sneak in on the action, making me think all the while that they too were shamans sent with a vision to teach me. Although I got hurt from my ignorance and encounters with them, they were an important part of my growth and development because I learned a lot from my mistakes. A person can't really learn to appreciate the good without knowing what the bad is like. Wherever there is light there is darkness, wherever there is positive there is negative, and the forces of light and dark, good and evil have been fighting each other since time immemorial. And the evil ones are tricky. They can come in any form, take on the appearance of anyone or anything, often fooling the best of the best, except the true Great Spirit of the Universe.

It wasn't long after I was hired at Humboldt that I started making more and more contact with Charlie. He was a cultural specialist and spiritual leader in the community. As a consequence I kept bumping into him at different meetings, activities, and events. We began to visit with each other more, although there was never any mention of me being his bastard son, and it wasn't long before I began to realize that he was also becoming my mentor.

After he was hired on campus in a grant project we became like two peas in a pod. He told me, "If you are going to serve the people, especially the local Indian people, then you have got to learn about your heritage and culture along with the other younger people. Don't feel embarrassed or ashamed that you have been cheated out of that opportunity all these years, because so have they. There will be times when you will be learning along with them but there will be other times, special times, when you will learn esoteric forms of knowledge in secrecy. Too much jealousy exists among our Indian people, in fact all over, even with other people in different cultures who you're interacting with. Therefore the spiritual experiences you have with me should be kept confidential for a long time. In the meantime, just call me Uncle Charlie like everyone else does out of cultural respect, okay?"

The apartment in Trinidad was really intense. My dreams became profound and even after all these years, my dreams and visions have never been so vivid as they were when I lived in the Trinidad area. Lilly and I both loved it, and although it was a prime vacation spot for tourists all over the world, mainly in the summer, it served as a resort year-round.

We spent many long hours on the beaches together and with the newborn, looking for agates, fishing off the rocks, gathering seashells, watching Sea Lions, Whales, Porpoises, and occasionally an Orca or Great White Shark. We also spent a lot of time together walking in the ancient Redwoods, observing Elk herds, Deer, Bear, Raccoons, Mountain Lions, Weasels, Bobcats, and every kind of bird imaginable. The region was lush with wildlife, on the coast, in the woods, up in the small surrounding mountains, and inland up the Klamath, Smith, Trinity, and Eel Rivers. But the environment also became a site for shamanic adventure and a school for me, and gradually my time with Lilly became replaced with quality time spent with Charlie. He even took me to sacred places and taught me how to pray.

Eventually we bought a small farmhouse in Trinidad, but my neglect toward Lilly caused marital problems. "Indians this, spiritual stuff that. You didn't marry me, you married the damn culture!" she would say. I felt bad but couldn't help it. I was being swept away in a current, one adventure after another, and constantly learning.

Charlie taught me how to hunt, how to fish, how to make cultural tools, weapons, and artifacts. We often went on long trips and stayed away several days at a time. He taught me how to sing local songs, how to dance in local ceremonies, and how to gather and use local plants and herbs. He also taught me how to make Indian cards and become a good gambler, and it wasn't long before he also taught me that it was okay to be a Coyote and have more than one woman to meet a man's needs.

His main powers were the Coyote and the Redtail Hawk, so he was always on the go, just like the Hawk and Coyote, and he was a trickster. Sometimes I got hurt from his teachings and adventures and had to go get doctored by Beeman, Rolling Thunder, Florence Jones, or Wahsek. But this was how I learned, the hard way, by making mistakes.

One time he took me hunting in the sacred high country, up near a place called Chimney Rock, and Lilly went with us. I didn't realize it at the time but it was the same place that I had seen in a vision after my deadly car accident when I was a teenager. It was also the same place that I had seen in dreams, and in visions while in the sweat lodge, dreams and visions that I'd consulted Beeman and Charlie about. They both told me that the spirits from that holy place were calling me, and that some-day I would have to go there and be tested, but they didn't know when. I didn't realize at the time that this was one of the test dates.

Charlie was an excellent hunter. He had both skill and a special kind of power for hunting. He had been hunting all his life, taught and trained by his grandfather and uncles, and he was always in the woods, watch-ing, listening, studying, and stalking something, especially Deer. In all the years that we hunted together, and it didn't make any difference what time of the year it was for him, I never saw him miss a shot. The concept of poaching was foreign to him.

He said, "That's the Whiteman's law. It's not the law of Nature. We have our own laws, aboriginal custom and laws. Under the Great Creator's Laws we, as Natives, have the right to hunt, to fish, to gather our tradi-tional foods and herbs, and to practice our rituals and ceremonies. Just because another race of people come to our country and use force to take everything away from us doesn't mean their way is right. It's not fair and just. The land in Indian Country will always be ours just as long as we pray for it and take care of it. The Whiteman can keep stealing it and the resources, he can put it into Forest Service land, BLM, or park systems, give it to timber and railroad companies, or whatever. It will always be ours. The White people never gave us a fair price and just compensation for the land and resources they took from us. They don't pray for it and care for it, so they will never really own it. All they can do is destroy it with avarice."

He paused, looking at me sternly. "But you mark my words. One day they will come to the Indian and say, 'We realize we really messed up here. We need your help to clean up the mess and survive. We realize that you Indians aren't so dumb after all. We realize that you are the original conservationists. We're sorry that we put you in jail for hunting, fishing, trapping, and gathering. We're sorry that we told you not to burn the land during certain times of the year. We're sorry that we didn't believe you that Nature is alive, that it has an intelligence, that it is full of spirits, and that it is sacred.' So remember these things I teach you, even if you have to go to jail. Remember what I am telling you because they will try to scapegoat on someone else for depletion of the natural resources, pollution of the world, extinction of the species in Nature, or the violent destruction of Nature as it tries to fight back. We have a right to carry on our heritage, culture, and religion. We have a right to survive. We have a right to believe in and follow our own laws."

Charlie truly believed that hunting was more than subsistence and religion. It was also like a game to him. It was not only a right in exercising a form of spirituality, but also a form of natural play. It was a way of understanding and using power, so there were times that he took me into the woods, mountains, prairies, creeks, and rivers just to teach me how to listen, observe, and learn.

He taught me how to use my five senses and he tried to teach me how to use my sixth sense, to be able to see the animal or other creature in my mind, in a clairvoyant way, and to use creative imagination, visualization techniques, and instinct to see, feel, hear, or smell the creature before it appeared physically. He said his grandfather taught him the art of hunting in the same way, but he also taught him how to use the sweat lodge for developing hunting power.

For example, he said, "My grandfather would take me into the sacred sweat lodge, you know, the permanent kind that is built subterranean, into the ground, and made from Cedar planks. He would tell me stories and make me recite and learn ancient hunting myths. He taught me how to sing hunting songs, along with other kinds of songs, until I could get my own song. He taught me how to concentrate and use my mind, and with certain kinds of mental exercises I was taught to prevision the hunt, preenact the hunt, and preattain the hunt. I sat in the sweat lodge for long hours, fasting, burning *keeshwoof* root (Grizzly Bear medicine, angelica root), and praying. Sometimes I had to rub *keeshwoof* all over my body or Douglas fir boughs to make medicine, to get the human scent off my body, and use those powers to help me concentrate and see mental images." Charlie looked toward the mountains and then said, "He also taught me how to offer buck brush and tobacco as payment to the Deer in exchange for its life, you know, what we call the Law of Reciprocity? You can't just take something without giving something good in return. Then he would take me into the woods to test my power. Sometimes I had to sleep all night in the same spot where a Deer had slept. This was to help me absorb its spirit, to absorb its energy, and to spiritually connect with it. And there were other times that Grandpa or my uncles took me up on top of Duzle Rock, Doctor Rock, Medicine Mountain, or Chimney Rock to fast, sing, pray, and give thanks to the Great Creator and the spirits, and the ancestors, and the animals, and all of Nature for the gifts they had given me. So after all that, don't you think I earned the right to hunt? Maybe someday I will do this with you, try to teach you how to get this kind of knowledge and power, if it is meant for you."

Charlie did try to teach me how to become a good hunter over the years but I never could get the hang of it. I was strong and agile, had excellent eyesight, made medicine like he taught me, sang the right songs, stayed clean while hunting, and tried to do everything the right way, just like he had taught me. I could see the Deer in my mind to the point of dreaming about them before we went hunting.

Dreams showed me where they were, but when it came time to shoot them I always seemed to miss. Charlie got so frustrated with me that after a while he simply took me along to help pack out the deer that he shot, even though he was very strong and in good shape for his age and size. My failure and shame bothered me so much that I hired Beeman to doctor me, to make medicine on me to find out what the problem was. Much to my surprise he said it wasn't a curse. He said that I wasn't meant to be a hunter because the Deer would become a spirit guide for me, and an ally in doctoring someday. When I told Charlie that he got mad. I think he wanted me to be more like him, especially if I was really his son.

With all this in mind I was quite surprised when he called one day on short notice and told me to prepare for a special hunting trip. He said I could bring Lilly along but to just make sure she wasn't on her moontime, and he told me to abstain from sex for a few days, and to fast. He also told me to use my own kind of sweat lodge, the type that is a temporary construction made from willow saplings, shaped like an upside-down basket, the kind that uses hot rocks and water to steam medicine and cleanse the people inside. He supposedly wanted me to make stronger medicine on the pretense that he was after a special type of Deer. He said he wanted to try and hunt a sacred White Deer or a very rare and sacred Black Deer. Sensing the seriousness involved I did as he instructed.

This was a great honor and the moment I had been waiting for, the opportunity to actually shoot a ceremonial Deer, the kind that is used in our sacred White Deerskin dance/World-renewal ceremony. Not only would such a bounty bring me great wealth, spiritually and culturally, but it would also raise my standing and make me a special person in the local Indian community. I thought that it would also make Charlie very proud of me and therefore compensate for the failure and embarrassment I had caused him. Lilly got a child-sitter for the day.

We met him over at Hoopa, visited with Velma for a while, and then followed him up to the town of Orleans. From there we went up past an old mill on Eyesee Road, past Donahue flat, and all the way up to the end of a paved road that was blocked by large boulders and construction. We turned into a small dirt road past a sign that read ELK VALLEY. We took a break in Elk Valley, smoked, drank coffee, and received instructions from Charlie.

We got out of the vehicles and I began to look around. I had a very strong feeling of déjà vu. I knew I had seen this place. I felt strongly that I had been here before, perhaps in a dream. Then it dawned on me that this place appeared in a series of dreams from the time I was a child up to the time I was mangled in the car accident as a teenager. And a number of months before, I had told Beeman and Charlie about a dream I'd had involving this place and a sacred White Deer.

In the dream I saw myself walking down a faint trail heading toward a large rock outcropping and a small pond. I was hunting with someone at the time but I couldn't remember who it was in the dream. I saw a White Deer and got excited, ran closer to get a better shot, and then all of a sudden saw a Flickerbird land on the antlers. The strange sight and behavior made me hesitate for a moment, and I was trying to decide whether to shoot or not. Then I heard the growl of a large Bear, turned to see which direction it was coming from, and couldn't find it. In the dream I also heard the cry of a Wolf, the scream of an Eagle, the squawking of Ravens, and a variety of Indian songs that were not familiar.

"Hey, Uncle Charlie," I said, "I know this place. This is the same place I told you I saw in a dream, remember, the dream with the White Deer. Beeman didn't understand it much except to tell me that the spirits were calling me to a sacred place, and someday I would meet that Deer and know why I had dreamed about him. Later when I told you about it, you just shirked it off and told me that someday I might get lucky and shoot a White Deer. What do you think now?"

He looked at me seriously and nodded. "Could be you're right about the dream because you are now right in the heart of the sacred High Country. This is where the old-timers went to pray, make different kinds of medicine, seek visions, and become ordained as medicine men. The women didn't use Chimney Rock. They used Doctor Rock, and sometimes

Medicine Mountain. Anyway, the road leading up to Chimney Rock is very rugged, so we can all go in my truck here. I want you to be careful because a person can get lost and never found up in these parts. You guys are still urban Indians so I want you to be very careful, okay? This is the only place left where I think the sacred White Deer can be found, or perhaps if we are real lucky, a very rare Black Deer. We can hunt it for ceremonial regalia but we can't eat the meat, and a very special type of ritual will have to be performed upon it. However, if you happen to see a regular Deer, especially a mossback [a fat old stag that's good for eating], then drop it."

The road was so beat-up and rough with rocks and deep holes and washouts that our heads kept bouncing up against the roof of the truck. We pulled off a sharp turn in the road into an open spot and got out and loaded the rifles. Charlie lit a piece of *keeshwoof* root, offered it to the Great Creator and the sacred mountains with a humble gesture, and then smudged all three rifles for good luck. He turned to Lilly and me and said, "I know it is getting cold up here and the weather can sometimes be unpredictable. So I hope you had enough sense to bring warmer clothes."

We both said yes, but it was warm enough for me just to wear a T-shirt and a wool hunting jacket. He continued, "Now Bobby, see this old trail leading into the woods? It's part of an ancient hiking trail that was used by the medicine people during their training and vision quests. Trails from the coast in Yurok territory, trails from the coast in Tolowa territory, and trails from our own Karuk territory below and to the east, all lead to this one spot and connect. But as you can see, the trail is faint and hasn't been used much over the years, so you really have to be cautious and keep an eye on it, or you could get lost. Also, it's full of spirits up here so watch your cussing and if you begin to feel something strange, get dizzy, or start hearing songs, then holler for me right away. Now I'm going to put you on this trail, I want Lilly to stay on the road, and I'll walk off to the side in the woods. This way we can flush the Deer toward each other, understand?"

We both nodded our heads in affirmation. I took out a piece of the sacred root, broke off a portion, and then started chewing it as I went vigilantly up the old trail. I sensed that Lilly was a little scared so I turned for a moment to make sure she was all right, waved to her, and got a very strange feeling deep in my gut. For a brief moment I felt as though I was waving good-bye forever, but I shook the thought and feeling off and proceeded into the clearing toward the forest and a very large rock outcropping shaped like a chimney. I heard the whistle of a Flickerbird ahead on the trail. Shortly afterward I started to get weak and dizzy and a heaviness began to fall upon me, the kind of feeling I always got when Wahsek doctored me. The trees began to shake and dance around me, and a strange Wind suddenly came up from behind as if a large, invisible presence was stalking me. I probably should have hollered for Charlie right then, but the spiritual power was hitting me hard and I began to go into an altered state of consciousness.

I could swear I heard people walking and talking on the trail but as I looked around I couldn't see anybody. My eyes started to blur, and all of a sudden I saw a large white buck jump out of the brush, run across the trail, and disappear behind some boulders. I started chasing after it, all the while staggering and trying to get my balance. I heard unfamiliar Indian songs coming in, and the sound of people singing got louder and louder. I managed to crash through the thick manzanita brush, which in turn flushed the White Deer into an open spot by a small pond. I did think of hollering for Charlie when I saw it, but I didn't want to scare the buck and spoil the shot. I had a Marlin .30-.06 rifle with a 3 x 9 Leipold scope, one of the best for hunting, so there was no reason for me to miss this rare opportunity. I said a prayer, made a wish, and had the Deer's head directly in my scope.

Just as I was about ready to shoot a Flickerbird flew in and landed on an antler. I got a very strange feeling all over me, almost electrical in nature. I was literally in shock, arguing in my mind whether to shoot or not shoot, when suddenly I heard the growl of a large Bear behind me. I turned and saw that it was a Grizzly Bear.

At first it was swaying its head back and forth while the growling got louder, and then it pawed at me and started to stand up. It was huge and terrifying. I started backing up to get away from it, all the while desperately looking for any way to escape. Then I tripped over a bunch of large rocks and logs, and I rolled down the side of a very steep hill into a deep ravine, crashing head over heel with my rifle tightly clasped in one hand.

I tried to grab hold of brush as I was falling and rolling with hopes of creating a buffer, but I was going too fast. A rock slide followed behind me. The impact of finally hitting flat ground knocked me unconscious.

When I woke up I didn't know how many hours I had been out, but judging from the way the Sun was now showing through the woods above me I figured it must have been at least half a day. I was battered, cut, bruised, and dizzy, with a severe headache. I tried to look around and get a sense of my direction but when a person is in a deep hole trying to look up for a way out, all sides of the hole appear to be similar. I had no choice but to take a guess. I thought it looked like I rolled down where there was a rock slide, so I tried to climb back up the same way. I didn't want to follow the ravine to get out because there was no telling where it would lead. It might lead deeper into the wilderness.

Unfortunately it's almost impossible to climb straight up the side of a mountain. I kept sliding back down while trying the straight-up approach. After about an hour of frustrating attempts I sat my ass down and smoked a cigarette, hoping to get a clear head and some composure. I heard a Deer and could barely see it through the thick brush, making a zigzag noise as it walked up the mountainside. That was the answer, so I followed it with the same approach.

Although I was in top physical condition, the few days of fasting, the impact of the fall, and the constant fight against thick brush all made the climb extremely difficult. I was exhausted by the time I reached an open clearing near the edge of a forest. I decided to rest and look around, hoping to find a familiar marker, such as the rock outcropping, a dirt road, a flat, or an open valley with a creek running through it.

The more I scanned the surroundings, the more scared I became. Everything looked the same. Nothing but trees and periodic acres of thick brush in every direction. I shot off my rifle hoping that Charlie or Lilly would hear it. I fired three times with a short pause in between for a response but there was no return. I only had two bullets left and decided to save them for later.

I tried hollering but every time I yelled out in a different direction a big gust of Wind would come in and drown it out. I thought it strange that the Wind only came when I yelled. Feeling deserted and trapped I then tried to study the position of the Sun, hoping for a sense of direction. I thought I had come in on the trail from the west so I started hiking in a westerly direction.

I walked for hours in thick forests and occasionally came out into more acres of thick manzanita and buck brush that covered large rocks. It got more and more discouraging fighting the brush, falling down, banging my knees and arms. The dust on the brush was blurring my vision and making my mouth dry. My thirst for water was becoming unbearable and the Sun was beginning to set. There was no water in sight for miles in every direction. I strained my senses to smell for water or to hear water moving. There was nothing but the smell of dry, dusty brush, a cold breeze coming in from the woods, and birds beginning to sing in preparation for their nightly roost. I hollered again until my voice became hoarse, but this time with tears of desperation.

Once again the Wind mysteriously came in and carried the cries away, and it got dead silent. I could feel the Wind penetrate through me and take possession. It was at this point that I realized I was lost, that I could wander around up here for days and nobody would probably ever find me, that I could die up here from thirst, starvation, and exhaustion. I lit the *keeshwoof* root and a cigarette, prayed with all my heart that the Great Creator and spirits would somehow help me, and fell asleep crying. I also felt that something had been trying to enter my body.

All night long the cold Wind howled around me. I tried looking for a log or cluster of rocks to crawl under, or an opening under the brush to find a way to keep warm. I was totally exposed, wearing only a T-shirt and a thin wool jacket, and mosquitoes devoured me unmercifully. I woke up at daybreak with sunlight hitting my eyes and birds singing. Still groggy and sore,

I tried looking around for a way out of my entrapment. I studied the position of the Sun and proceeded to head in a westerly direction but found myself being forced to crisscross over brush, rocks, and old dead trees. I also tried hollering and at one point I thought I heard someone holler back. I decided to go in the direction of the human sound.

Several hours later I finally realized that what I'd heard was an echo. I was more scared than ever and found myself trying to fight the panic. I realized that my only way out of here now was to keep a level head, have faith in the Great Creator and spirits, and try to think more like an animal than a human. I was hungry and very thirsty. I only had a few cigarettes left for relaxation and prayer. I decided to try and follow the thick forest that served as part of a backbone for the mountains. I thought I would have a better chance of finding water where there were trees.

I hiked all day through the woods and never saw anything except a few Blue Jays once in a while. Everything was so dry I couldn't even scrape moisture off the leaves to drink, but I did manage to suck the juice out of some roots, which only made me more thirsty. The sky was getting cloudy and appeared to be bringing a storm. I knew that it could possibly snow up here at this time of the year and the thought of freezing to death ran a chill of desperation up my spine.

I had to find a stream someplace, even if it was dry. As I looked around I finally realized what my former college professor had meant when he said that some people can't see the forest for the trees. All I could see were trees in every direction. I couldn't find a natural marker, such as a ridge or a rock outcrop or a logging road, because the forest was too thick and the trees too tall.

It wasn't long, however, before I discovered an old stream. It had been dried up for quite some time but I knew that water runs downhill. I rationalized a plan to follow it at any cost because a small stream will eventually run into a creek, which in turn should run into a pond of some sort, or into a larger creek, which in turn will eventually run into a river. Sooner or later a river is going to run into civilization.

This was the second day of being lost, and I had given up all hope of being found. Now it was up to me, and the powers that be, to save my own life, and I really wanted to live. Down the dry streambed I went, over rocks and dead tree limbs, under tree limbs, down, down, and down until the stream began to fork. Then I had to decide what direction to take. One direction might turn into a dead end, the other might lead to water. I had to sit down and think about it. I couldn't afford to flip a coin and leave it up to luck.

Suddenly a small doe broke through and ran down into the dry streambed to my right. I grabbed the rifle and aimed, hoping to get something to eat, fired, and missed. *Damn,* I thought, *maybe it was a sign or omen, a spirit in Deer form trying to help me and I screwed up.* I apologized to the Great Creator and the spirits, and to the Deer. I hollered for her to come back, to pity me, and to help me. I was crying, I was so sincere. I heard someone singing and looked up to see who it was.

The doe had returned and was staring very intently at me with her large, dark brown eyes. I could swear for a moment that I saw her change into a young Indian woman with long hair wrapped in mink hide braids, a basket hat, and a ceremonial shell-type dress. It had to be my imagination going wild, I began to reason, but I continued to try and communicate with the doe anyway. She turned and waited and seemed to indicate that she understood me and that I was to follow.

The dry streambed gradually got wider and deeper until it turned into a creek, but still there was no water. I could hear the Deer's hooves pounding slowly upon rocks and breaking sticks ahead of me but I couldn't see her. I kept following until sunset. Somewhere along the way I came up with the idea to use a small pebble to suck on while trying to fight thirst. And for some strange reason it seemed to work, but I was still craving water to the point that I didn't care if it rained or snowed. It was so dark I couldn't see my way around anymore, and it was getting colder by the minute. I needed to find some sort of shelter for the night.

I figured it would be all right to build a small fire in a dry streambed that was buffered by rock and sandy sides. I didn't want to do it while I was up in the high and dry brush because the Wind could have caused the fire to get out of hand and create a different kind of death trap for me. The cigarette lighter was getting low on fuel but it had enough left to get a fire started with dry grass, dry pinecones, and a few twigs. I found a natural hole in the dry streambed buffered by a logjam behind me. It served to create a small, semishelter from the Wind and possibly Rain or Snow.

I sat inside the shelter for hours warming myself, thinking about my life, wondering if I would ever see Lilly and my son again, and about the dreams I had been having during the past months. I also thought about the power I felt in the sweat lodge, how it really served to purify and strengthen me physically and spiritually, and about the visions I had been getting since using the sweat lodge. And I thought about the dreams and the strange encounters I was having with the Deer.

I woke up at daybreak, cold and wet, realizing it must have rained during the night. I was stiff and sore and still bruised, but the headache from the concussion had diminished. I had one bullet left, two cigarettes, and very little lighter fluid. I saw drops of water on plants and tree leaves and began sucking them like crazy. At least I finally got some moisture in my mouth, just enough to give me the strength to push on.

A few hours later I smelled and heard water! The dry streambed I had been traversing suddenly came to an abrupt halt on the edge of a cliff. About twenty feet directly below it was an active creek. I climbed down the steep bank in joy, with rocks and sticks falling behind me, and dropped on the sandbar. I prayed and gave thanks to the Great Creator and to the spirit of the water, and drank until I choked. After resting for a while I started the hike again, wading through intermittent pools of water that got deeper as I progressed farther down the creek, and over rocks and logs that got bigger the farther I went.

All day I hiked, climbing over slippery logjams, over treacherous boulders, oftentimes sliding down miniwaterfalls. Occasionally small Wrens, Flickerbirds, Blue Jays, Robins, Sapsuckers, and Finches came around, and I found tracks of small animals that were probably Squirrels, Weasels, and Pine Martens.

At a few hours before sunset I encountered another serious problem.

The creek ran into a river. It was partially blocked by logjams, boulders, and a fairly good-sized waterfall. I tried to climb up the steep cliffs hoping to get above it, follow a ridge along the riverbank, and then work my way back down, but the sides were too steep and soggy. I couldn't get a grip on anything. Then I tried to climb over the slippery logs and boulders and finally got to a point where I was looking down the waterfall, which cascaded into a water hole approximately thirty feet below. The water hole was surrounded by sharp rocks and more boulders.

I was sitting there trying to decide whether to jump and take a chance when all of a sudden I smelled what seemed to be a large animal, perhaps a Bear, but the stench was horrible. I turned to look around and directly behind me was this huge, hairy, manlike but also apelike creature. I didn't hear him come up behind me because the waterfall was making too much noise. The statue of Bigfoot that I had seen in the town of Willow Creek flashed in my mind. *No, it couldn't be,* I thought. *I'm just delirious and exhausted. I must be hallucinating.*

Then it looked at me and screamed, sending chills up my spine. The scream was similar to that of a Mountain Lion but ten times louder. The huge, hairy creature started to walk toward me in large strides, appearing to be slumped over to gain momentum. I only had one bullet left and I didn't want to take a chance and wound him. Terrified, I jumped into the waterfall.

The pool below was deep enough to soften the fall and luckily I didn't hit any rocks. But the current was swift and upon surfacing I was carried downstream while I fought desperately to keep from drowning and crashing into rock outcroppings. Gradually the force of the current began to taper off and I grabbed hold of a log and pulled myself up on the side of the bank. As I stood up the water appeared to be approximately four feet deep, and I assumed it got shallower as the river was getting wider.

I was soaking wet and the rifle was soaked and banged up, but the clouds had disappeared and the Sun was warming up everything around me. I looked around for a flat, dry spot along the riverbank that had a lot of Sun exposure and decided to take off my clothes and let them dry. I also looked behind me to see if that weird creature, that Bigfoot, was following me. He was nowhere in sight. So with a sigh of relief I decided to lie down on the warm sand and sleep. I was dead tired. When I woke up it was already dark and I was getting chilled from the dampness. I got dressed even though the clothes were still a little damp, then started looking around for a place to build a fire.

A little way down the river was a cave-type opening, probably carved out by a former flood, and it appeared safe enough to use as a shelter. The Moon was full and provided ample light for me to see while I foraged around for dry grass, bark, pinecones, and dry sticks of wood. The lighter was soaked and out of fluid. *Now what?* I thought. I remembered how my Uncle Earl had taught me how to start a fire with chert flints when I was a kid. After trying different kinds of rocks I finally got a spark going.

Cold and shaking, I kept dropping the rocks, couldn't seem to get the hang of it all, and out of frustration started to cry like a lost little kid. Yeah, me, the tough guy, the macho man, the guy who pumped iron, who stayed in top shape, the lover boy who was always popular with the women, and who wasn't afraid to fight anyone.

I cried because of memories about a bad childhood that kept surfacing in my mind. The loneliness, social isolation, fear, and depression I was now experiencing evidently made me regress psychologically. Sitting inside a dark, lonely cave in the middle of nowhere reminded me of the many times I had hidden behind the couch or in a closet as a child, neglected or abused. Suppressed memories and feelings of anger and resentment toward my mother and father or fathers, and uncles and aunts came pouring out with the tears.

All these years I had hated all of them, except my Uncle Earl, who had been kind enough to take me into his home and temporarily raise me like a son. And now he was dead. He had died from diabetes. He was the only person in my life when I was growing up who actually showed me love, caring, and respect, and who took the time to teach me things, little but important things like how to start a fire the Indian way.

My stepfather was an alcoholic and beat the hell out of my mother all the time until finally one day he just left. I heard stories that I had a real father in California but I never got to know him as a child. My mother and her sisters were sirens and floozies who ran around constantly with different men, and they didn't care who I saw them screwing. Their mother, my grandmother, was even worse. When I was hungry, sick, hurt, scared, or in pain, they didn't give a damn. They didn't have time for me. They were all too busy drinking, flirting, and fornicating. So I developed a habit of hiding in a closet to get away from the drinking, the domestic violence, the rejection, and the neglect.

During the years of abuse I had subconsciously absorbed their negativity. In the fear and darkness I had learned to hate women, and swore that one day I would get even. That was why sex mattered so much to me and why I had this attitude that women were created just for the pleasure of men. Love them and leave them, that was my motto. Be a macho man, as Gina had called me, a tough guy who likes to impress women by his fighting skills and dominating masculinity, just like the young bucks during mating season. And now, even though I had the best wife a man could ask for in life, I still cheated on her. The dysfunctional family syndrome and imprinting had been made at an early age. Could it ever be broken or replaced?

Hidden childhood fears and secrets can haunt people all their life. Hate, jealousy, fear, shame, guilt, and selfishness can destroy people if they are not confronted and eliminated. Sometimes they can be tamed, and sometimes they can be suppressed, but sooner or later they become a poison to the human mind and soul if not released. These emotions sneak into impoverished families the way a poisonous Snake takes possession of a nest. It devours the young and lays eggs of its own. Unnoticed, it coils in a circle and perpetuates the cycle of a dysfunctional family for many generations.

Here, in an isolated place in Nature, in another small dark corner of the world, I had finally found a way to release the psychological hedonism that for whatever reason had not been released during my suicide attempt, that had not been released when I got doctored by Wahsek or

Beeman, and that had not been released during all the times I prayed for a purification in the sacred sweat lodge.

This accident had not really been an accident. The dreams about Deer, a doe coming to my aid, the problem of not being able to hunt skillfully, and this constant relationship with the Deer were not just a coincidence. Sitting there in the dark cave with a warm hypnotic fire, I came to the realization that the Deer I had been encountering in my life were, indeed, spiritual messengers. They were supernatural symbols, or what Carl Jung called ancient archetypes from the unconscious mind, and for me they were female symbols. They were the spirits' way of telling me that I was sick and contaminated, and that I could not progress any further in my spiritual or shamanic development until I had purged myself by redemption.

With the help of Nature and by some strange design of the Great Creator I had finally found a way to go deep into my subconscious mind and find that abused little boy. I had found a way to reach out to him with a caring and loving hand, and to help release him from that closet so he could go forward and mature. I pulled him out of the dysfunctional family nest that had entrapped him all these years, caught like a bug in a spiderweb. In the process I had found something that was lacking in my life all this time. I finally found myself. I also learned at that point in my life that Nature was both a teacher and a healer, not just a killer as Western society had taught us to believe.

In a therapeutic way I had made contact with my own soul, and at that moment I knew that I would walk back out of the wilderness as a different person. I continued crying, thinking, purging the negative thoughts and experiences from my mind, letting it all flow into the current of an ancient, pristine river. On this mental journey inward, I had found the negative symbols that had shaped my bad thoughts, feelings, and behavior in life. Through this moment of realization, I also found the courage to forgive my mother, aunts, grandmothers, and all the many women I had exploited for sexual pleasure, or whom I had blamed for my pain and problems in life. A feeling of peace and harmony came upon me, and I slept like a Bear in hibernation.

I woke up in the morning from the loud squawking noise of a Raven. He was sitting in a tree hollering like crazy, then he would fly over toward me, then back down the river several times, as if he were saying, "Come on, let's get out of here. Let's go this way." The river was a beautiful emerald green color, the color of healing, the same color as a Hummingbird that flew by. A very good omen!

The long hike along the river provided me with ample time to think. I could feel the flow of the water pulling thoughts from my mind. I thought about my son Kanawha, and about Lilly, and about going out and getting drunk, celebrating while she was suffering in the hospital in labor. Maybe that was why my son was born with a few white spots on his body and a crooked foot, like a wounded fawn. And maybe that was why Beeman, Rolling Thunder, and John Fire Lame Deer couldn't get my child healed. I had them try their powers and knowledge when the leg-brace approach and medicines used by the White doctors failed. Perhaps children do, indeed, inherit the sins of their fathers and forefathers. Would I ever be able to reconcile and redeem this violation and Karmic debt? Perhaps that was why I'd gotten lost up here in Nature.

I kept looking for a trail opening on the sides of the riverbank, hoping it would lead to a logging camp, wilderness camp, or some sign of civilization. A number of hours had passed and I was getting tired and sore again, a little weak from all the hiking and fasting. Once again I heard the calls of the Raven, looked to the left, and saw a small herd of does run up a trail leading from the river bar. I got excited and followed them. Sure enough, about two hundred yards later the trail came out into a meadow. I could see an old shack, and the trail continued on the other end of the meadow. I went into the shack and sat down, and prayed, giving thanks for the chance of salvation.

Approximately an hour later I heard human voices and saw a forest ranger coming up the trail toward the shack with a two-way radio. He looked at me, surprised, and said, "Are you Bobby Lake?" I nodded in acknowledgment, too choked up with tears to talk. "Man, am I glad to see you. Do you know where you are? You're about sixty miles on the other side of Chimney Rock area, just the opposite of where everyone has been searching for you. I don't think anyone expected you would possibly be over in this region. They had Forest Service personnel, helicopters, the sheriff's posse, and all kinds of volunteers, but nobody could find you. A storm came in and it snowed up in that area so the search was called off. Don't you know that other people have gotten lost up there and died, that they were never found, or that their bodies were found thawing out the next spring, half eaten by wild animals?"

I could see tears of happiness coming down his face while he was talking, and then he started transmitting the good news over the walkie-talkie radio. He told me we were about a three-mile hike away from the paved Forest Service road. "By the way," he turned and said while we walked briskly, "how did you get lost in the first place?" I told him about the Deer and how a Grizzly Bear had suddenly come up from behind, and that while trying to escape I fell down a steep cliff and into a ravine. He said, "We don't have Grizzlies up here anymore. Haven't been any since the early nineteen hundreds. It must have been a very large Cinnamon Bear, but they can be dangerous and maul a person, too."

Lilly and Charlie were waiting for me by the truck at the end of the trail. They both came up running, excited and crying with arms outstretched to hug me. "God, I thought you were dead," she said. Charlie hugged me and whispered, "Yeah, I almost lost faith too, but I knew better. You did real good, son. You passed your test. I'm very proud of you." He said he realized I was hungry but he wouldn't let me eat yet. He wanted to take me back home, put me in the sweat lodge, and sing and pray over me all night. He made medicine on me to cook and strengthen the newly acquired power, and to prepare me for future development. Charlie said a ceremony was needed to heal me from the traumatic experience and to help me with the psychological transition. "Anytime a person goes through something terrible such as you did, an accident, a death in the family, a divorce, or a sudden life change, there should be a ceremony."

Stories and Legends about Shamans

Charlie must have known something I didn't know because shortly after that, Lilly left me. I guess she had just had enough of the neglect, capers, and constant worry. My adventures had just been too much for her. I knew she also probably got fed up with my cheating and running around on her. I didn't see much of Charlie either for a while because he quit his job at the college and moved back home, back up to Quartz Valley Indian Reservation and the Mt. Shasta area. Lilly had been secretly seeing a car salesman down the street from where she worked while I had been flowing with the current. I wasn't too surprised because I had dreamed about it in the High Country.

We were on different roads in life. Spiritually and culturally the dividing line had already been drawn; therefore, when the divorce became final, I just let her have everything without challenge or remorse. It was the least I could do as partial payment toward an ongoing Karmic debt. After all these years I still realize how stupid I was to lose such a good woman, but like Gina once said: payback time is a bitch. The car salesman turned out to be a good man and wise choice for Lilly's needs in the long run. They became happily married and prosperous and have stayed that way.

Our son Kanawha eventually grew out of the crooked leg but he never got rid of the white spots. And although I didn't get to see much of him during the next decade, I did make sure that I bonded him with the

Earth, his culture, his spirituality. And I tried to provide him with a much better imprint than I had been given when I was a child.

My job had been a grant-funded position and the grant ran out that year. By the summer of 1976 I had lost my wife, my family, my job, and everything I owned. Broke, destitute, and having nowhere to turn, I decided to go up on the mountain and visit Wahsek. I figured I had been made a victim of sorcery. After all, isn't it always easier to blame someone or something else for our problems? Or was sorcery really the cause of my troubles?

Wahsek, like so many of our other tribal Elders, always had a way of teaching and perhaps preaching by use of parables. The old 1966 pickup I bought from my Apache friend Jerry was in good enough shape to meet my basic needs, and it got me up the hill to Wahsek's house with no problem. I guess I was stupid but I gave Lilly the new car and all the furniture and appliances, plus the money she made from selling the old farmhouse. Hell, the way I figured it at the time, I was paying off a debt for insult and injury, according to Indian custom and law.

Wahsek was working in the garden but I saw him looking up at his patroller, the Chicken Hawk, just before I came into the yard. I also noticed for the first time that a lot of Blue Jays were flying around raising hell, squawking and making continuous noise. Then I saw some Flickerbirds come in and try to chase the Blue Jays away, then a Deer, a doe, suddenly appeared out of the woods and walked up toward the garden, where Wahsek was now studying it.

He was happy to see me and came up with a greeting, shaking his head. "Now what kind of mess have you gotten yourself into this time?" He stopped and placed the hoe on the fence and tried to scare the Deer away, but it was persistent. It couldn't get into the garden but it still kept hanging around, looking at us. Then a few minutes later a number of does came to get the first doe while the dogs pursued, barking at their hooves. The first doe split from the herd, jumping around erratically, as if confused. Then she ran directly over toward a buck that was standing in the clear-cut area. The buck and doe greeted each other affectionately, and then they ran up the hill out of sight. At the same moment, the herd of does ran in an opposite direction, into the woods.

Wahsek motioned for me to come into the house. I reached into the front seat of the truck and grabbed a large can of tobacco, some spotted Eagle feathers I had found in the woods during one of my former adventures with Charlie, and a can of coffee that was with the other groceries in a large box. I also grabbed the checkbook.

Gina was sitting and smoking in her usual spot at the small table facing the front door. She looked up as if coming out of a trance and said, "I see you brought your friends again." I turned around to look behind me but I didn't see anybody. I laid the groceries down on the old picnic-style table next to the kerosene lamp. Wahsek sat down in his old blue chair, his throne, as I called it, and started laughing. I turned to Gina and responded, "I don't see anybody. Who are you talking about?"

"Well, to begin with," she said while pointing with her eyes closed, "that big Grizzly Bear, the Black Bear, the old Indian man from back East who is always with you, the white Wolf, and that Indian chief I always see dressed in white buckskins and a white headdress, and a few other things such as the Raven, Eagles, Hummingbirds, a white buck and doe. But now this time you got a whole gang of women following you around, including this one young woman who looks to be about only sixteen. She's the main one hanging all over you, and man are you in trouble!"

"Yeah," Wahsek confirmed. "It's getting pretty crowded in here and a lot of action going on outside, too."

Gina got up and got me some coffee and told me to sit down. I reached for the Eagle feathers and tobacco, including a carton of cigarettes for Gina, and got out the checkbook. I said, "According to Indian custom and law I would like to make this offering, this donation, and ask you to doctor me." I wrote out a check for three hundred dollars and handed it to Wahsek. I handed the cigarettes and a fifty-dollar bill to Gina. "I also brought some groceries," I said, "and I am willing to perform labor in exchange for your help because I think I need a lot of help this time."

Gina started crying while Wahsek looked at me for the longest time, studying me in a psychic way, as if trying to make a decision. She said, "It seems you lost that good woman you had, huh? I told you that Coyote was going to get the best of you sooner or later. Damn, you have a hard lesson to learn this time. When are you going to stop trying to be a macho man, or is it just in your blood?"

She was so upset that it made me start crying. Half stammering and in a state of humiliation, I confessed, "Yes, you're right once again, as usual. This time I lost everything, my wife and child, my home, my job, my new car, and all the furniture. I don't have anywhere to go, except up on the mountain to talk directly to the Great Creator and cry for penance, that is, if Wahsek will help me." I got sullen for a moment, and then continued, "I don't think just doing a ceremony in the sacred sweat lodge will handle the problem this time. I need higher spiritual guidance and a cleansing."

Wahsek and Gina both agreed to doctor me but Wahsek said he would need to study my situation carefully before deciding to take any additional action. He wasn't the kind of person who ever took a Band-Aid approach to any problem, nor was he a quick fixer.

The role of shaman is diverse, demanding, and dangerous. The highest-ranking shamans usually fill a number of roles in their sacred profession. They are a multifaceted combination, often serving as physician, psychologist, philosopher, mystic, priest, and warrior all rolled up into one package. That's what makes them so unique, but this also requires caution in their work for the people. Their extraordinary talent and skills, combined with rare and ancient knowledge and training, can be traced back to the beginning of time, when humans were first created and became sick. The shamanistic approach is natural and holistic, although some shamans do have fields of specialization, whereas Western medicine is still in the embryonic stage of development.

Wahsek leaned back in his seat with eyes half closed, appearing to be meditating, and then he reacted. "It is, indeed, unfortunate that you lost your wife, but it was inevitable. I really liked her, what little bit I did know about her. She was a very good woman, probably the best a man could hope for in a marriage. She was pretty, intelligent, educated, caring, devoted, and a happy person. She also had power but you didn't know it. She never really knew it either, and never showed it openly. She could have been a darn good dreamer or seer with training, but that wasn't her destiny. So she did what any smart woman would do under the circumstances. She surrendered to her fate and to your destiny. She has a good spirit and she is a very clean person so the Great Creator and spirits from her own heritage will take care of her. But the bottom line here is that an Eagle can't marry a Crow."

I was quite taken aback by his statement at the end. It just didn't fit the preceding compliments. "What do you mean?" I said defensively.

"Let me tell you an old myth, a teaching that might help you understand." He paused as if searching for the right words, and almost started talking in the Yurok language until he caught himself and proceeded in English. He reached down and picked up the handful of spotted Eagle feathers, all tail feathers, that I had given him as a donation.

"A long time ago, Talteth, the Golden Eagle, was the most beautiful bird in the world. He was the biggest, the strongest, and the bravest of all birds. He was probably considered the most powerful of all the birds. That is why all Native people around the world want his feathers. He is used in all our different ceremonies and in doctoring, even for war dance medicine and protection.

"He can fly the highest, and therefore be closer to the Great Creator. He can see the farthest, thus having foresight and vision. He also represents wisdom, wealth, and high spirituality." He hesitated for a moment in his talk and affectionately stroked the feathers.

"One day, the birds all gathered together for an annual ceremony, a tradition that they had been doing for centuries. They talked about world affairs, visited with old friends, were cautious but friendly with old enemies, and made plans for the sacred dance. It was also a fine time for one to select a mate.

"The females grouped together, taking care of their affairs and probably gossiping, while the males sat in council talking about more serious matters. Eagle was a leader, but perhaps also a little too proud, apparent by the way he strutted around. This in turn caught the attention of the women, especially those who were seeking a possible mate.

"A female Hawk spoke up first, saying, 'See how handsome he is. I would like to have a man like him.' 'Yeah,' said the Buzzard, 'he is about the right size for me but prettier than my people.' 'I don't think I could get along with him,' said Turkey, 'because I wouldn't be able to keep up with his constant flying around all over the place, but I wouldn't mind having him as a secret lover.'"

With a sly grin on his face, Wahsek continued, "In a short while they all started arguing and fighting over him. Big and small, young and old, it didn't matter. It was obvious that Eagle was the most popular and most wanted man. Blue Jay jealously squawked at some of them. 'Yeah, but none of you have enough power to get him.' Crow, who had been silent and listening, reacted, 'I bet I can get him, I've got power, too.' Then they all laughed.

"Well, to make a long story shorter," Wahsek said, "Eagle fell in love with Crow. Eagle and Crow got married and had a baby. The baby got sick. One day, Eagle told Crow, 'I will go to the brush dance and get the people to sing, dance, and pray for our child.' Crow was concerned and said in return, 'I will go with you and help, too. You are always leaving me at home!' 'No,' said Eagle firmly, 'you don't belong there. That's not your kind of medicine.' So Eagle went to the brush dance. Crow stayed at home and got her feelings hurt. She got mad.

"'I know how to make medicine too,' she said defiantly to herself. And she did, but the baby died. Eagle came home and found out what went wrong. He beat her and threw her out of the house, saying, 'Go back to your own kind. I should have known better.' He then flew up into the sky, higher and higher, farther and farther away. Crow tried to follow but she couldn't fly that high. She wasn't strong enough to catch him."

I had listened carefully to the lesson Wahsek was trying to teach but my rational mind tried to deny the message. I said in response, "I think that story is racist and sexist. It just doesn't make sense."

Wahsek was patient with me. He replied, "Sure, in some ways it might teach that it is best to keep the race pure, and that women have their proper roles to follow, but the message involves power and spirituality. Human values, beliefs, and practices can't replace the Natural Laws of the Universe. There is law and order in the Universe, as I have told you so many times before. A man or woman of knowledge and power knows that and lives by the laws with discipline and principle. To live by the laws will create balance, to violate the laws creates an imbalance, and eventually causes problems such as bad luck and sickness."

He became silent, waiting for the teaching to penetrate the right side of the brain where the subconscious, spiritual, and ancient forms of knowledge are hidden, that part of the mind that we are rarely taught to use and develop in Western society. Evidently, such ancient and symbolic teachings just don't seem to register with the left-brain, scientifically oriented, conscious way of thinking that uses logic and reason to comprehend the world. Wahsek had told me once before that he believed Western society was culturally and spiritually deficient, and as a result, he felt his perspective about certain phenomena could not be comprehended easily by the new generation of Indians.

That is why he said he was so patient with me all the time, because he realized I was a product of Western society, with my Indian way of thinking glossed over, but he felt I had potential. Thus, he often used parables as a way to create a new lens for me to perceive reality beyond the frames of Western thought, social beliefs, and values.

He said Nature was constantly in a state of change, growth, and development but the laws and certain functions remained static, unaffected by human beliefs, perspectives, or actions, which often changed in Western society. Consequently he firmly believed that myths and rituals were needed as a natural tool for learning to develop both the mind and the spirit. He often argued that tribal myths might be ancient but they weren't archaic. They still had relevance in a modern world that was governed by the laws of Nature, not by humankind. He believed in using both hemispheres of the mind-brain complex in order to survive, and as a means to develop critical thinking, creative intelligence, and higher learning.

Gina and Wahsek stayed silent for a long time while I smoked a ciga-rette and seriously thought about my situation, what could be done about it, and the meaning of the myth he'd used to help soften the suffering. I say *suffering* because I had come to the conclusion that going through a divorce was probably worse than grieving over the death of a spouse. I wondered if we had a ritual for dealing with divorce in our Indian heri-tage and culture. If anyone knew, it would be Wahsek.

He broke the silence with assuring closure. "Like I said, an Eagle can't marry a Crow. Evidently the Great Creator has something else and someone else in mind for you, and you now have the free time to figure it out. An Eagle should marry an Eagle; and even a Raven mates with a Raven. It doesn't mate with a Crow because power has rules. In order to pursue power, acquire power, and apply power you must follow the rules. It's as simple as that. Now what else is wrong with you?"

Gina starting laughing like crazy and hollered, "He's got crotch rot from all those nasty women he's been running around with!"

I wasn't about to embarrass myself any further and ask her how she knew. She was definitely clairvoyant, a seer. "Yeah, you're right. I do have a bad rash and I've been using everything on it, including old-fashioned cornstarch."

"That was stupid," she retorted. "All you did was start a garden down there. You just added fertilizer to the problem."

"How do you figure that?" I said defensively.

She drank a sip of her coffee and looked at Wahsek, smiled, and turned toward me. "If you have a yeast infection, or what the coach calls jock itch, the cornstarch will just add more yeast to it. It won't dry it up. So you need herbs, especially if the Whiteman's medicine at the pharmacy won't work. But more than likely it's spiritual in basis." She took a ciga-rette, smoked it for a while, closed her eyes in meditation, and then continued, "For example, the spirits said you got it from women, from having sex with women on their moontime, and from having sex in a Whiteman's sweat house."

Damn, I thought to myself. *A person can't hide anything from this woman. She's incredible.* "Well, I guess I have to *pegasoy* tonight, huh?" Wahsek preferred to doctor at nighttime, after the sunset, not only because it was more convenient for him, but also because he said the power was stronger. Over the years I had seen him doctor during the day, especially during emergency situations, and he once told me, "I have daytime spirits and night spirits, but I'd rather doctor after sunset. It seems stronger and more effective."

I had lunch with them and they said I could sleep on the front-room couch if I could handle the fleas. I hated the fleas. I must have been allergic to them because they always ate me alive. One time they devoured Kanawha so badly I had to take him to the hospital and got thoroughly scolded by Lilly and the White doctor. Wahsek refused to use any kind of poisonous sprays against the bugs in his house or the garden. He had just developed a living style and evidently some sort of agreement with the parasites because they never seemed to bother him or Gina, only visitors.

I saw a similar phenomenon occur with Rolling Thunder when I went out and visited him over the years. The mosquitoes never bothered or bit him but they always ate me and other people alive. When I asked R. T. about the relationship he said he just used his shields to keep them off, meaning his aura, a natural energy field that surrounds the human body but isn't visible to the human eye. I never did learn how to keep the damn insects off, although Rolling Thunder had tried to teach me how to use his secret method using prayer and visualization.

I think Wahsek had a similar secret but he also used a lot of pepperwood and some other herbs. Charlie was the same way, perhaps from always being out in the woods. He had learned how to adapt to his environment. He said that his body just naturally took care of the problem in the same way that it didn't react to poison oak. I guess he had just built up an immunity to it.

Anyway, I had a lot to think about while I spent the major portion of the day cutting and splitting wood, working in the garden, repairing fences, and sorting out haystacks in the barn. There was always work to do at Wahsek's and that was probably what kept him in such strong, well-muscled physical shape.

They doctored me that night in the same style, and I had to confess for my violations against the spiritual laws, for having sex with women on their menses and while in the sauna. Wahsek scolded and said the Whiteman's sweat house was sacred, just like the Indian sweat lodges, and although the White people had forgotten that reality, he said it should be respected and used properly. He said all sweat houses, no matter from what culture, were originally designed for spiritual use, to be used for purification, healing, and religion, and were not to be contaminated with drugs, sex, alcohol, or blood. They were allegedly given to the people, by the Great Creator, as a spiritual tool and form of knowledge to prevent sickness and disease, not promote it. Wahsek also said he felt very sad that modern people had forgotten so many sacred teachings. Once again I had learned the law of physics—for every action, there is a reaction—and I had to redeem my transgressions in order to achieve a state of homeostasis.

Gina had already boiled mugwort herbs for me on the woodstove while she was cooking dinner. After the healing ceremony I was instructed to thoroughly wash my crotch with old-fashioned lye soap, and then pack a poultice around my crotch filled with hot herbs. It was raw and burned in pain but I did as instructed, and I slept all night long with the homemade diaper. By the next morning I could feel and see the rash was clearing up. I also figured out that mugwort was the same medicine used in Absorbine Jr., a pharmaceutical ointment used for skin rashes, sprains, and muscle aches. It was also the same medicine they'd had me bathe in a number of years before when I first came to get doctored for the suicide attempt and arthritis.

I had a bowl of oatmeal and a cup of coffee and visited with Gina for a while and talked about doctoring, how a person became a medicine woman, or shaman, and what she really thought about me having so many strange dreams, visions, and spiritual experiences. At one point she suggested that I go out and visit with Wahsek, who was over by a water spigot, near the end of the fence.

I knew he frequented the same spot when in deep thought or praying. There was a small campfire just at the end of the fence some distance from the water pipe. I had felt drawn to the spot when I first came to his house to get doctored, and I'd developed a habit of instinctively going over there to smoke and think during the past years and visits with him. He had noticed my behavior and made mention of it, so that I almost felt I was intruding into his personal space. I liked the spot because it felt peaceful, and sometimes I could faintly hear Indian songs there.

He was looking sadly at a spot on the other side of the fence, a spot that had obscurely been fenced off, as if to separate it from the old hog pens and other fencing. "Do you feel that spot over there?" he said, studying me. "I know you like it here. I gave up a long time ago trying to keep you from it."

In a humble tone of voice I said, "Yes. I have always been attracted to it, although I never bothered your prayer pit. It just felt natural to come over here and smoke, talk to myself, or just sit and feel the peace and quiet. Sometimes I thought I heard faint singing around here. I'm sorry if I intruded or insulted you."

He looked at me seriously again. "Well, at first you looked suspect but then I had to study the situation. After giving you a couple of hints I began to see, in a spiritual way, that you were being guided. If you try to look in a psychic way, perhaps by first closing your eyes and trying to use the intuitive side of your mind, you might be able to see an old plank sweat lodge there in the ground. It's obviously all covered up now but it's still there in spirit form, and remnants of it are buried underground."

I told him I had dreamt about an old building being there quite some time ago. I tried to use his suggestion, and I did see with the mind's eye, in a clairvoyant way, an old Redwood plank sweat house. But I saw it burning up, that it had caught on fire, and a person was trapped inside of it. He was impressed with my ability and accuracy, and he appeared to become excited.

"That old sweat lodge belonged to my grandfather, Lucky, who used it for *hokep,** for spiritual training, vision seeking, and religious practices. My mother also used it for her doctor training, my father for ceremonial use, then my older brother. I got to use it when I was a child, up into my early teens, but my brother burnt it up. He evidently did something wrong while making medicine. It caught on fire, and not too long after that he died. That's how serious the power can be. A person can't play games with such matters."

He paused for a long time while wiping tears away, closed his eyes and prayed, and tried to get his composure. Afterward he said, "Yes, we do have a ceremony for everything, even divorce, because sudden life changes can be traumatic and cause sickness. But like you said, sometimes the sweat lodge ritual isn't enough, so in that case a person must enter *hokep.*"

I was totally shocked, flattered, and caught by surprise. "Are you saying that you are willing to train me? Do you really think I am meant to be a medicine man, like you, or is my mind playing tricks on me again?"

"Well, let me put it this way," he stated flatly. "You're already an Indian doctor in spirit form. You just need the right kind of teaching, training, tests, and experience to become what you were destined to be. I told you when we first met that I didn't want to doctor you because it would lead to a long-term, complicated relationship, remember?"

I nodded and remained humble.

"I knew then that you were my successor, and that I was destined to help you. And remember when you came up here half crazy to get doctored because that mermaid, Wohpeckameth, was tormenting the hell out of you? She's the Great Creator's wife, and when she chose to give you her songs and seeing powers that was also a sign, an omen that you were special, and destined to be a shaman. I don't know anybody else except according to legend who ever got to see her like you did, especially so many times. And, remember, a couple of years ago, you came up here to get doctored after the ancestral spirits abducted you, and there were four flying saucers positioned over my house? Now that was

*Hokep is a Yurok word for shamanic training, that is, training in doctoring and power acquisition.

one hell of a job getting rid of those guys, the *wogey*, but they too gave you power. All of these mysterious encounters, omens, and experiences were ways that the Great Creator was testing you and guiding you. So who am I to stand in the way?"

I was speechless. I idolized this man and saw him work natural wonders and miracles when the other medicine men or women had failed. He was probably the highest-ranked shaman on the continent, and definitely the last of his species. What a great honor—but I didn't think I was qualified or worthy.

"I feel lost for words and so honored," I told him. "I never expected this to happen. Why me? Why not someone from your own family or tribe?"

"Like I already told you, because I knew in a spiritual way and because of the signs and omens, even though I procrastinated and tried to ignore them. I have been teaching you all along, and I'm sure you understood this; it was a subtle given in our growing relationship. You didn't see too many other young Indian people hanging around my house trying to learn, did you? I've never met anyone who got so sick, hurt, into so much trouble with spirits and forces, or into so many different mysterious capers as you have, even more than what I went through. Besides, now you have nothing to lose. The timing is right."

I was still dazzled but anxious to get on with the program. I had felt in my gut, for a long time, that there was a reason I'd met this extraordinary man, and despite any detours in my life, growth, and development, I always came back to his cave to get healed.

He made a prayer and invocation to the Great Creator, the doctor spirits, the ancestors, and Nature. He made a pledge to put me under his tutelage as a shaman apprentice. In return, I had to promise to keep the apprenticeship, and what I had learned, a secret for at least ten years, or until after his death. He said that after he died he didn't care what anyone knew, but while alive, he didn't need any more problems.

I asked him if I could build my own style of sweat lodge, the steam-and-rocks style, since it would be impossible at this point to salvage and use his family *wogel-urgirk*. He said he didn't know much about that kind but he was willing to try, as long as it was isolated and out of sight from visitors. He also instructed me to follow a discipline that required fasting for a period of ten days straight, a process of packing my own wood while crying to the spirits for pity, and no contact with any other humans during the training process. He said he would teach me how to pray, what herbs and medicines to use for the training, how to meditate in the sweat lodge as a means to seek visions and guidance, and the proper way to sit by the sacred fire while repeating ancient prayer formulas needed to make contact with certain spirits.

Wahsek also made it very clear that I had to prepare my own food, since I did not have a woman to help me as was the custom, and the religious food required for fasting was acorns, dried Salmon, and Deer meat that could not be touched, cooked, or shared with anyone else. In this way I could avoid all contact with menstruating women, unclean people, sick people, jealous or flirtatious people, or people in general who in turn might interfere somehow with my training.

He also instructed me how to fight evil spirits that might challenge both of us, as we had been previously warned by an omen involving Blue Jays, and to be very cautious about having dreams involving women. He said if I dreamt about having sex with a woman and ejaculated or masturbated, then the flow of power would be broken and my training ended. I was to focus completely on the training objective with solid determination, and the goal was to make contact with a special kind of spirit on a nearby power center that would help me with my predicament.

This type of training was like an entrance exam. It wasn't a form of doctor training, although it was similar to the type of training used in becoming a doctor. This training was being used to prepare me for possible future *hokep*, to see if I really had what it took to handle the suffering, sacrifice, and rigor required as part of an ongoing apprenticeship. But by the same token, I was preparing myself for purification from divorce and its related psychological, physical, spiritual, emotional, financial, and social effects. According to Wahsek, if I did everything right, I would be accepted by the spirits in a certain place, and they would grant my wish and change my life and luck for the better. I therefore had not only a rare opportunity to learn esoteric knowledge, but also a chance for a new start in life. He visited with me at my training camp on a daily basis to check on my progress and provide additional instructions and teachings, and he deliberately spent time telling me stories and legends about shamans. It wasn't until many years later that I fully realized the purpose, meaning, and value of these stories, some of which follow.

Wahsek

Wahsek said he knew he was born with special doctor powers because he was a bloodline hereditary village leader, ceremonial leader, and healer. His mother was a doctor, his father a ceremonial leader, his grandfather a ceremonial leader, and so forth back many generations. He began to have special spiritual experiences as a child, such as the ability to see and hear spirits, the ability to communicate with animals and birds, and the ability to make accurate psychic predictions. His grandfather and other relations started training him at birth, and he was constantly exposed to the teachings, myths, religion, ceremonials, sacred dances, and doctoring sessions by his immediate relatives and shamans from other tribes.

One time his grandfather offered to train him for wealth and good luck. He was only about ten years old at the time. For ten days straight he fasted, gathered his own wood, prayed in the sacred sweat lodge, and prepared for the vision quest up on Kewet Mountain. (Kewet Mountain is Burrill Peak Mountain. At the base of this mountain is where a man named Patterson took the only authentic video and photos of the alleged Bigfoot; they generated international controversy.)

His grandfather stayed in the sweat lodge with him the whole time, giving him instructions, support, and encouragement. On the ninth day he started hiking up toward the mountain, which took him a full day. On the tenth day he ascended the mountain, built a prayer altar, smoked his sacred pipe, and wished for wealth and a vision.

According to his story, he heard strange and heavy footsteps just before daybreak. When he got up to see what it was, he got scared and tried to run, falling around in the darkness. But it was too late. The legendary Bigfoot was upon him, and he had to fight for his life. He tried to bend and run between the creature's legs, but the creature growled and wrestled with him violently, and then threw him over the side of the mountain where he continued to fall, rolling into rocks, log debris, and bushes.

He was crushed beyond repair, bleeding from broken bones and large gashes on his head, arms, legs, and chest. He was dying and surrendered himself, but first he prayed and cried with all his heart and soul. That night when he died his soul was taken inside the mountain by ghosts, Native people who had been former shamans. They did a ceremony on him in Bigfoot's lodge. They sang, prayed, smoked, and used their herbs on him. They told him someday he would do this too, and that he was now alive and had to return home.

He woke up with lightning and thunder cracking over him, the rain pouring down. He could see fresh dried blood upon his body but did not feel any pain. The cuts he had previously seen were all gone. He got up, staggered around, and looked for shelter.

In a semipartial cave he found safety and by instinct proceeded to sing kick-dance songs until he achieved a trance and felt pains in his stomach. All day and all night he sang, and occasionally slept, only to be awakened by the spirits and made to sing and dance some more.

A few days later he woke up and felt that he was being carried down the trail, and much to his amazement, it was the big, hairy creature that was carrying him home. At first he tried to fight and get away. He was terrified from the previous ordeal, but he passed out. He said Bigfoot laid him alongside the sweat lodge, stood there for a long time, looked sadly at him and his grandfather, and then let out a bloodcurdling scream and ran back up the trail toward Kewet Mountain.

His grandfather was scared and shaking from the encounter but helped him get back into the sweat lodge, where his grandfather started singing, praying, and doing the *remopho*—doctor-making dance—on him. His other family members heard the singing and joined in to help, and the ceremony went on for about five days. Wahsek said that during this time he went crazy because he could see the spirits and hear many loud songs.

He asked me if I had ever seen the famous documentary film of Bigfoot that was taken at Bluff Creek by Mr. Patterson a number of years ago. I told him I had seen the documentary. The film had been scientifically scrutinized, and yet people refused to accept it as legitimate.

Wahsek claimed he was responsible for helping with the making of that film because he agreed to use his doctor song and call Bigfoot out into the open. He also said that our Indian people did not ever fish at Bluff Creek because they knew it was Bigfoot's traditional fishing spot. He showed me plaster castings of the footprints, some pieces of hair, and dung. In closing, he confessed that he never should have tried to help the scientists because he got deathly sick for a long time afterward from the transgression. And with that he warned me to be very careful on my planned trip to the same power spot.

Wahsek knew all the "old-time doctors," probably the last in their day, when earlier anthropologists such as Kroeber, Park, Lowie, DuBois, Spier, Harrington, and Dixon came in to study them in the early 1900s.* Doc Thomas was Wahsek's primary mentor. He was half Wintun and half Achomawi. But there were other Indian doctors that Wahsek got to meet, learn from, or get doctored by, including Charlie Klutchie, Nes Charles, Fanny Brown, and the Wah Fan family. He also talked about some of his experiences with a Rattlesnake doctor over at Hayfork known as Ida Cyst, a Karuk doctor from Quartz Valley by the name of Benoni Harrie who helped train his mother, Nancy, and the famous Fanny Flounder of the Yurok. He said there had been other doctors a little before his time, such as Weitchpec Susie with the Yurok and Pi-ker-una with the Karuk, but he had little knowledge about them except from legend, stories, and rumors told by his family members during Kaamus, the time of the year in winter when such stories are normally shared and regalia repaired.

He seemed to have tremendous mistrust for the old-time doctors, claiming that they were very competitive, egotistical, and often prone to using both good and bad power. The exception, he said, was probably a Pomo sucking doctor by the name of Essie Parrish, his mother, Nancy, and the legendary Fanny Flounder of the famous Spott family lineage. Otherwise, he said, "Most of the older doctors at that time were facing acculturation and assimilation. The Indian way of life as they knew it was being wiped out by federal policies and Christian missionaries, and the notorious Bureau of Indian Affairs boarding schools.

---

*The dates for some of these anthropological studies are: Park, 1922; Kroeber, 1928, 1944; Dubois, 1936; and Dixon, 1938.

"So I guess they got desperate or something because the power went to their heads. They figured they were going to be the last, and they were under tremendous psychological conflict. Money became a big issue because of the poverty they faced, while they saw the White doctors being paid big money for their services. More and more new diseases kept coming in that they didn't know how to handle. A lot of them reverted to drinking *mespa,* whisky, and became mean and prone to domestic violence. I think the effects of the alcohol also broke down their traditional morals, values, and religious ethics because they became very abusive, began to doctor while drinking, and began to ignore the spiritual laws and codes. The power turned on them and their families. It wiped out whole families for many generations, and it created survivors who were products of incest, molestation, insanity, and alcoholism, who were sometimes diseased, mentally retarded, or crippled.

"A tremendous amount of ancient and secret knowledge concerning the healing arts had been lost by the time World War Two rolled around, so eventually even I became a drunk for a few years and was often found rolling around in the gutter on Second Street in Eureka, Redding, or Ft. Jones. Our Indian people not only became 'terminated' by the BIA and government in terms of land, language, and culture, but we were also becoming spiritually and physically terminated as a result of Western society. I suppose that is why so many of the earlier doctors reverted to using sorcery. It was a way of trying to get back at the system. Hopefully I learned from their mistakes, and hopefully you will, too."

Doc Albert Thomas

"Doc Thomas was one of my main trainers. My mother wouldn't help me because she said I was a brat, incorrigible, and she favored my older brother and sister. I looked up to the older Indian doctors like they were gods or something. I was constantly hitchhiking around the country, following them, acting as a slave just to be around them and learn. I was drawn to them like a magnet, like a moth is to the light. At first Doc Thomas was very strict with the religion and would go long periods without eating, stay clean, and do whatever the spirits demanded of him. The people had respect for him and trusted him a lot. But in time that began to change.

"That is why I hung around Doc Thomas so much. He said he had trained over in Wintun Country (although he was also a Pit River Indian), up at Yolla Bolly where he had entered into the mountain when it opened up. His main power was the Lizard, although he also worked with the Mountain Lion, the Moon, a Pike, dwarfs, and even a Whiteman's ghost. He was a trance doctor, like most of them at that time. According to his story, he kept feeling pulled to this one sacred place. He was always swimming in lakes and sacred creeks, and praying to different mountains.

"He had been camped there for a number of weeks and had heard from older doctors about a secret entrance, I suppose what people today would call a dimensional doorway—a doorway into a spiritual realm unseen to the naked eye. He entered and found himself inside a cave. Once inside he met different shaman ghosts who gave him two choices.

"On one side of the cave was revealed a life of hardship, suffering, and sacrifice but rewarded with the power to heal anyone of any kind of sickness. On the other side was a dead person hanging with blowflies all over it, claimed by a two-headed Snake, and this power could do anything. It could heal or kill, but it would bring a person great wealth, fame, women, and very strong protection. Doc Thomas was known for praying to sacred places for good luck and wealth, so it wasn't any surprise when he revealed to me which power he accepted.

"It drove him crazy. He became very sick, died with his body covered with flies and maggots, but in a few days awoke in the meadow alive and stronger than ever. He said he couldn't stop singing day and night until a month had passed. Then he went back home. He was so powerful that he could make it lightning and thunder and bring sudden storms on a perfectly clear day, or throw balls of mysterious fire across the sky, like torpedoes, and set a person or house or car on fire. It was very, very powerful.

"That is the way he became wealthy and famous, and a womanizer. The women were crazy about him, and when he used his mouth to suck, they would have orgasms and go crazy. He would doctor them and get them well, but he would always find a way to sneak them outside away from their husbands and family and fornicate with them. They would do anything for him, wait on him hand and foot, and take money and rifles away from their husbands and give them to Doc Thomas. They would travel long distances to see him to get doctored, even though they weren't really sick, and they would give him all their money, baskets, regalia, anything. A lot of them were so in love with him that they became a bother. When this happened he would send a bad spirit against them and kill them. The husbands and family members were so afraid of Doc Thomas that they wouldn't do anything in return, and the other shamans also feared him.

"He even tried a couple of times to seduce my mother but that Karuk Indian doctor, Benoni Harrie, and my mother were best of friends. He protected her. That is when I pulled away from Doc Thomas, and a number of years later I heard he died a horrible death. While singing and dancing he fell on a very hot wood heater. It blew his guts wide open and he died in excruciating pain. So you see, not all the spirits you might encounter are representing the Great Creator. The Evil One has workers, too. Not all shamans are mediums for the Great Spirit, although they might have great spiritual powers."

Nancy

"A lot of the doctors back in those days wore Flicker feather regalia when they doctored or did ceremony, both the red-shafted and the yellow hammer. That's the way my mother was also meant to be, to work with the Flickerbird, Hummingbirds, Woodpeckers, and certain mountain spirits (ghosts of former shamans). One time she kept having dreams about a large Sea Serpent up in a big lake. You know the kind, like the famous Loch Ness monster, with horns on its head. That's how the power comes, through dreams about different kinds of spirits in different places. Strange, though, how some of these places can be so far away in a different tribe's territory.

"Well, like I said, this Indian doctor from up there at the Quartz Valley/ Ft. Jones area was helping my mother, teaching and training her. He used to call her his little spirit sister. But the spirits, good and bad, can play games with a human. They like to tease, lead a person on, and test them to see if a neophyte shaman has what it takes to endure the pain, suffering, and arduous training.

"Such spirits can take away a person's mind. They can make you *ker-pey-it,* or what the White people call paranoid schizophrenic. You can feel terrified seeing and hearing these things coming after you, but other people can't see them. Such phenomena are real, and they can torment a person day and night, as you yourself have come to learn.

"Well, Mom kept looking for this big lake. She would wake up singing and go in a trance talking to it, pointing up there, back east. Whenever she got the urge she would drive everyone else crazy until we got in the car and went looking with her. This adventure, of course, led to other shamans and different lakes, which in turn led to new encounters, then new dreams, and more spirits, and more singing and craziness; she was caught in a vicious cycle.

"Benoni doctored her and talked to the Sea Serpent. He found out it came from way over there in Washoe Indian Country, from Lake Tahoe. So that's where he took her to find it. She fasted all the time, with the trip taking about a week. Just a little smoked Salmon and acorn soup, no water. Then when she got there she had to find a place away from all the White people and casinos and motels. They built a fire, offered *walthpay* root (Grizzly Bear root, angelica in Western English, *kooshwoof* in Karuk language), and they all sang kick-dance songs.

"Mom got so crazy she jumped in the ice-cold lake and almost drowned, but that Serpent with the horns saved her, it pushed her back up on the beach. After that she had a connection with Indian people from other tribes and could doctor long-distance, meaning she could use that Sea Serpent to soul travel and doctor, often flying with the Flickerbirds or traveling through the water. My mother was a righteous person and led a good life. She refused to accept the Blue Jay doctor power, or any other bad powers, and she never charged much for doctoring. She didn't have to. People liked her work so they always gave her a lot in donations."

Benoni Harrie

"Like I said, he was a Karuk Indian doctor and his wife was one of the best basket makers around up in that part of the territory. One time my mother got very sick. She was running a very bad fever, broke out in spots, and shook with chills. She also started spitting up blood. My sister sent for Benoni to come down and doctor. You would always know he had arrived because you could hear the Woodpeckers and Flickers making all kinds of noise and jumping up and down in the yard. Then he would walk in and say, 'Now my little sister, ah, what kind of trouble did you get yourself into again this time?' And he would always laugh and then scold her.

"He didn't use much in terms of regalia, just a headband made from Flicker feathers, armbands, and a necklace, but sometimes he did strip down to his underwear and wear Flicker feather anklets.

"He told my mother she was being made sick by the Flickerbirds. He scolded her for not taking care of her doctor regalia. For example, he said that she kept her feathers and pipe under the mattress, for convenience and protection while she slept, but the younger female relatives often came and sat on the bed while they were on their moontime. Thus, he claimed Nancy had feathers in her chest that had to be taken out, cleaned up, and pleaded with. She got well after that but only lived a few more years.

"Benoni didn't live much longer either because he was hell for sneaking around and drinking. Our Indian people are allergic to alcohol. I don't care if you do consider it a stereotype. It's a fact. We didn't have it in our heritage and culture, and it acts like a poison on us. It begins to take control mentally and spiritually, then it spreads all over the body, and it gets passed down to the offspring, so they too inherit the poison as well as any transgressions that go along with it.

"That's what happened to Benoni, and it wasn't long before he went downhill. He became a drunk, sex crazed, and there were rumors of him supposedly molesting young girls. The power itself was driving him crazy. Otherwise he had been a damn good seer and a strong doctor. One day he got so drunk he lost his doctor bag, with his pipe and medicines in it. He died shortly afterward with a curse upon his family. I don't think that any of his children, grandchildren, or great-grandchildren will ever become doctors, although they might (genetically) inherit the power. The alcohol, jealousy, anger, fear, and bad spirits will get the best of them, or they might become small-time sorcerers on the pretense of being spiritual. That's how strong Benoni's power was and the restitution associated with it."

Other Shamans

"Some of the other shamans I had contact with and learned from included Charlie Klutchie, Fanny Brown, Ida Cyst, and Tilly Griffin. I didn't actually train under them as an apprentice; I just got doctored by them a few times and stayed with them occasionally while getting doctored because they were so far away. Tilly had a good reputation and was well respected by everyone, but Fanny Brown was feared and despised. The way I understood it, Fanny had lost a number of her children. They died by accidents in a bad way. People said it was because she used evil power and spirits on people, especially on some of the other shamans who she tried to blame for the death of her children.

"I know Doc Albert Thomas didn't like or trust her. He could take a fire, or make a small spark of electricity by grabbing the back of his head and flicking it like a flint, then he would light his pipe, a woodstove, campfire, or anything. Some people thought it was magic but it was just pure fire power, something that the White people will never understand. Anyway, Fanny was really jealous because he could do that.

"So she sent Rattlesnakes against him, not only in spirit form; physically the Snakes would show up out of nowhere and try to bite him. Sometimes they even got into the house in a mysterious way. She was also jealous of Charlie Klutchie but he mostly avoided the shamanic power trips as he called them, the jealousy games that the doctors over in his country often played while witching and deviling each other. I heard that they even had contests in the old days, at cultural gatherings, and challenged one another with their power. For example, they might throw spiritual objects at one another such as feathers that shot like arrows, or flints, or things that could not be seen by the human eye that were similar to electrical currents. At other times, people such as Charlie Klutchie and Albert Thomas would pick up red-hot rocks from the fireplace, or even a whole burning woodstove, and they never got burned, probably because they had power from the fire. Some of the Indian doctors could dance in a big fire on hot coals and logs and never get burned. The White people (anthropologists) called this ability magic. They didn't believe it.

"Charlie Klutchie was a good person with a good reputation. He came from a long line of doctors. His powers got much stronger, though, after one of his boys died. That boy got stabbed in a fight. Charlie went up to

Mt. Shasta and grieved. He stayed up there about a month fasting, praying, bathing, and crying. The strongest power, Grizzly Bear power, comes from that ancient and holy mountain. The Shasta Indians had good doctors, and even they will tell you that the strongest doctor power, the highest in rank, is the Grizzly Bear. And I understand the traditional Indians in other tribes across the country have the same belief and understanding about the ranking of doctor powers.

"The belief is similar to that of our people, the Yurok, and our neighbors, the Karuk, but not too many people alive today know that kind of knowledge. I met some Sioux and other Plains Indians years ago from over there in Montana and South Dakota. I guess they have a similar belief, or understanding, that the Grizzly Bear is the highest doctor power, but also the most difficult to get. It is also the most feared, I guess, and whoever has that kind of power will always have a very hard life. People get jealous of a Grizzly Bear doctor. They don't understand the lonely and moody-type behavior of such a person. They fear that kind of doctor and don't trust him.

"So they tried to gang up on him, the Grizzly Bear, and cause trouble for him all the time. Our old Indian myths tell stories about that, from the House of Talth, the secret doctor society. So Charlie Klutchie was highly respected but also feared, and misunderstood because he was quiet and humble, reflective, you might say, and not very sociable. He preferred to live by himself and not be around other people too much, just like that Grizzly Bear. If a person acts that way the community thinks he's strange. They will find excuses to talk bad about him, ways to spread lies and rumors, and cause trouble until that Bear gets mad enough to fight back, then watch out! Nobody wants to deal with an angry Bear, and they begin to hate it. When people hate something, they try to destroy it, just like they have tried to do to the Grizzly Bears in this country. Just like the White people in their religion did to the man called Jesus who also went up in the mountains to talk to God, to make a special connection with the Great Spirit, and who tried to use his power and the Great Creator's powers to heal people.

"That's why Charlie probably lived such a strict and righteous life in comparison to the other doctors. He didn't drink or fool around with women, although he got accused about it a lot. He died in a good way because he was close to the Great Creator, just like that Grizzly Bear who is from Mt. Shasta, high up beyond the other animals and birds, close to where the Great Creator sometimes lives or comes and visits the Earth and the people. The higher a medicine man goes to acquire his knowledge, power, training, and pass his tests, then the higher his spirituality will be. The more he suffers and proves himself, supposedly, the more he will be rewarded, sooner or later.

"The strongest doctors in all the local tribes always trained in the sweat lodge and got their first powers, dreams, and songs that way. Then they were tested and sung over by the older doctors. As they gradually progressed, they would eventually be required to go on a vision quest at different places such as alpine lakes, smaller mountains, caves, then higher mountains. It's like going through school or college to higher grades and degrees of learning. More dreams lead a person to more and different spirits, to more encounters and adventures, and of course, more exams to prove they are qualified. The Elders and older medicine people, or who anthropologists call shamans, did the evaluation and ordaining.

"Therefore, any person who has not followed this process to the letter is a half-assed Indian doctor, or quack. Or what we call today a Shake 'N Bake shaman, plastic shaman, etcetera. They might have some power and knowledge but they are not genuine, legitimate, or bona fide. A person has to earn the knowledge, powers, ability, status, and recognition. To simply be born with it, the potential psychic powers and abilities, is not enough. All medicine men and women are constantly tempted by the evil spirits. The bad powers are easier to get and use, so be careful about what you dream, what you encounter, what you choose, or what you let enter you.

"Sometimes it is better to have failed, to not receive anything, than it is to accept lesser powers or evil powers. Sometimes it is better to be humble, to act like you are afraid and not fight when challenged, to just walk away. Otherwise anger, fear, jealousy, and ignorance will seriously interfere with your potential and ability to achieve higher spirituality, knowledge, and powers. Be careful of the enemies you might make. Also be careful of your role models, mates, and certain friends you choose in this life; and be especially careful of your mentors. They can help make you or break you in what you are destined to be."

For nine days straight I fasted, sweated, gathered wood, prayed, meditated, and thought a lot. I had plenty of time and isolation to think in privacy, except for the periodic interruptions caused by the spirits, heavy footsteps around me day and night, the feeling of a strange presence and that someone, or something, was scanning me. There were growling sounds and strange birdcalls late at night when I fell asleep. I strained my eyesight each time an incident occurred but I could never see anything, only periodic apparitions. They were in the vague forms of large animals, birds, people, dwarfs and gnomes, and other things that were so weird that I can't describe them.

I left on the eighth day while trying to find an old trail that I learned later had not been used in fifty years, since Wahsek had done his *hokep*. It started from behind the hog pens, on the other side of the fence, cut a faint path through a clear-cut field, then gradually headed into a thick Douglas fir forest. I frequently got sidetracked by Deer trails but kept my direction focused by certain landmarks that Wahsek had told me to look for, such as a large displaced boulder, a creek, remnants of an old farm site, and then some crisscrossing over old logging skid trails that eventually disappeared as the terrain turned into patches of thick buck brush. I was to follow this up to a flat that came out by two twin ponds, then proceed up the west side of Kewet Mountain, past an obvious prayer altar and naturally formed seat, then over through the cedar woods to Fish Lake. According to myth, Fish Lake is where a legendary ceremonial leader trained as a child. He was a bastard child, from a very poor family, and an object of community ridicule. The ancient myth or legend tells how he overcame his demise and became a famous man of wealth, power, and stature.

Before I left, Wahsek wanted to loan me his pistol. He had tears from reminiscing in his eyes. I told him I didn't think I would need it, that it would probably be an insult to the spirits. But he was stubborn, indicating that his brother had made a similar attempt and got attacked by what he called "wild Indians." Evidently they were a band of prehistoric indigenous people who had somehow managed to survive all these years with hardly any contact with the outside, modern world.

Wahsek claimed his forefathers knew about them, as did other Elders, but by legend. The "wild Indians" were supposedly midgets who ran around naked, but they were extremely dangerous because of their cunning, their special hunting and survival skills, and their magical powers. He further advised that they were not to be confused with dwarfs or "Little People"— Indians allegedly the size of human toddlers and gnomes who could appear in solid physical form or as spirits in specter form. I took the pistol just to appease him but later hid it on the other side of the fence.

I wasn't really worried about anything wild hurting me except the drugged-up hippies, renegade Vietnam vets, and ex-cons who had been seen hiding out in our reservation woods and wilderness areas from time to time.

I was pretty exhausted at about midway and decided to stop and pray when all of a sudden I got attacked by hundreds of Blue Jays. It was worse than Alfred Hitchcock's movie *The Birds*. They came in from every direction, screaming, squawking, and diving, trying to peck and claw me. I was terrified and fought for my life. I used sticks, rocks, a broken-off piece of Douglas fir bough and just kept fighting for what seemed like hours. Then a very large Raven came in hollering and fighting in my defense. Soon a flock of Crows came, and the Blue Jays scattered like snowflakes melting out of sight into a warm winter Wind.

I got out my pipe and prayed for my life, giving thanks to the good spirits. There were beautiful Blue Jay feathers all around me, tempting tools of power. I didn't want that kind of power, however, and I refused to accept it. I clearly stated my defiance verbally and symbolically to the powers, and after regaining my composure, I proceeded to a nearby stream to wash up. I was craving a drink of water but kept disciplined. I didn't give in to that temptation either.

By sunset I was at the flat, near the base of the mountain. I had a very difficult time finding the flat because the old trail from Wahsek's house had been obliterated with time; it was overgrown or distorted from prior logging activity evidently done a couple of decades before. The forest was cool and refreshing but the flat was hot from the summer-afternoon Sun.

I couldn't remember what pond Wahsek had told me to bathe in. The twin ponds were the home of two twin giants, spirits who lived there and were known to grant special wishes to humans under certain circumstances, and upon training properly for the quest. But one spirit was mean and vicious, and the other giant brother was kind and generous. I got out my pipe, smudged myself with *keeshwoof* root, chewed a piece for good luck, and closed my eyes in meditation, hoping to "see," in a psychic way, exactly which pond to choose.

I looked for a sign, an omen of some sort, but I had no cooperation from the spirits or my relations in Nature. It was a very perplexing situation because the right decision could get me prosperity, and the wrong decision could wipe out my family. According to myth, one of the giants was a cannibal who took out his revenge by devouring humans. He could sneak in on the unsuspecting prey during the middle of the night, in phantom form, and leave behind a bloody mess, an attack so terrible that not even the best detective could figure out what or who had committed such a gruesome act. There was a history of this kind of rare, unsolved murder mysteries in the local county during the past century.

I walked up to one of the ponds and looked in the water. I saw a reflection of myself but older in age, as an Elder. I walked up to the other pond and didn't see any reflection at all. Hoping that my intuition was reliable enough to make the right choice, I chose the pond where I saw my reflection. I then proceeded to strip down, offer the tobacco as instructed, and make a wish while totally submerged under water. I could feel something large turn me around and around several times until I floated to the top. Although I was dizzy, I managed to crawl out over the muddy bank and get dressed.

After checking for landmarks I hiked up the side of Burrill Peak and got to the old prayer altar just before sunset. I had to strip down naked, reconstruct an altar, pray with my pipe, burn angelica roots, and lament all night in spiritual discussion and pleas with the Great Spirit. I asked for sincere forgiveness for any prior misconduct or immoral behavior in my life. In repentance, I pleaded for forgiveness for any prior violations

I may have made against the Natural Laws or Indian custom and laws. I begged for protection against any enemies I might have made, and stated very clearly that I did not want any enemies in my life. I forgave those who may have done me wrong. I wished for a chance at getting another good job, a good woman, and a prosperous life. But I also made sure to thank the Great Creator, the good spirits, and all of Nature for the many gifts and good things that I had already been given in this lifetime and former lifetimes.

All night I stayed awake and prayed, cried, and pleaded. I had to cut myself with a piece of sacred white quartz rock as part of the ritual, and as a symbolic act to let the bad blood and negative energy flow out of my body. It hurt terribly and the mosquitoes swarmed in for a feast, but with the release of bad blood also went the discharge of bad luck, toxins, and stress-related sickness. The ritual and form of self-mutilation were intended to simulate the natural purging that a menstruating woman experiences during her cycle.

Afterward I used herbs, positive thinking, bathing, and prayer to achieve a balanced state of spirituality. This esoteric way of thinking and medicine making was a male's approach to achieving homeostasis. In other words, women were given the natural gift of bleeding for purification, and although one part of the menses is negative because it serves to release toxins and bad power, it is also positive in the sense that it affords the woman a unique opportunity to regenerate herself both physically and spiritually. Men are not that fortunate. They have to suffer in a different way, to find a different means to achieve balance.

In this sense men are considered inferior. They are considered less powerful than women spiritually, but they don't want women to know it. That's why some men resent the menses to the point of making it a curse for women. They fear it and despise it, so they teach their wives, sisters, and daughters to look upon it as a negative phenomenon. But the women weren't born stupid. They know intuitively that it is a unique source of power. The traditional woman knew that if the power was handled properly, in a ritualistic way by using a moontime ceremony, it could bring good luck, good health, and good fortune to her family. If handled improperly, however, it could and often did have an adverse effect. Indian men did not have such a ceremony, and therefore they had to create one of their own as a means to acquire good luck and wealth. That is why menses can be considered a curse or a blessing. It is naturally powerful, and power deserves respect.

Gina said the original cultural attitude and understanding of menses as a source of power, both positive and negative, had been replaced, distorted, and suppressed by Western superstitious thinking, lack of morals, and discrimination against women. To support her analogy she often referred to the concept of marriage and bride price. According to Indian custom and law, a man was required to buy his wife with a lot of regalia and money. She said this was a way of showing respect to the woman, her family, and the community, as well as a means to compensate that family for the loss of something very valuable. It was the Law of Reciprocity. On the other hand, she stated, the Whiteman didn't pay anything for his bride, so therefore the woman was of no value to him, and he assumed that he could do whatever he wanted with her, which usually led to mistreatment and abuse. A man who did not pay for his wife had no respect for his wife. Gina was perplexed and outraged about the Western-European concept whereby the father was expected to pay the groom a bride price for taking the worthless daughter off his hands!

As I sat by the fire lamenting, I thought about God's Laws, Natural Laws, aboriginal custom and laws, and the Whiteman's laws. I thought about my past life and actions, about my past marriage and divorce, and about future reconciliations. I swore that if I ever got married again I would do it the right way. I would make payment for my bride as part of a traditional Indian ceremony. I would try to be a respectful and righteous person.

I cried myself to sleep but was awakened just before daybreak by the sudden crashing of brush and wood debris. At first I thought it might be Bigfoot, or a Bear, or perhaps the wild Indians. As I scanned the area I heard it come closer but it sounded a little softer upon approaching. It was a pure White Deer, a buck with red eyes. He was awesome. I could feel his spirit move out and touch me, just before he turned and headed over to Fish Lake. I picked up my gear and proceeded to follow.

A couple of hours later I got to the lake. I did take the time to stop, build a small fire, and smudge my body with fir boughs as part of the training and preparation. The closer I got to the lake, the more I could see that it was crowded and contaminated with campers. There was no way I could do a ceremony and expect to make spiritual contact with a mythological Whale, Sea Serpent, or any other creature. Tired, frustrated, and discouraged, I decided to walk and hitchhike down the narrow paved road that was the easiest way off the mountain. It wasn't long before I caught a ride down to the bridge by Pearson's store, then walked from there along the Klamath River up to Wahsek's ranch, then up the old dirt road to the house.

I checked from a distance to make sure that no visitors were at his house, and then I tried to sneak through the woods past the rear of the house and up to my training camp. After resting for a while, I started building a sacred fire for the sweat lodge. I was despondent. I thought I had failed, and I was ashamed. I just wanted to be alone in my misery for a while, but a person can't hide anything from Gina or Wahsek. They have radar around the place.

I caught him checking up on me but ignored it. I wanted to heat the rocks before sunset and have privacy to think. When the rocks were hot and ready, I placed them inside the lodge, finished making my medicine, and dreamed all night, trying to rest and regenerate.

Learning How to Deal with Demons, Ghosts, and Sorcery

A couple of nights later I had a dream about a giant Indian. He came and picked me up, holding me up high while I shook in fear. He asked me if I knew him, and I said no. He responded by saying gruffly that I had come to his house and visited with him, up at the pond. He talked to me firmly and said that some of the things I wished for would come true, but not all of the wishes would be granted. I also dreamed about a young, beautiful, and very spiritual Indian girl. At first I thought it was a young girl I had met down at the Tule Indian reservation while doing ceremonies with Charlie a year or so before. She kept following me everywhere I went, and I couldn't get rid of her. She was only fourteen and too young for my interest. The dream about the young girl kept coming in stronger and stronger, each time more clear. She lived down near the Ocean and was from a ceremonial family. I saw her dancing with a Redtail Hawk and the Morning Star. I also saw her crying in pain, loneliness, and abuse, pleading for someone or something to save her.

I had dreams about mountains and spirits other than Chimney Rock, although earlier visions I'd had in years past involving Chimney Rock kept flashing in my mind. I also had dreams that I had acquired a lot of regalia, obtained some minor wealth, and secured a good job in teaching. The last dream I had was about fighting a heavyset, dark-skinned Indian man who was dancing with Snakes, Blue Jays, Spiders, Water Dogs, Owls, Skunks, and flints (obsidian stones that are used to make arrowheads and spears).

Wahsek was pleased with my performance. He said it wasn't my fault that I couldn't access Fish Lake, that Western civilization was not only destroying the Earth, but also traditional Indian religion and culture in the process. He said I'd handled the situation with the Blue Jays as a warrior, and that I had made the right decision not to accept the offer of becoming a sorcerer. Such feathers, he said, were tools of the trade in sorcery.

He warned me, however, that I would be locked in a deadly battle with a very powerful sorcerer and his apprentices for many long years, the same sorcerer who was partially responsible for ruining my marriage and causing me to lose my job. He knew who it was but he wouldn't tell me because he said it was my fate, not his, to find out and learn how to deal with it.

Lastly, he appeared to be concerned about the dream involving the young woman. He said it was a premonition of my next mate, and that according to myth and legend, the best women came from Requa, a historically significant village near the Ocean. But he also strongly warned me that this woman would be an extremely powerful and temperamental temptress who could either advance my spirituality, shamanic development, and success in life, or eventually destroy me. He said she was a young shamaness but she didn't know it yet, and he reminded me that power always had a price involved, and that sometimes it couldn't be tamed.

I stayed for another week to heal my cuts and seal the new envelope of spirituality. I didn't want to chance anything that might break my medicine. I was lonesome to see my son and take time out to just fish, relax, and enjoy regular life before starting an intensive job search and possible career change. It was during this time that I met the young Indian woman, down at Klamath, while stopping by to visit with her father, who was a traditional fisherman, canoe maker, and cultural specialist.

I first saw her while getting out of the truck. I also saw the Flickerbirds, Hummingbirds, Ravens, and Woodpeckers dancing around in the air, as if symbolically mating. She stood in the doorway, then started nervously pacing back and forth. I was halfway to the porch when I caught her staring at me with the piercing eyes of a Hawk, and then suddenly I felt a profound force fly into my body and I began to shake all over. I could see that she was also in a state of convulsion, vibrating at the same rate.

I tried to stagger back to the truck and leave. I wanted to get the hell out of there but her stepmother came up and grabbed me. "Hey Bobby, you can't leave yet, or you'll violate custom and law. It's time for lunch so you better stay and eat or Chuk-chuk will get mad at you, and you know how his temper is."

I thought this woman was about sixteen but soon discovered that she was going on nineteen years of age. We were both nervous and couldn't keep our eyes off each other. She kept dropping food on me while she was trying to set the table, and I kept spilling the coffee. It was the same spiritual feeling I had when I first met Lilly, but this feeling was more forceful. It had power in it. In fact it was so strong that I creamed myself. No woman had ever caused that to happen before.

I was still shaking when I excused myself from the table and went into the bathroom to clean up the spontaneous ejaculation. I had never encountered a woman who could strike me this way, with such a strong electrical current and profound sexual bonding. It was not only embarrassing but it was humiliating and frightening. I ended up staying a week before finally tearing myself away to take care of personal business.

I visited and fished the traditional way with her father, with gill nets and a boat, sang songs, and practiced the hand game called "Indian cards." I had known her father and brothers and other sisters for a number of years but I didn't know he had a younger daughter, the youngest of the family. Her name was Tela. She was extremely beautiful, well built, dark skinned, with jet black hair and the eyes of a Raven. She also had the mystique and profound aura of a Raven, or some other kind of magical bird. I spent every free moment I could with her, talking, laughing, embracing, and romancing. I wanted to sneak into her bedroom at night but I was afraid her father would catch us. His room was next to hers. Every night I dreamed about having sex with her, only to discover the next day that she had been having similar dreams. But she also told me about the many other kinds of dreams and visions she had been having all her life, including the dream about me before we met.

By early July I had spent some quality time with my son, Kanawha. I had also applied for different jobs, including a newly created position at Humboldt as coordinator of the curriculum program I had previously created.

I couldn't stop thinking about Tela. Day and night she was constantly on my mind. I had bad dreams about Owls trying to attack her, dead people pestering her, and a young Indian man beating her up. I figured it was the Pit River guy she had been living with and left, prior to the time I met her at her father's home. I called and found out she had been in the hospital, very ill, and the White doctors didn't know what was wrong with her.

When I called her on the telephone she seemed scared, lonely, and languid. She told me that she wanted to sleep all the time and that she was feeling her strength wane. She said she had been attacked several times by Blue Jays during the day, and sprayed by a Skunk, that Owls were screeching around the house every night, and that a Fox kept coming around whistling at her, until her father had killed it. She also said she had nightmares involving ghosts and dead people. I knew these were all bad signs that Death was stalking her. She pleaded with me to come and help her.

I intuitively knew that she would die if I didn't go back and get her, but it was too tough a case for me to handle. The only salvation was to get her to Wahsek. I still had a couple of checks in back pay coming from the college that had already been transferred into my bank account. So I figured I could make Wahsek a worthy donation and still take care of whatever basic needs we might have while trying to relocate to a mountain cabin up on the *rancheria*. I stopped at my friend's house and picked up my full-blooded pet Wolf named Tobacco, gathered up some regalia, and took a bunch of cash with me. When I got to the house her father was half drunk.

"What are you doing here, Coyote?" he growled. " I already ran one asshole off, that Pit River dude."

"I came to get your daughter," I said firmly. "I fell in love with her, and I know she loves me, and I'll take damn good care of her. You know me real well. We've done a lot of good cultural things over the years. You know I'm special, not like that trash she was living with that beat and abused her."

Tela came walking up to me very listless when I first entered the house. She could barely stand up, and she held onto me, crying. "I'm going Chuk-chuk. You never gave a damn about me anyway. You never cared anything about your kids. You haven't done anything to help me since I've been here anyway, and I don't want to die here!"

She already had her clothes and personal stuff stacked up on the couch, waiting to leave. I told Chuk-chuk I knew he was a traditional man and as a result I had respect for him. I told him I wanted to buy his daughter according to Indian custom and law, and that I could only make partial payment, but I promised to make full payment at a later date. At that time I offered him a large-sized, handmade Navajo rug that was worth a lot of money, several pieces of Indian jewelry, including some expensive silver and turquoise, and local Indian dentalia and abalone necklaces. I also gave him a large can of tobacco, a rifle, some animal hides, Eagle and Hawk feathers, and my Wolf. All in all this bride payment was probably worth about seven thousand dollars. It was probably the first time in a long time that any man had bought his wife locally.

Tela fell asleep on the way up to Wahsek's house. It was getting close to sunset. I stopped and picked up a can of tobacco and coffee, some cartons of cigarettes, and basic groceries, enough to feed several people for several days.

From the town of Orick I proceeded over Bald Hills Road and crossed over the bridge directly to the Wahsek ranch just a little farther down the river. As usual the Hawk came flying in to greet me but Wahsek was busy in the front yard trying to fight off a flock of Blue Jays with a broom. They all took off just as soon as I pulled up to the house, next to the old fruit trees, with the Hawk screaming at their heels in downward attacks.

Gina had already smudged the house and had been praying with pepperwood leaves, and it was quite smoky by the time I followed Wahsek into the house; I had asked Tela to stay in the truck until I got permission to bring her in.

Sitting in his blue chair and looking disgusted, he said, "I don't know who the hell you got in the truck but it doesn't look good at all. A large tree just fell before you got here, and well, you saw all the damn Blue Jays I was fighting, plus the Owls have been screeching every night. A war is breaking out around here!"

I told him about who I met, what kind of condition she was in, and that she had been experiencing similar problems. He seemed pissed off and growled at me, "Now why in the hell did you go and do that, wind up with another woman at a time when you really should be focusing all your time and energy on spiritual development? No, I don't think I want to get involved."

In desperation I turned to Gina, who was already crying. She also scolded me. "I told you that a young woman was following you. Damn it, you're really in for it this time. This one has got her claws in you and there ain't no way you're going to escape, so I guess you better learn how to start dealing with it. She's a beauty all right, very special, but with her is also coming a lifetime of problems and trouble. She's like a diamond in the rough, and you best believe you're going to pay one hell of a price to get her polished and shining, that is, if you have enough tenacity and power. Go on now. Go get her and bring her in the house. Poor thing, she's scared to death!"

Tela was shaking like a leaf in autumn while I tried to carry her into the house. Wahsek and Gina were arguing with each other but stopped suddenly when I brought Tela in and introduced her. "Damn," Wahsek said curtly, "she's the spitting image of her grandma Alice, huh, Gina?"

Gina looked and just shook her finger at me, but then in a tone of compliment she said, "Yeah, she's the runt of the Wolfpack but the best out of the whole litter. Just like her Grandma Alice, but she's also got the powers of her Great-Grandma Nellie, and her Great-Great-Grandma Tipsy, and even that mean old witch, Pi-ker-una, the last of the female shamans from upriver."

They both laughed and kept shaking their heads in disbelief. I was so scared for Tela's life that I offered five hundred dollars cash, the standard protocol of tobacco, and more Eagle feathers, and I promised labor in return for their doctoring her. I gave Gina a carton of cigarettes, the coffee, and two fifty-dollar bills.

They acted as if that was the first time anyone had ever donated so much money. Somewhat reluctantly, Wahsek agreed. "Well, I guess I really don't have much choice. Hell, man, I don't know what I would do if she died up here in my house. Besides, she's probably the last of the Talth female species; out of respect and cultural preservation I am obligated to try and save her, but I'll need your full cooperation and doctoring assistance, okay?"

Tela looked like a trapped Rabbit. She didn't know what to say, what to do, what to expect, or where to run. She sat there shaking and crying, listening to the negotiation. It was the first time I ever saw Gina reach out and hug anyone in an affectionate way, except her adopted son. She pulled Tela into her loving bosom as if embracing a lost and returning daughter. "You're not on your moontime, are you?" she said softly. "I believe you know about that custom, right?"

"I'm clean and not due for a few more weeks," she said. "I know some things about it but I never went through the Flower Dance."

Gina smiled and in a motherly tone responded, "That's okay, just as long as you follow the spiritual laws. I don't think any of the younger women have had the good fortune to train in the Flower Dance because the Whiteman's religion tried to wipe it out. I think I'm the last woman in the area to actually go through it, except maybe Velma who married that Coyote, Charlie Thom."

Tela helped Gina with the cooking while I helped Wahsek feed the hogs and chickens. We ate a late dinner because the Sun stays up longer in early summer, and it is too hot to cook on a woodstove. I had already explained to Tela the way Wahsek doctored, so she had some idea of what to expect. Gina added to the knowledge partly out of conversation and partly to help Tela feel more relaxed. Wahsek kept looking at Tela, obviously reading her aura and piercing into her soul. He said, "You know your great-great-grandfather, Captain Spott, is a legend around here. He was a very powerful and religious man, a true high man, but as a consequence you have inherited the good, the bad, and the ugly. For example, did you know that there is a terrible curse against your family?

That's the cause for some of your sickness. The curse was made against your family generations ago by an old witch, a Tolowa shaman, who lived up past Crescent City."

I could feel the cold chills run up Tela's spine when he said that, and she became very uneasy. The Sun had gone down and we heard strange birdcalls and whistling around the house. Coyote could be heard howling up on the ridge, and then the Owls came in hooting.

Wahsek turned toward the window and said nervously, "Well, I see we have a visitor outside, a challenger, in fact a number of challengers. We've got an *uputawon*, bad spirit, out there from upriver and an *umaa*, sorcerer, from downriver, a *say-gap*, or Coyote, from Pit River, and a bunch of deceased people coming to get you. So you see, that's some more of your problem, but don't worry. Let them have their fun. We'll soon take care of it."

Gina interrupted, "Yeah, Tela, you've really got to be careful where you leave your hair, especially your pubic hairs. Those men over there in Karuk, Pit River, and Wintun Country are hell for making love medicine against a woman. They'll drive you nuts, break your heart, and steal your spirit if you're not careful. I've seen a lot of women end up as slaves in a relationship, trapped and lovesick with no way out."

Wahsek laughed and reacted, "Yeah, you should know, woman, but they're not as bad as the Hupa men, are they?"

"Oh yeah, well, the Hupas aren't as bad as those damn Karuks, like that Pi-ker-una and the rest of those witches."

"Wow, Gina," Wahsek replied. "Why do you hate those women up there so much? You know you're talking about some of Tela's relations. Pi-ker-una was a damn good doctor, the last of her kind up there."

"Doctor, my ass. Yeah, she might have been a good seer, and that's about it. All those women up there had *uputawon* power and love medicine. I ain't stupid, you know. I know that. I know you got a kid running around up there someplace. You can't hide it from me. You couldn't give me a child of my own but you sure as hell could Coyote around up there, until you got your ass nailed, huh? I know your kid is a girl too, even if you do try to hide it from everyone else." She was obviously hurt and slightly vindictive.

On that note Wahsek got up and said he had to go outside and make medicine, confront the challengers, do mortal combat if necessary. I knew a person could die from fighting sorcerers and dead people if they didn't have enough power. I was worried about him because I heard footsteps. Someone had been walking around the house. "Want me to go out there with you?" I asked. I was afraid that someone might jump him in the dark, stab or shoot him, or worse.

"No, I'm fine," he said. "Just help get the room set up for doctoring. When we're done Tela can sleep in here and you can stay up there by your sweat lodge. I want you to stay up all night keeping vigil. I want you to help pray and make medicine for her."

The women cleaned up the kitchen, came into the front room, and then sat silently smoking, waiting. It was dead silent for a while, then the birdcalls and whistling got louder, more Owls came in hooting and screeching, but the Coyote, *say-gap,* could be heard crying in the distance while the dogs chased and barked viciously after him. Then all of a sudden a big *boom* noise hit and shook the whole house. The impact was so strong that it knocked Tela off her chair and I jumped to keep the kerosene lamp from crashing. It felt like an earthquake.

Gina just laughed and told us, "I guess they wanted to play rough so Wahsek called in stronger protectors. He works not only with Lightning and Thunder Grandfathers, but also the Earthquake Brothers. They're all spirits, you know."

Although there was no sign of Rain, Lightning began to flash all over the place, Thunder got stronger and louder, the house shook a couple more times, and a Mountain Lion screamed, sending chills up the backs of our necks. Tela ran over and desperately held onto me.

Shortly after everything got calm, Wahsek came back into the house and started in doctoring. He lit his pipe, sang and danced, and used his hands all over Tela but he didn't suck on her. This went on until just before daybreak. She fell asleep on the couch and never got an opportunity to confess for any sins or violations. I went out to the sweat lodge, built a fire, prayed until sunrise, and then went inside the lodge and slept. I could hear Wahsek and Gina's songs bounce off the mountains and drift down the river.

The next day herbs were made up for Tela. She spent most of the day in misery between puking and shitting, then finished with an herbal bath. Wahsek sent me to get his sister Bunny up the road to come and help with the doctoring. He explained to both of us that he needed stronger female support and he felt it would be in my best interest if I wasn't present when Tela had to *pegasoy* for certain affairs, activities, and transgressions.

Apparently this wasn't his normal approach in doctoring, but I realized he was trying to be thoughtful about a very sensitive subject matter, some things that a man or woman needs to keep private until a trusting relationship has been established. It was obvious that certain things might come up that could upset me or shame her. I agreed to cooperate, and although Tela was a little puzzled and reluctant, she also agreed.

I was still bothered for a long time into the marriage about the secrets that had been kept from me. It wasn't until years later that I discovered for myself, when doctoring her for an entirely different ailment, why the problems and related illnesses required confidentiality as a buffer against potential shame and guilt. It wasn't her fault that she had been physically, mentally, and sexually abused by her own relations, and by other men while confined to foster homes. The impact of these unfortunate affairs left serious wounds that would take a long time to heal, and perhaps scars that could never be removed.

Wahsek had me join in on the third night of doctoring and I helped Tela *pegasoy* for inherited violations, and other things that were tormenting her beyond her control: for example, a history of using sorcery in the family, a curse against her family because sorcerers had dug up the family burial grounds, her forefathers' misuse in handling ceremonial regalia, and her own violations involving menses power and certain traditional foods and sacred places.

On the fourth night, Wahsek said he had to visit a cemetery in order to pray and break the curse. He asked if I would go with him to the cemetery where Tela's relatives were buried. I was scared but felt honored. It would be a good opportunity for me to learn more about the dark side and how to deal with demons, ghosts, and the vile art of sorcery.

Preparation for the task required special, secretive, and strong medicine making, an ancient ritual that can only be shared with the higher shamans, those who were righteous spiritual healers and who had a definite holy commitment to the profession. There could be no mistakes while making this kind of medicine, no room for fear, and no substitutes for the remedy.

It had to be strategic, synchronistic, and complete. If the ceremony wasn't done properly and according to specific rules and formulas, a backlash could occur causing serious supernatural consequences beyond human imagination. Violent death in the practitioner's family for many generations was just one example of possible repercussions.

We stopped at a very sacred place and made our medicine. We prayed for protection, we prayed for higher powers needed to fight special kinds of evil power, we prayed for courage and strength. Then we proceeded up the highway, through a mysterious shield of fog, toward the cemetery that was sitting on a bluff overlooking the Ocean. I could hear the sounds of Whales crying an ancient song and Sea Lions barking frantically, and I could feel the strong salty air tingle my skin and nostrils.

Wahsek instructed me to turn off the truck headlights as we began to ascend a very narrow, winding road. It was treacherous. One wrong move and we could crash over the cliff into the Ocean. I tried to have faith but couldn't help but ask how he expected me to see where I was going. "With instinct and guiding spirits," he retorted, "and perhaps with a little stroke of luck." It wasn't long before I could see the old Spott family house up on the hill, and several figures standing in the graveyard. Sparks of light flashed through the dense fog.

We got out of the truck, being careful not to slam doors or make any unexpected noise. Like two stealth warriors we silently crept up on the perpetrators. In a circular motion we went, imitating two Great White Sharks circling their prey, while Wahsek kept singing in a low voice.

We weren't more than twenty feet from them when he stopped and motioned for me to lie down on the ground, being careful not to lie upon any graves, or any spot that might feel extremely cold, eerie, and dead.

I could not see the faces of what appeared to be an older, heavyset man and two younger men digging up a grave. I couldn't believe that people would actually be so evil as to desecrate the dead. I got so disgusted and angry that I wanted to jump up and run over and beat the hell out of them with their own shovels. Wahsek touched me to quiet me down, whispered that I had to control my emotions, otherwise they could sense we were here—or at least their evil spirits could sense we were present.

They dug up a body and I could hear the older man giving instructions for the younger men to remove rib bones, sinew from the legs, and any available regalia or artifacts. He was singing very strange birdsongs and smacking two flints together. Sparks circled counterclockwise around them. I then saw what appeared to be zombielike creatures rising from graves. They walked in a stupor, staggering for a sense of direction, then gathered around the humans as if waiting for instructions.

A slight sea breeze carried the older man's voice toward us and I could hear him say, "There aren't going to be any more Indian doctors, ceremonial leaders, or medicine people in this family. I'm going to put an end to it all. I'm going to be the ceremonial leader. Everyone will look up to me and I will become rich. My uncle did it to his enemies and I am going to do it to mine. Then you boys here can continue the ritual to the next generation, just in case the curse gets broken."

The older sorcerer turned to the dead people, offered them food and tobacco. He pleaded with them, crying for them to help him. He wanted the deceased to torment and capture the souls of the living family members. At one point he stopped, extended his arm and hand as if trying to feel something in different directions. I thought he was also trying to listen by the way he cupped his ear. He immediately went back to shoveling and covering up the graves.

We waited patiently for them to finish their diabolical work. Then just at the moment they started to depart, I heard Wahsek let out a high-pitched war scream. He stood up and started dancing frantically, imitating the movements of a Hawk diving and swooping in combat. I burned root while he screamed and danced, then suddenly out of nowhere a strong Wind blew in from the north. With it came a ten-foot skeleton, walking fast in a jerking motion, while sparks of fire were shooting out of its mouth and eyes. I think I got more scared than the sorcerers so I started to dance, sing, and scream hoping to work off my anxiety.

It was extremely cold but my entire body was burning up. I noticed that we had a red-hot glowing light encircling us, some sort of supernatural shield. The giant skeleton that Wahsek called So-oh in his song moved in for a fast attack. He busted up zombies left and right, then threw their bodies over into the Ocean, and I could swear I heard the crunching of large teeth tearing into bones and meat, while screams wailed in a frenzy. A group of phantom warriors gathered up the remaining deceased and forced them back into their graves. The entire scene was like watching a horror show at the movies. It was incredible. I just couldn't believe all this was real.

Then I heard the loud scream of a giant bird and saw its silhouette. It had the appearance of a large Condor as it swooped down and grabbed the older man and carried him off into the night. He violently fought the huge bird, with arms and legs waving frantically in the air, but in just a matter of minutes his screaming subsided as the mythological creature disappeared into a distant patch of fog. The two younger men ran down the road screaming like banshees while the skeleton pursued.

With a sigh of relief and a new song, Wahsek began to point to and pray upon different graves in the cemetery. He sprinkled crushed pepperwood leaves and salt in every direction, often making circles within circles. He cried and pleaded for the deceased while iridescent entities danced upon the cemetery in a holy way. He pleaded to the Great Creator to forgive the violation and desecration that had been committed against the deceased and their family members.

He pleaded for the family's protection, for a blessing, and for restitution according to the Natural Laws. We stood on the outside of the cemetery, beyond the fence boundaries, while he smoked his pipe and carried on a lengthy conversation, apparently with spirits. I heard Tela's name mentioned a number of times, and a reference to any children she might have in the future. Then we quietly left.

We went down the other side of the Klamath River until we approached the beach. We got out and Wahsek pointed at a large split rock. He said it was a very evil place and to avoid it at all costs whenever I came down here to fish with my brothers-in-law or friends.

He got out and prayed, then sang another song, and talked in both English and the Yurok language. I heard him warn the evil spirits of that place to leave Tela's family alone because they were from the House of Talth. Otherwise he would have no recourse but to obliterate them off the face of the Earth. Wahsek evidently served as avenging angel as part of his profession.

Suddenly a strange creature appeared in front of the rock. It appeared to be half bird and half human, a short, fat, furry creature with large bird-type feet and a long nose. It was cream colored with large, protruding, iridescent red eyes. Behind it a huge Octopus-type creature was crawling out of a large crack. Wahsek said the creature was an *umaa*, an Indian devil, and the sea monster was its ally. Such a monster was extremely dangerous because it had only one purpose in life, and that was to eat; and it thought it was a god so it feared no other gods, not even the Creator. They stood defiantly, ready for the challenge.

Then all of a sudden I saw Orca, the Killer Whale, jump out of the water some distance behind the large rock, crying out a death chant. It rushed toward the rock and rammed itself on the beach. A mini–tidal wave followed directly behind it and engulfed the rock, pulling the horrible creatures back into the Ocean.

I suspect they were devoured by sea spirits. Wahsek hollered, "*Skuyeni, ca-wees-cha,*" which means "Thank you and good-bye." We left feeling it was a job well done. As we went further down the road, past Orick, Wahsek told me to stop at a sacred place near the Ocean so we could bathe and purify ourselves before returning home.

We stopped at Tsurai (Trinidad Mountain), and since it was late at night and foggy, there didn't seem to be any problem with intruders or spectators. The fog was extremely thick, but an opening cleared for us just a few feet from the incoming tide. Once again Wahsek lit his pipe while I burned root, and we prayed asking for permission to bathe, and for a spiritual cleansing.

We both stripped down naked and plunged into the water like two Otters, and although it was icy cold, I felt a strange warmth as we both churned over and over in the waves. All of a sudden I felt a strong undercurrent pull me under the water, pushing me into depth and darkness. I also felt a large fish, or at least what I thought was a large fish about the length of my own body, brush up against me and then, with a jolt, push me toward the shore. Wahsek was already standing in the sand and laughing. I hoped it wasn't a Shark.

I saw a Porpoise stand up in the water and make strange crying noises while he appeared to be gliding backward. As I turned to swim back, I also saw the Mermaid swimming away with two Porpoises toward a very large albino Whale. Exhausted, I crawled up on the sand and rested while Wahsek got dressed and kept singing.

Our clothes were damp as we drove home but I felt totally refreshed and recharged. A couple of times I tried to question Wahsek about what I had seen and experienced. At first he snapped sternly, cautioning me to be silent, to let the dead rest in peace. But halfway over Bald Hills Road he made us stop at a rock outcropping he called Chilula Doctor Rock, where he prayed and then decided to explain things to me. He said we would be safe because the protection against the sorcerers couldn't be broken here.

He began, "Indian devils, or what you call sorcerers, have their own special form of supernatural knowledge, rituals, and power. For instance, here is a good place for Indian doctors to pray to good spirits. Now down there, over near Redwood Creek, is a bad place where they can go and make medicine. Wherever there is good, there always seems to be the bad lurking close by.

He looked intently into the dark distance over the fields and continued. He said sorcery was an ancient art and that all cultures probably had some form of it, although it might not be apparent to most Western people. Wahsek also explained that sorcerers had their own places to pray, tools of the trade to use, and rituals to perform as a means to activate the evil power and summon the evil spirits.

"For example," he said in a pedantic manner, "they have different levels of development, a ranking of their own requiring certain qualifications, powers, abilities, and skill, similar to the way it is for Indian doctors. They also have their areas of specialization. In fact, some of them can be shamans, as in the case of a Blue Jay doctor or an Owl medicine man."

He paused and looked around the area. A couple of Raccoons came over and sat on the rock listening, then a Ringtail Cat ran by and he laughed. "They're okay, they're good powers. Remind me to tell you the story sometime how the Raccoon people saved the Sun from drowning down at Orick. That's how they got their burnt markings."

He talked to them in Indian and then tried to enlighten me further. "So they might make poisons and use power objects such as Blue Jay feathers, Owl feathers, Water Dog eggs, Toads, Skunks, Snakes (but not the King Snake), flints, rocks, herbs, just about anything, even things from the Ocean, such as certain kinds of fish and shellfish.

"They could put their poison in a person's food and cause that person to get very sick and slowly die, or to have a sudden stroke or heart attack, or to be killed in some horrible way. The White doctors wouldn't have the slightest idea what caused the sickness and death, even if they performed an autopsy; such forms of supernatural poisoning, although used in physical form, are untraceable to the human eye or medical machines. Remember what happened to that young healthy man up in Crescent City a few months ago? That's an example. Nobody could account for his death. There was no logical explanation."

Wahsek paused to let me digest the information, and then he went on. "A sorcerer might have as many as ten different poisons that can be shot into a person in a supernatural way, and he makes them by hand at a very powerful place, like Bad Place up near Doctor Rock in the High Country, and he strengthens the poison by secretly laying it on graves, or in graves, or by using poisons made from different concoctions, such as Rattlesnake poison, Owl shit, Skunk hair, and deadly nightshade-related herbs.

"He can shoot that poison into his victim in a supernatural way. It's like the Blue Jay, who can shoot a worm into its victim and make different degrees of sickness. The Indian devils can send miniature flints, spears, worms, or bugs such as Spiders, Centipedes, Crickets, Ticks, even Scorpions, to bite a victim. Others might send Snakes, Salamanders, Toads, even Dogs and Cats.

"All such horrible things can leave behind a poison that will stay in the human body for years, then reactivate because these things are sneaky in spirit. If you think this stuff isn't serious and deadly, then think about this for a moment. How many White doctors have you ever heard of that could cure Lyme disease or Rocky Mountain spotted fever?"

"Not too many," I said. "By the way, can I interject here for a moment and ask you a question? Why would the Great Creator let such vile creatures and people continue their diabolical work?"

He looked all around him, studying the environment, and responded, "Because the Great Spirit didn't create these things. The Great Evil One did, the Imitator, and it is pretty damn powerful, too. Like I told you before, the forces of Light and Dark have existed since the Beginning."

He looked at me firmly, then proceeded to elaborate. "The Evil One came in the Beginning, just after Creation, and he was jealous. He wanted to imitate the Great Creator, God if you will, so he went along and spawned his own evil things in many forms. Hence you can have two plants side by side, and one is a healer while the other is a poison. That's why shamanism is such serious business. Not everyone can become a good medicine man. There is just too much to learn.

"But let me finish," he said humbly. "That is why there are so many different kinds of bizarre creatures, ones like you saw tonight, demons beyond human imagination and perception, and evil entities that even reside in other dimensions on this Earth. They can stalk, kill, and devour a human, capture the human soul and feed on it to strengthen their own power, and they are all over the world."

He went on to tell me that what these sorcerers were doing tonight was worse than tricking someone to pick up a feather, step on a worm, get bitten by a bug or poisoned by food. He said that most sorcerers, even those of different ranking, had knowledge and skills to send evil spirits to cause a person to get sick, or have an accident, or get into a fight and get shot or stabbed. Wahsek claimed that some sorcerers could even cause their victims to mysteriously die in a car accident, or drown in the river, or burn up alive in a house fire. He explained that the grave robbers we saw here, the head sorcerer and his apprentices, were digging up deceased bodies in order to get a human rib and sinew to make a magical bow, which in turn would be used to shoot poison at unsuspecting victims. But even worse, they were cursing the grave, using it as a lethal weapon against the family.

I reminded him of the story he once told me about Fanny Brown, and how she said the sorcerer-type shamans used human hair, fingernails, defecation, clothes, or even the intended victim's blood, such as from a woman's sanitary napkin, to make bad medicine and a curse; and I asked him if sorcerers also used their special knowledge in making love medicine to possess and control other people, or to split couples up.

He said that was a reality, and often the case, but the love medicine approach was used by lower-status sorcerers, and even regular human beings who had some basic knowledge in medicine making, but it could and did work on most people, whether they believed in sorcery or not. He also claimed that with the right kind of knowledge average people could protect themselves or even cure themselves from the lower acts of such black magic.

He went on to explain that highly trained sorcerers, however, took human parts and blood to their altars in Nature and made stronger medicine. And they too had spirit allies and powers from Nature they used in their evil work, and for self-protection, and they had places of power where they went to pray, in the same way that Native healers and good medicine people went to the sacred places to pray. In order to commit the intended injury, the sorcerers would place something of the victim's on a negative node while making supplication, pleas, and curses in an attempt to conjure evil spirits who resided at such places. That way the practitioners could walk around unsuspected in society. He finished by saying that the strongest evil powers always wanted human blood, and a human's soul, to the point of human sacrifices if necessary, as part of the sorcerer's bidding and negotiation. Sometimes the price might even require the death of a sorcerer's children as payment in exchange for the Evil One's service.

As we started to leave I asked him in a concerned way, "Then what was I doing during *hokep*, when I used white quartz to gash myself? Was I feeding or attracting bad spirits?"

He laughed. "No!" he said. "The true Great Creator of the Universe and the good spirits don't feed on blood because they know it is the human life force. They might work through your blood in a spiritual way to strengthen your life force but they are more concerned about giving than receiving. What you did was a purging, a cleansing similar to what a woman on her menses goes through. You used an ancient concept and method to release the negative energy, toxins, and bad luck from your body, providing your life force with an opportunity to be rejuvenated, to be recharged. You might say you were trying to get a good spiritual transfusion."

He laughed and laughed almost all the way home. "Oh by the way," he recounted, "things might not be as bad as they appear in the world of sorcery. The Great Spirit has provided us with the knowledge, tools, and means to fight evilness. Remember the story I told you about Blue Jay and Chipmunk, how the Blue Jay deviled Chipmunk to get all the acorns? Well, remember it was Flickerbird and Hummingbird that came and doctored Chipmunk. They sucked out the worm and destroyed it, removed the poison the worm left behind, and used their good power to cure the Chipmunk. So in this respect, for everything evil there is a counterpart. Eagles eat Snakes, Hawks can beat up Blue Jays, Sharks can devour Octopuses, certain good herbs can cure poisons."

It was just about daylight by the time we got to his farmhouse, but we still weren't finished. He told me to build a small fire by the sweat lodge while he gathered fresh Douglas fir boughs. Then he made both of us, individually, lie down in the bed of smoke. I stayed until I couldn't stand it any longer. I was suffocating and choking. I crawled into the lodge and slept half the day while he went back into the house and went to bed. This was the first time I ever saw him sleep so long. Normally he was up at sunrise even if he worked late.

I couldn't tell Tela what we had done and what I had experienced. Otherwise it could break the pledge and medicine making. Her health improved tremendously, and I could see a real change in her aura, the way she moved with vigor, and the way she laughed. She also looked more beautiful and transcendental, and still very enticing. I could sense and feel the excitement in her, and the eagerness she displayed while making this transition.

We stayed with Wahsek throughout the summer. I continued to learn new things while doing farmwork with him, and Tela evidently started an apprenticeship with both Gina and Bunny. Gina happily teased Wahsek on several occasions with taunts like, "Hey grouch butt. Now I've got someone to do things with me too, and I think I've got a better student than you do." Tela absorbed both spiritual and cultural knowledge just as fast as they could give it to her.

At one point during our visit and training, she had to be excused from the house and chores. She had to focus on her moontime ceremony and use it as a source for self-purification, self-development, and healing. I think the ten days of her isolation seemed longer to me than they did to her, and although I was anxious for her return to social life, I was very proud of her.

In the meantime I was busy with Wahsek, learning to gather herbs and wild tobacco for healing, ceremony, and protection; and I was given a new lesson each time we passed a mythological or legendary site. Some of the places, he said, were used for making different kinds of medicine, such as hunting power, good luck wishes, love medicine, gambling power, or medicine for acquiring wealth or long life. Other specific places were used by Indian devils for sorcery. It seemed there were more sorcery places than there were good places.

Our conversation focused on the concept of spiritual training and vision quests, or what was more commonly referred to as power quests in northwestern California. He said that he wasn't that knowledgeable about the processes for becoming a sorcerer because he had not trained in that particular field of expertise. He had learned, however, from his mentors, some of whom specialized in dealing with sicknesses that were caused by sorcery, that the process for becoming a sorcerer was significantly different, except in the cases when a shaman might turn to sorcery as part of his or her professional activity.

Wahsek said that a person just couldn't wake up one morning and say, "Gee, I think I want to be an Indian doctor, a medicine man, or a shaman." He claimed it didn't work that way. He explained that the path to shamanhood was a combination of many complicated affairs, that the training was arduous, the learning never ending, and further, that it required tremendous sacrifice and suffering. Both the spirits and the Elders would test the shaman.

He admitted that there was ranking within shamanism and sometimes fields of specialization, but he said the highest, purest, and most powerful—and hence the most effective—shamans were those who had been fully accepted and spiritually blessed by the Great Creator on the highest mountains. These he called *Pay-lin Skuyent Kay-Gey,* meaning "Great Indian Doctors" or "High Men and Women"—the kind that had been associated with the House of Talth. They were the only ones who had experienced the ultimate quest and connection with the Great Spirit, which was extremely difficult to define other than calling it *mer-werk-ser-gerth,* which means "total power, beauty, and bliss," or "one with the Universe."

They were the ones who had qualified to ascend the Golden Stairs leading to Doctor Rock, Chimney Rock, Peak Eight, and Sawtooth Ridge. And he emphasized that such rare people walked, crawled, starved, and cried every step of the way. They weren't conveniently driven up there in a Jeep or truck to get a quick nirvana. He further added that he hadn't known anyone in the past fifty years or so, not even himself, who had made such a pilgrimage to become ordained.

He hesitated, then said, "If there is anyone left, it might be Dewey George, the Yurok holy man, who has been celibate all his life. I know his grandfather, Sregon George, was ordained up there, but I don't really know about Dewey. My brother insulted him when we were younger so I haven't seen him since. I think he has been living over on the coast and must be getting pretty old by now."

Wahsek enjoyed elaborating on the part about becoming an Indian doctor before finishing his discussion about sorcerers. "Thus, the process is basically like this: you are born with the power, spiritually and genetically, you inherit the spirit and potential, then you are usually called to the profession by dreams, an accident, profound sickness, disease, or a death experience. The dreams might be about an ancestor who was a doctor, or they might involve ghosts of former doctors, or they might be about certain birds, animals, fish, and so forth that are doctor powers. With the dreams usually come pains in the solar plexus.

"Of course a person can have more than one dream. Each new dream, each new mystical experience or supernatural encounter with powers, spirits, and forces requires diagnosis and testing for validity. When that happens you are usually guided to an older medicine man or medicine woman who will interpret the dreams and pray on you.

"This in turn might require a *remopho,* the kick dance, or what some call the doctor-making dance, usually held in the old-style sweat house. Inside the sweat lodge with a very hot fire, you fast, sweat, sing, go into a trance, and cook the new power, try to regurgitate the pains up, show it to the older shamans for confirmation, then swallow the bloody phlegm and synthesize it with your soul and spirit. The kick dance usually lasts five to ten days.

"So the pains and power might hit you through a dream, which in turn must become physically manifested. But at other times, it might be necessary for the neophyte shaman to continue arduous training, similar to what you did through *hokep,* then go to the mountain, cave, waterfall, or sacred place where a particular kind of spirit lives. In this way the shaman makes a spiritual connection.

"Remember the story I told Tela about her Great-Great-Aunt Fanny Flounder? Well, it's like that, and once you make the right connection at the sacred place, the *tsekstel,* doctor seat and altar, the power will shoot into you, or surge like an electric current throughout your entire body. In other situations the neophyte might be required to fight the power-spirit and overcome it, or let the power-spirit devour him. This is the case with the powers of the Bear, Wolf, Mountain Lion, Bigfoot, Shark, Whale, Orca, or Condor.

"With that kind of doctor power you become repossessed, reclaimed, so to speak, by the forces of Nature and the Great Creator. In other words, you become one with that spirit, power, force, and all its other connections and allies. For example, the Grizzly Bear works with the Sun, Moon, Big Wind, Lightning and Thunder, Hummingbird, Wolves, Golden Eagle, Hawks, White Deer, Frog, high mountain spirits, and other creatures.

"The Frog works with the Moon, the fire, the Grizzly Bear, the water, Little People, certain plants and rocks; and the Wolf works with the Raven, the Wind, the Snow, and certain little birds. With the higher powers, everything is connected to something else in Nature, and the good powers do not fight good powers. Physically there might be some territorial spats but spiritually they are synchronized and harmonious, and usually work as a team of spirits."

He paused as if trying to get off the tangent and back on track about the part concerning sorcerers. "So with true shamans, good Indian doctors, there is no easy way out. A person who doesn't follow this spiritual process precisely to the letter will just end up becoming a quasi shaman, a man or woman of knowledge, who may even have some power. But such a person will not qualify as a full-fledged medicine man or woman, understand?

"Now to conclude the lesson about sorcerers," he said, laughing. "Just about anyone can qualify, I guess. Of course sorcerers are stronger if they inherit evil power and train to develop it, but basically a person can even buy an *uputawon* [in Karuk language], or an *umaa* [in Yurok language, used to identify and describe a sorcerer's power and regalia or medicine bundle]. Older sorcerers are always looking for some naive person to recruit, exploit, and train in their dirty work. That's why they look for people who are full of jealousy, anger, fear, hate, or grieving, or people on alcohol, or even better, on drugs.

"They want people to look up to them. They are selfish. They feed on fear, they are bent on avarice, they are prone toward violence, they usually have no morals, no ethics, no respect for authority or laws of any kind. They have a tendency to be temperamental and mean people, to the point of being tyrants and dictators. There is no honor in being a sorcerer, or amongst sorcerers themselves, no matter what you have heard or been told. Evil is evil.

"But they are also very daring and adventurous, thinking they have nothing to lose and everything to gain. So they will use narcotic plants to develop their psychic powers, or use narcotic plants to achieve temporary trance states or to acquire and exert negative power. They get pleasure out of controlling and inflicting pain on others, and even on themselves. They can be used in the culture like a hit man, what the Mafia calls a mechanic, an assassin. That's also why they are dangerous—because they're crazy, often beyond reason."

I had often wanted to talk to Wahsek about the concept of shapeshifting. I had been told that some medicine men had that kind of knowledge, power, and ability. Charlie Red Hawk talked about it some but he said that it was *uputawon* power. I had dreams about going through a metamorphosis and changing into a Raven, Eagle, or Bear, but I didn't really understand the dreams.

I talked to some older medicine men about the unusual dreams and they just shrugged it off, except for Rolling Thunder. He got excited about it and said that a long time ago some of the shamans could do it, but he was more into soul travel so I didn't learn much from him about the phenomenon.

One time Wahsek and I went to Duzle Rock to gather wild tobacco and other herbs. He liked to make a special pilgrimage there every summer, set up camp for a few hours at the base of the mountain, and then go up and pray. On this one particular trip I saw a Bear suddenly appear while we were praying at the campsite near a spring.

Wahsek liked to reminisce, saying, "This is where I came with my mentors, sat, prayed, and learned stories. We recharged ourselves. Duzle Rock is a strong doctor-training site, a vision quest place of power. It is exactly lined up between Mt. Shasta to the east, and all the other doctor seats and altars to the west, south, and north."

I told him that my dad Charlie—the man I'd believed for years to be my dad and who finally agreed to go to court and make it legal—once took me here to pray. I said, "He wasn't as strict as you, Wahsek, but I was required to fast for a couple of days and cleanse myself in the sweat lodge. Then we came up here to make special prayers. It was during a time that he was trying to teach me how to defend myself against my enemies, including alleged sorcerers."

I paused for a while waiting for a reaction because I knew he and Gina didn't really care for Charlie. They said he was too much of a Coyote, a trickster. They never accused him of being a sorcerer, and they respected him as a man of knowledge and power. They considered him a ritual and formula type of medicine man, which is different from a ceremonial dance leader or Indian doctor. But because he had Coyote power and was hell with the women, they felt his morals were questionable.

"Anyway," I continued, "he had me make an altar, burn tobacco and Grizzly Bear root, and pray in a certain way. Then I had to walk out on that far point, the one shaped like a large spearhead, and I had to stand there and holler for the ancient ones.

"I could barely walk by the time I got out to the point, it was so narrow." I explained how it was very dangerous because it stuck out like a skinny diving board, with nothing but a straight four-hundred-foot drop on either side. "I knew if I slipped I would fall to an instant death upon jagged rocks, and each time I hollered a big gust of Wind came in. I fought like a tightrope walker for my balance, wavering back and forth, crying, desperately trying not to slip over the edge.

"Then at one point, only for a moment, the Wind started blowing in both directions at the same time and lifted me like a kite in the air. Two Falcons were crisscrossing in front of me. I was literally suspended in midair, held by the crosswinds. Then I fell backward, frantically grabbed the ledge, and with a minimum of balance, miraculously crawled as fast as a Lizard to safety."

Wahsek was fascinated with my account and looked at me with an expression of disbelief. He turned and pointed and asked, "You mean those two Falcons up there?" While the sacred birds came in to visit he talked in his language, saying, "Well, I guess you had quite an experience. There is the confirmation for my doubts."

He sat respectfully for a while watching the Falcons at play, and then he turned and said, "Yeah, that's a form of doctor power too, but more in the realm of warriors, and every good shaman can use additional protection. Good work, kid."

At that point I made reference to the large Black Bear that had been walking around the periphery. He stood up and looked at us with very human-type qualities, then walked away with a manlike limp. He even had this particular kind of human smile. He kept reminding me of someone I knew but I just couldn't seem to remember who it was. Wahsek laughed and greeted him, talking to him in Indian language, calling him Uncle.

I said, "Wahsek, I've been wanting to ask you a serious question for a long time. Do you know what a shape-shifter is?"

He looked at the Bear, and then he looked at me and laughed. "Now you're not going to accuse me of being that Bear are you? By now you should know that he's not my kind of power, but yours."

We both laughed and continued studying the Black Bear as he walked down the road, all the time standing in an upright position on only two legs, humanlike. *"Choot-ney Cher-urie kay-gey,"* or "Good-bye, Doctor Bear," he hollered, getting up in preparation to leave.

Then he answered my question. "Some of the old-time Indian doctors had that ability to change into a Bear, Wolf, Buck, Raccoon, Mountain Lion, or even an Eagle or Raven. But I never learned that kind of medicine. I guess it wasn't meant for me. Besides, I don't really see the utility of it outside of being able to impress people, or perhaps in the need for doctoring in a special way.

"I have heard of Bear doctor medicine men among the Shastas or Pomos, and the Plains Indians doctors being able to do that in front of their patients, as if by magic. But it wasn't magic, it was a very strenuous affair. They had the power and knowledge to actually change completely from a human into a Bear, then back again."

He started scratching his head in puzzlement. "Well, if you really want to learn that kind of medicine then go down there in Quartz Valley and see your Uncle Lester. As you know, he ain't an Indian doctor, and he ain't an Indian devil, but he does have his own special kind of cultural knowledge and power."

He was still pointing downhill, toward the visible valley, while we gathered wild tobacco from the upper Forest Service road. "But as you well know, I don't like hanging around that place. Too many Shasta Indians massacred down there. Too much evilness down there, too many mysterious deaths in a bad way, too many Indian devils live down there. I know because that's where Doc Benoni Harrie lived. His wife still lives there but she's quite elderly and in poor health. Sometimes I wonder how she manages to survive with all that drinking and fighting, rough-necks running wild and stealing, and all that evil going on down there." He stopped and stared at the valley and the towns of Ft. Jones and Quartz Valley for a long time, and then continued, "Personally, I think the whole area is cursed, nothing but bad news and bad medicine, families killing each other off like crazy. Something ain't right down there, and I don't think those Indians will ever get their act together, no matter how much they try to start up a reservation again. You're better off staying away from it."

I was still curious and accepted the forewarning and advice, but that was where I was enrolled as a tribal member, that is, if they ever managed to form a legitimate tribe again. That's where Dad Charlie, Uncle Kelsey, and Uncle Lester grew up and that's where I had a lot of relations, although I was ashamed to admit it. I had tried to stay away from the place as much as I could, for my own protection.

"Yeah," he said, motioning for us to leave, "go down and see your Uncle Lester sometime. He knew that old man Ben Richards real well. Ben was his grandmother's brother, his great-uncle, and he was probably the last of his kind, what you call a shape-shifter. Come to think of it now, that Black Bear we just saw resembles old Ben with that limp, but your Uncle Lester has the same kind of limp, doesn't he?"

I kept getting a strange feeling in my stomach. I could feel something trying to pull me back to Quartz Valley, and I couldn't keep it out of my mind.

On the way back to Wahsek's house I thought about finding a job. Summer was coming to an end, money was tight, and I had to worry about Tela as well as myself. By the end of summer she had learned how to pray, make medicine for certain types of ceremonies, cook and can food, prepare traditional food sources for survival, gather and use specific kinds of herbs for healing, and protect herself spiritually from demons, ghosts, and sorcerers. I am sure she was also provided with an opportunity to learn ancient and esoteric secrets concerning women's affairs.

Though I already considered Tela to be my wife after making the traditional trade with her father, when we left Wahsek's home we stopped at a justice of the peace and got married a second time. Now we were married in both cultures.

I must have passed my interview at the college because I received notice that I was hired for the new position, with an increase in salary, rank, and status. Tela and I found a neat little rustic house in Eureka to rent, surrounded by a farm and Redwood trees for privacy.

We had a couple of weeks before classes started up at the college, and I had received a late state tax refund, so we decided to go on a belated honeymoon at Lake Tahoe. We thoroughly enjoyed ourselves, got lucky and won a little over seven thousand dollars between the two of us, and came back with a new start in life.

We had a home, a better vehicle, a good-paying and stable job, and some money in the bank. Plus we had our health and happiness. Apparently the spiritual training and quest—the *hokep*—had been worth the sacrifice. The Great Creator and his good spirits evidently heard my pleas for help because my life completely changed for the better. My belief that there was, indeed, a Great Spirit was also reinforced and strengthened. Not only had I passed another shamanic and spiritual test in my life, but I had also passed a test in the reality of faith.

The Changing Art
of Native Healing

Tela and I became partners in pursuit of spiritual growth and development. During the fall, winter, and spring months we trained down low, in the sacred sweat lodge, along the coast, and in the smaller mountains as our mentors had instructed. We focused on developing our dreams, pursuing our dreams, and acquiring new knowledge while our psychic powers became stronger. I taught Tela how to use the sweat lodge as a spiritual and cultural tool for psychic development, as a vital means for protection and self-healing, and as a way to doctor patients who began coming to us.

Her clairvoyant power and ability progressed much faster than my own. It was apparent that she was a bloodline hereditary doctor, and a natural-born shaman, but the path and training to become a fully qualified shaman takes a long time. It requires a very disciplined life, it can be lonely in the social sense, and it is a never-ending learning process. It is also kept secretive in order to protect neophytes from psychic and social or cultural harm.

As a result, we found ourselves going up to visit with Wahsek, Gina, and Bunny quite often to seek answers and guidance. We also went inland and visited Charlie and Velma for additional learning and to cultivate family ties, and on a couple of occasions we went over and spent some time with Rolling Thunder to expand our depth and breadth of knowledge.

I always liked Rolling Thunder, although he could be a stern person at times. He had a tremendous amount of knowledge and power and a good heart to share with the people, and he was a strong doctor. As long as I knew him he never charged a fee for doctoring.

But it made me sad to see how poorly certain groups of Indian people treated him, just because he was very light skinned and didn't fit their stereotype of what they thought a medicine man should look and act like. He was often called a rainbow medicine man or Shake 'N Bake shaman behind his back by people who didn't understand his mission, and because a lot of White people looked up to him as a guru and flocked to his national lectures.

In retrospect, however, I think some Indian people had resentment toward Rolling Thunder because he was willing to share his knowledge with people of other races, cultures, and backgrounds. His lectures and popularity evolved at a time in history when urban Indians were just waking up to Nativism and trying to learn more about their own heritage and culture. Some of them probably got jealous, became territorial, and wanted to keep Native spiritual teachers and Native religion for themselves, perhaps fearing they might lose it again to Western society.

Rolling Thunder had a vision to share and truly believed he was on a mission for the Great Spirit. After all, as he put it, "Someone had to counteract the whitewashing by Western missionaries and their devastation of the Indian people and their religion." He wasn't, however, a spiritual huckster, as some Indian people falsely accused. He never got any royalties from the books that were written about him, and whatever honorariums he acquired for lecturing were usually donated to Indian groups and organizations in need, including a cross-cultural camp he was trying to support near his home for displaced Indians and their families.

He was a very powerful psychic and healer, probably one of the most knowledgeable medicine people on the continent concerning the art of using plants and herbs in healing. He was also highly effective against sorcerers, who seemed to multiply until they were coming out of the woodwork. As Tela and I strived to lead a righteous and spiritual life, we kept encountering more and more challengers and challenges, which, although very dangerous, also led to the expansion of our knowledge and skills.

The evil spirits, powers, and forces have been here from the Beginning of Creation. Where there is light, there is dark; where there is positive, there is negative. Unfortunately that's just the reality of life. The dark forces and evil ones want to take over the world. They want control, and they can always find someone to trick, entice, control, and work through—especially when there is a breakdown in morals, ethics, and the value system in society.

The human ego is susceptible to it. Everybody wants power, especially if it is easy to obtain. Too many people don't want to work, suffer, and sacrifice for good spirituality. They don't want to earn it the right way. It is much easier to pursue psychic-type spirituality and get recognition, status, and wealth. The negative side is exciting, mysterious, challenging, and competitive, and I suppose it has its own kind of rewards. But it is also convenient, like anything else in Western society. It can be bought, sold, and marketed, while ignoring the Natural Laws and the Great Creator's Laws.

With a breakdown in values and an increase in alcohol and drugs, the evil entities begin to run rampant. Tela and I found ourselves trying to use old ways and forms of knowledge to survive in a New Age current. New Age spirituality made shamanism popular, but sorcery became popular as well, and the "how to become" type of books, workshops, and seminars started flooding the market.

Shamanism became as popular as the martial arts, but to use an analogy, somewhere along the line people forget that a ninja is an assassin. A ninja is an evil person with special training, skills, abilities, knowledge, and power. Ninjas have their own laws, which are much different from the Great Creator's Laws, the true spiritual laws of the Universe, and they believe they are above the law. Sorcerers, black witches, wizards, and shamans from the dark side operate on the same premise.

Consequently we couldn't help but notice that wicked challengers started coming out all over the place, initially like wanna-be gang members, but eventually as qualified diabolical members of their sects. And although we tried to keep our own apprenticeships secretive, humble, and obscure, they somehow managed to find out about us. In this regard we became a threat to them. They probably regarded us as competitors. As a means to test and sharpen their skills, they had to find adversaries.

Rolling Thunder and other Native spiritual leaders we personally knew all said the situation was comparable to the "gunfighter syndrome" in the days of the Wild West, or the Bruce Lee syndrome. Once people found out who or what we really were they wanted to get a reputation for taking down the best. Tela and I had to gain new knowledge and skill in order to protect ourselves.

Wahsek and Gina lived an isolated and reclusive life. They were the last of the old guard, perhaps similar to some of the Indian doctors and medicine people who hid from Western society on the Navajo, Hopi, and Cheyenne Indian reservations. Sure, they too had their share of demons, ghosts, and sorcerers, but it was in their specific cultural context and domain. The good shamans in such places had the knowledge and skill needed to handle such phenomena.

But they weren't prepared to deal with the cross-cultural diversity that Tela and I were now encountering, as part of our predestined learning experience. Rolling Thunder was, however, because somewhere along the trail he had acquired the cross-cultural training, knowledge, and experience. He was an invaluable support system and mentor for Tela and me, and he helped us when we found ourselves under attack.

For example, we had felt sorry for a certain person who lived in Santa Rosa. She was a good person, but during her quest for spirituality she became involved in local black witchcraft. This in turn made her sick. She was developing arthritis, chronic migraine headaches, and problems with her menstrual cycles.

Tela and I agreed to doctor her although we weren't really fully qualified and ordained ourselves. We just felt sorry for her, which was our first mistake, and second, we felt it was a calling and an opportunity to exercise our unique spiritual knowledge and skills.

The patient was required to follow the laws of being clean. We purified her home with cedar, we made protective medicine on ourselves, we smoked our pipes and diagnosed her condition. We had her confess for certain sins and violations, and then we both took turns singing and dancing on her. We didn't charge a fee for doctoring but we did accept gifts and a small money donation. Everything seemed to work out just fine. The patient had to dispose of certain power objects that were tormenting her. We taught her how to give the objects back to nature by using a ceremony. She burned the objects so the spirits and negative energies connected to the objects could not return.

The woman reported a few days later that she felt great and that her good health had returned. But Tela and I began to experience problems of our own. We started getting severe headaches and we had tormenting dreams. Tela, who was pregnant, was developing toxemia, and I fell down and got a herniated disc. The house kept filling up with those large, dirty blowflies that are typically associated with garbage and defecation. We knew that the flies were a very bad sign.

We made medicine to protect ourselves, chased out the flies with cedar and sage smudge, occasionally killed some of them and burnt them up, and used other methods of protection we had been taught by our mentors. Nothing worked.

As a result, we decided to go over the mountains into Nevada and get doctored by Rolling Thunder. Tela had to drive because I was in too much pain. We called ahead of time and asked for his assistance, giving him the normal three-day grace period. His form of protocol required waiting three days while he decided whether he wanted to take a case or not, and it also gave him time to prepare himself for doctoring. We almost got into several car accidents on the way over; thus, it was obvious that someone or something was trying to block us from getting to see Rolling Thunder.

The whole trip took about twelve hours one way. Rolling Thunder worked for the railroad as a brakeman so we also had to make sure that he would have time off for the doctoring. We got to his house late. We were screened by his wife Spotted Fawn and his son Mala, we offered our gifts, Indian blankets, and money donation, and we were instructed to spend the night in a *wickiup* at the camp.

R. T., as he preferred to be called, was a little more elaborate than

Wahsek in his shamanic approach and preparation. He preferred to doctor people outside in Nature, away from his house. I remember Wahsek preferred the same approach, often claiming that the old-timers never doctored in the house, but he couldn't afford to build a ceremonial lodge or doctor shack for his services, so he always used his home.

R. T. said he liked to be closer to Nature when performing healing because it was more powerful and more effective, although he admitted that there were times when he was on the road traveling that he had to do the best he could, often using a patient's home. He also said Native shamans always used Nature in healing.

His regalia consisted of Eagle wing fans, an old pipe, a Badger hide, a bag full of herbs, and a number of power objects that he kept discreet. His regalia symbolically reflected tools of the trade, all from Nature, and I knew his main powers were the White Rattlesnakes, Spotted Eagle, Lightning and Thunder, and the Badger, but I am sure he had other spirit guides and protectors.

He was also a sucking doctor but in this case didn't need to apply it. However, we were a little apprehensive because we knew that sometimes he actually doctored while holding live Rattlesnakes. For Tela's sake, and because of her pregnant condition, he substituted Rattlesnake buttons and skins.

The *wickiup* was dark and earthy, with a barren dirt floor, a few handmade wooden beds, and a wood heater in the center. A few skylights and candles were used for lighting, but otherwise it seemed fairly dark and primitive. The atmosphere gave the ceremony a feeling of integrity and mystery, and a certain bonding with the Earth matrix.

His assistants told us to sit next to the woodstove on the ground. They built a fire and proceeded to smudge the room with cedar and sage. They prayed and sang songs, and then shortly afterward R. T. appeared painted up in colors for protection, an old-time practice that some Plains Indian people still use. He then lit his pipe, prayed to the Great Spirit and his own powers, and asked for permission and help to doctor us.

Rolling Thunder sat for a long time and studied our condition. His eyes were half-closed, Snakelike in appearance, with a profound radiant reflection. It was the same kind of inhuman, supernatural light I often saw in Wahsek's eyes, especially when he was under the power or in a trance state. He then recounted our attempt to doctor the woman in Santa Rosa, although we had told him nothing about that ceremony, and he firmly stated that it was the cause of our sickness and problems. R. T. didn't use confession as a catharsis.

He claimed we had been witched up by a black magic type of witchcraft ceremony. He said we were victims of Whiteman's sorcery, an ancient form of satanic religion from Europe. He also said that it was becoming a popular form of religion with White people in this country, but that it was also attracting people from other races and cultures. He scolded us for not taking more precautions and for being too ambitious. Then he related how he had gotten into a similar situation years before while trying to doctor the Grateful Dead, a famous rock-and-roll band, while visiting the Bay Area.

He proceeded to talk to the Great Creator and good spirits on our behalf, pleading for our protection, and asking to have all evilness and sickness removed, and to not let it return. Rolling Thunder then sang over us with a rattle for a few hours. He used a piece of raw meat on my spine to entice out an evil power object, and then he had one of the assistants take the meat outside and burn it up. He massaged my spine with his hands and I could feel the healing power and heat being transmitted. He wanted us to drink herbs for three days.

By morning Tela's headaches had disappeared, the pain and swelling in my spine had disappeared, and the swelling in her body from toxemia had subsided. We felt great and spent the remaining part of the day visiting and learning new forms of doctoring knowledge from R. T. We were also impressed that everyone in the camp and his household followed the moontime laws. So we didn't need to worry about abstaining from food, and we got a chance to visit with other people in the camp. We left the next morning in good spirits. Afterward, though, Tela had a relapse.

We didn't notice until we'd gone two hours down the road toward Reno that she had been bitten by a Black Widow Spider. I tried to call

R. T., hoping to return for his help but he had already left for work. So I took her to the hospital. The physician in the emergency room was not very cooperative.

He identified and confirmed the poisonous bug bite but he didn't know what kind of medicine to use on Tela. Evidently he was afraid the Western medicine could cause the fetus to abort. So he just gave her some Tylenol and some antibiotic ointment for the punctures. He advised us to get back home as soon as possible and let Tela's ob/gyn deal with it.

We were both scared that her fever would get worse and that she might lose the baby. I finally had to stop on the other side of Susanville and pray on her in an isolated and private spot near the creek. I sang the Flickerbird song, used Flickerbird feathers, and tried to suck the poison out. While I sat praying in meditation I heard and saw a grandmother spirit in my mind. She told me to use an herb that was growing along the creek.

I was apprehensive about using any kind of concoction on Tela, fearing that it could cause the fetus to abort, but once again I realized we were being tested in our faith. I prayed and gathered some stinging nettle, and then called an Indian friend who lived in Susanville and asked him if we could use his house to rest up from the trip.

When we arrived at his house I asked if we could use his kitchen to make up some herbal tea. He was happy to see us, realizing it would be a short visit, and he was very cooperative. I boiled up the nettle, packed the warm leaves as a poultice on her stomach, and had her drink two cupfuls. We took the remaining nettle tea with us just after she started vomiting and getting loose bowels.

It didn't take Tela's physician long to meet us by the time we got back to Eureka and the hospital emergency room. He diagnosed her condition and said, "I don't know what you did, but whatever you used apparently worked pretty well. Most of the poison is out of the wound, and internally she and the baby seem just fine." He was a little worried, however, about the toxemia and her weight gain, so he put her on a special medicine as a follow-up.

Several years later, Rolling Thunder told me that his path to shamanhood wasn't an easy one either. He said that strange encounters with spirits, both good and bad, had pestered him since he was old enough to walk. He became very ill when he was only about seven years old, and he was living with his grandmother in the Ozarks of Arkansas. His family were Cherokee remnants from the notorious Trail of Tears. They belonged to a small pocket of the eastern tribal people who had managed to break off from the death march and revert to Nature for survival.

R. T. explained that his family and small tribal community had tried to retain their cultural beliefs, practices, and knowledge. As the generations passed, they in turn passed down teachings to each new generation. He apologized for the fact that they never received enrollment status and recognition as Cherokee, but they had managed to maintain their identity with pride despite the forces of acculturation and assimilation. He was also part Shawnee.

That, he claimed, was the basis of his shamanic inheritance, knowledge, and spiritual potential. He said his Indian background is what probably saved his life when he became deathly ill with pneumonia and tuberculosis. He remembers lying in bed with a high fever, coughing and hallucinating while his grandmother tried to make him inhale herbs, drink herbs, and bathe in an old washtub full of herbs.

His grandmother had been praying to the Great Spirit to pity her child, and somehow, someway, send a healing so he could live. At one point, feeling half dead, he saw a large, strange-appearing, pure white Frog, about four feet high, at the side of his bed. The Frog was licking his face, and each time it licked, Lightning and Thunder cracked four times. His grandmother, who had cried herself to sleep, suddenly awoke and discovered the creature. Rolling Thunder followed it outside into the pond, as if hypnotized, and drowned.

All he remembered after that was a series of strange dreams that kept pestering him, and an elderly Indian man who sang on him in a hut for several days. He became completely healed and very psychic after that experience, demonstrating an ability to communicate with reptiles, birds, mammals, and plants in a telepathic way. He learned how to work with so-called home remedies all his life, and when in doubt on how to use an herb, he simply placed it in front of his forehead, and the spirit of the plant told him, in his mind, how to use it in healing.

Rolling Thunder said that when he was a young man in his twenties, he got burned up in an accidental home fire; his children at that time got killed. His Christian relatives had him convinced that Satan had caused it, when Satan allegedly took the form of a Rattlesnake and came into his house just before the fire started.

R. T.'s story has it that the fire started while he was trying to kill the Snake. In later years he realized that he should not have done that because it was a spirit coming to warn him, it was an omen, and it was really trying to protect him against an enemy, not harm him. As a result, he traveled the country grieving, trying to run from the fear and shame he felt, all the while blaming the Great Spirit for allowing such a tragedy to happen. At that time he said he had cursed God and the Rattlesnake.

He ended up in Arizona and pulled into a small town. He had been trying to doctor himself with herbs after the experience. Two elderly Indian men saw him when he pulled up to the trading post. They told him that they had been waiting for him. They offered to teach him about herbs and help him heal from the burns of the fire. Rolling Thunder said that while he lived with them, they had a habit of teasing him for cussing at God.

"They said to me, 'So you don't believe that a Great Spirit really exists, huh? Is that why you blame God for your problems? Someday you and that Rattlesnake are going to meet again. You have unfinished business with him. Maybe we should let you meet God in heaven. Now wouldn't that be something if you found out he was a giant Rattlesnake, or something else? He can take any form, you know.'

"And they would just laugh at me and sometimes say, 'Here he comes. He's coming to visit you,' while pointing at a Rattlesnake. I would get scared and run, thinking it was really evil. Then they would say, 'Maybe he shouldn't have tried to come in the form of a burning bush in your house.'"

As the story goes, the old men adopted him, taught him the art of medicine making, and then a couple of years later put him on a vision quest. They told him they would help him meet the Great Spirit in person, so he could seek answers to the questions that had been haunting him in life. They also told him that God was protected by Rattlesnakes.

The vision quest required going into a sweat lodge for purification and preparation, and then they took him way out in the desert, then up on some plateaus to ancient Indian ruins. They made an old rope, stripped him down naked and painted him, and then lowered him over the cliffs into a cave. The cave was about one hundred feet from the top of the cliff and about two hundred feet from the bottom of the gorge.

He had to swing into the ancient cave, being careful not to miss the entrance. Otherwise he could be pulverized. He had to stay in the cave for a period of ten days with no food or water, and with hundreds of Rattlesnakes around him. R. T. claims he was tested in the areas of fear and his belief in a Great Spirit, and that he learned how to confront and deal with his own worst enemy, himself (his soul). He also claims that he got to find out for himself if there really was such a thing as God, or a Great Spirit.

He was bitten numerous times, died, and was taken into the spirit world in the heavens, into the home of Lightning and Thunder. When he woke up he was alive, healed, and charged with power. On the tenth day he saw the rope dangling down in front of the cave entrance. Lightning and Thunder raged in every direction while he was being pulled up.

He was then placed in an old Earth-type sweat lodge and remained in isolation for another month while eating moderately. Ever since the experience he has been followed by Thunder wherever he goes; and that is how he got his name, made his connection with the Great Spirit, and became a medicine man.

He finished the account of his shamanic training by laughing and then said, "You might have seen parts of it in the Hollywood movie called *Billy Jack*. I guess I shouldn't have shared that shamanic experience in a movie, though, because some Indian people bad-mouth me for it. I was hoping that I could use that experience as a way to teach other Indian people a very important part of their heritage and culture.

"Strange how things get twisted around, even the best of intentions.

But I guess they have been brainwashed by the system. Some of them are ashamed of the real religion, especially the shamanic part. Too ancient and too unbelievable I guess."

Tela and I had numerous opportunities to learn from a variety of Native shamans as the years progressed. The experiences we had with different Indian doctors and medicine men and women provided us with cross-cultural and intertribal learning. It also provided us with a means to acquire depth and breadth that would be needed in the future as we progressed into the New Age and a different era from that of our mentors.

Wahsek and Gina and Bunny, and eventually even the Wintun doctor Flora Jones, were the old ties to the past, and they had a lot to teach us. Rolling Thunder and Charlie Red Hawk Thom were reflections of Native shamanism and transition into the New Age, and they too had a lot to teach us with their philosophy, their experiences, and their unique knowledge; they also served as role models to emulate.

They all taught us that becoming an Indian doctor was a matter of facing extinction against overwhelming odds. They taught us that it was a never-ending learning process because the world was constantly changing. In order for us to survive and become effective in the sacred profession, we would need to change, adjust, and adapt. They taught us that a true shaman, a good healer and spiritual person, is a reflection of his or her time in history.

For example, the old-time shamans dealt with sicknesses mainly caused from violating traditional custom and laws, accidents and injuries, bug- and Snakebites, and deliberate acts of sorcery. There came a time when they encountered the effects of a new race and society that brought war, genocide, diseases, and alcohol, in addition to the older generation's causes of human illness. Indian doctors in this era now found themselves trying to learn how to cure measles, small pox, venereal diseases, influenza, and new forms of mental illness brought on by forced acculturation. They didn't have any grants, research teams, laboratories, hospitals, and new resources to help them find a cure. They watched their husbands, wives, parents, children, and family members die all around them while they desperately searched for the knowledge and means to serve the people.

The path and function of Native shamanism is full of suffering and sacrifice. Shamans are not only technicians of the soul, but they also become technicians of physical and mental pain. New knowledge and learning come the hard way with very little support. Medicine men and women from the old days became exposed to the new problems and diseases of their time in history, and they were forced to find a spiritual way to heal themselves. I suspect that their faith in the existence of a God, Great Creator, or Great Spirit was probably strained and tested to the limit. Experiencing the sickness, and learning how to cure themselves of the sickness, gave some of them the new knowledge needed to cure others, but many of them died in the process.

The shamans that Wahsek trained under and looked up to as role models were also a reflection of their time. Doc Thomas, Charlie Klutchie, Nes Charles, Fanny Brown, Benoni Harrie, Ida Cyst, and later his mother, Nancy, and the famous Pomo sucking doctor Essie Parrish all carried on their learning and practices in a particular part of Indian history. As a consequence, they had their share of problems, challenges, new learning, and bouts with personal illnesses reflective of their time. With it probably came a new philosophy about shamanism and doctoring that was different from the ancient ways.

The government and Christians had outlawed shamanism and traditional Native religion. The religion went underground in order to survive, and some of the shamans at that time converted to Christianity and used Western religion as a cover while they made a living at sorcery. A number of Indian people during that time turned to sorcery to fight Christianity because traditional Native religion was overt, while sorcery was historically conducted in a clandestine fashion.

That was easy to do because Christianity refused to accept the reality or possibility of sorcery. It wasn't in the mainstream of the Western belief system. The Great Spirit concept was dying, true Native spirituality was dying, Nature was under attack for its resources, but God, the Christian

God, was apparently alive and well. Where did the Indian spiritual leaders and shamans fit into the new scheme of things?

The old-time Indian doctors and shamans asked: But what kind of God? What kind of God condoned war, massacres, rape, murder, slavery, racism, prejudice, desecration of others' religions, genocide, stealing, violation of the Natural Laws, and immoral conduct, all under the justification of Manifest Destiny, White supremacy, and salvation?

By the time Wahsek and Gina became full-fledged, bona fide shamanic professionals of the sacred, they found themselves confronted with a profane inheritance from both Native culture and Western society. Western science and medicine were making significant progress, and people, including Indian people, were developing a dependency on it. Western religion had also made a tremendous impact. However, there was still some need and value for their shamanic knowledge and services. Strange things happened to Indian people that could not be handled by White doctors and religious leaders. Thus Wahsek's services became a supplement to Western medicine and were sometimes used as an alternative to Western medicine—or, as in my case at the beginning, as the last resort for dealing with a medical problem or sickness.

Wahsek, Gina, and Native shamans in their generation had managed to survive through all the former problems their predecessors had encountered, but they now inherited a society that was saturated with transgressions, genetic backlashes from former diseases, and people who were culturally deficient and spiritually ignorant. Wahsek's reservation land had been busted up, sold, and scattered. The termination act did the same thing to his neighboring tribes, except for the Hupa. The role and function of shamanism as a former honorable profession and the shamans' status as Indian doctors now had very little meaning or value to the more assimilated Indian people, or non-Indian people in Western society.

Wahsek's generation had its share of new sicknesses and problems to deal with in the form of alcoholism, diabetes, domestic violence, incest, mental illness, gallbladder ailments, urinary and kidney diseases, heart diseases, obesity, arthritis, strep throat, influenza, viruses, herpes, vaginitis, colitis, ulcers, cataracts, bronchitis, tumors, measles, chicken pox, allergies, unusual skin rashes, and more people experiencing migraine headaches. He believed these new illnesses were being created by Western society as a result of stress, pollution, and lack of religious values and spirituality.

The termination of Indian land and aboriginal rights, such as fishing, hunting, gathering, and trapping, caused severe stress and mental anguish for Wahsek's generation of Indian people. Although the former generations had also experienced sheer poverty, at least they could use Nature, their land, and their culture for subsistence and survival. Stress, he said, was therefore becoming a serious secondary cause of people's illnesses.

Wahsek often said, "The mind is a healer or it can be a destroyer. Nobody really knows the potential of the human mind, and like everything else in Nature, it can be positive or negative. But in order for us as humans to be healthy, our mind, which in some ways is a miniature creator and reflection of Creation, must be kept balanced."

Stress as he defined it could be a result of life crisis, financial worry, poor diet, poverty, pollution, ghosts, bad spirits, and entities from Nature penalizing people for their desecration and violations against the Earth and Nature. It could also be a result of negative thoughts and actions that people were directing against one another, intentionally or unintentionally. Stress caused an imbalance.

Wahsek further stated that certain mental illnesses, physical sicknesses, diseases, injuries, and the many different kinds of human ailments that he treated could be attributed to spiritual, cultural, and natural transgressions. Some of the modern illnesses could also be blamed on sorcery, but Wahsek said the majority of the illnesses he was now doctoring were a result of human sins and violations against the Earth, Nature, the Great Creator's Laws, and one another.

He therefore defined sorcery in new terms. The first kind he said was traditional and deliberate, meaning trained sorcerers had been hired in the Indian cultural context to use their knowledge, evil power, and bad spirits to harm, hurt, control, or kill people.

The other kind of sorcery he said was a consequence of jealousy, fear, greed, vindictiveness, lack of proper upbringing, lack of values, and perhaps an effort by some to preserve a portion of the Indian culture. He explained that this kind of witchcraft was really unintentional. It just happened because people were insecure and sometimes tried to take matters into their own hands. Thus, such people made reactionary mental curses, or they had learned a few ways of making bad medicine from elderly family members, or from reading anthropology books.

Wahsek had an interesting theory. He said all mental thoughts were energy, both positive or negative. He said bad thoughts created bad images and symbols that in turn could be transferred and transmitted, or sent unintentionally or deliberately, against another person.

He was always warning me to watch my thoughts. Part of my shamanic training required sitting by a sacred fire for hours on end. He tried to teach me how to use meditation and prayer formulas that were a form of affirmations as a means to tame and control negative emotions, thoughts, and feelings such as anger. He taught me this technique so I would not make others and myself sick, and as a means of learning how to develop self-protection.

He said that anger, fear, hate, and jealousy were forms of negative energy that the human mind could and did create into a force that could consciously, or unconsciously, be transmitted to another human being, creature, or object, just as a radio could transmit unseen wavelengths of varying force. He made another comparison by stating that bad words could and did hurt people's feelings. The negative energy associated with anger and bad words could not be seen. It wasn't visible to human eyes, but it could be felt by the recipient—for example, the other person might get a sudden headache, upset stomach, or a pain that usually appeared in a weaker part of the body.

He also said that the human body had a form of protection around it but most people rarely used it. That field of protection was an aura, an energy shield that could be strengthened with knowledge, spiritual practices, visualization, and prayer.

However, he believed that most people he was now doctoring in his generation had a weak aura and ill disposition because they lacked specific cultural and religious knowledge and spirituality. They were therefore more susceptible to the impact and effects of negative energies; that is, they were mentally and physically weak and prone to sicknesses in their relationships to other human beings, supernatural entities, and natural forces.

Wahsek believed the positive use of Native or primitive religion—as in the case of prayer formulas and affirmations, myth, ritual, sacred dances, ceremonies, and spiritual practices—served to strengthen the human mind, body, soul, and aura. The lack of spiritual knowledge and practice weakened most modern Indians, and other people, thus inclining them to sickness.

In Wahsek's generation of shamanhood, typical ailments associated with poisonous bug- and Snakebites, wounds from fights, injuries from accidents, alcoholism, and illnesses requiring surgery of vital organs were handled by Western physicians. Domestic and psychological ailments and problems were normally handled by Western therapists. Religious and spiritual principles, morals, values, and beliefs were normally provided by local Christian leaders, or not at all. His shamanic profession had become a supplemental service, but as more people began learning about alternative medicine and taking an interest in holistic healing, he became more credible and sought after.

10

Case Studies and Examples of Indian Doctoring

Tela and I came into Wahsek's life at a time when Indian people were waking up to Nativism. Indian people began to realize that there was a need for learning their heritage, culture, traditions, and indigenous religions. Local Indian people and tribal people across the continent started seeing the value of a culture they had almost lost, and as a consequence they started searching out tribal experts and spiritual teachers.

These experts were the few remaining Native shamans, some of whom had to be enticed and transported from the reservations into the urban areas so they could share their teachings. As stated earlier, medicine men such as the Hopi spiritual leaders, Rolling Thunder, Beeman Logan, Mad Bear Anderson, John Fire Lame Deer, Philip Deer, Julius Murray, Twyla Niche, and Thomas Banyaca, along with some of the Iroquois Six Nations chiefs, were at the forefront. They were very influential in raising spiritual consciousness, helping people return to Nativism, and giving credibility to shamanic knowledge and skill. Behind them came a new wave of Indian medicine men and women, including Stanley Smart (a peyote priest), Wallace Black Elk, Archie Fire Lame Deer, Crow Dog, Martin High Bear, Florence Jones, Buster Yellow Kidney, Bear Heart Williams, Charles Red Hawk Thom, Raymond Many Bears, and Red Cloud from Canada, and eventually Charles and Geoffrey Chips. In the meantime, those originally in the Red Power movement with Richard Oaks, or those involved with Lehman Brightman in United Native Americans, eventually got replaced by American Indian

Movement (AIM) leaders, such as Russell Means, Dennis Banks, Clyde and Vernon Belcourt, Carter Camp, Russ Redner, John Trudall, Leonard Peltier, and their followers, all of whom contributed to the social and cultural consciousness.

This new Indian spiritual awakening and movement gradually worked its way back to the reservations and into rural Indian communities. Ancient rituals and ceremonies that had become dormant, suppressed, hidden from the public, or almost extinct now began to resurface. The sleeping giant of combined Native nations was beginning to wake up and come out of the den, to reassert its rights and sovereignty.

Thus, the need for preserving ceremonial sites, sacred places, power centers, and aboriginal natural resources became a serious concern in many places across the nation. Indians began fighting back for their aboriginal rights, their land, and their religion. It was in this context that Tela and I began to make more public appearances, not as an ego thing, but as our spiritual obligation to preserve and protect the places that were considered invaluable and sacred to us, our mentors, and the Native people. Without the protection and preservation of such ancient sacred and aboriginal sites, Native healing and resources would become extinct.

I had made a commitment to the sacred profession, and hence I had no choice but to put my job, secret apprenticeship, and life on the line, if needed, in order to protect the Native religion, sacred places, and natural resources. I tried to get Wahsek to become involved in these issues and concerns because he was a vital link to the past, and more knowledgeable as to the actual significance of the environment, sacred sites, natural resources, and ecosystems.

As a consequence, he gradually started getting recognition in his local area, and his services to the people increased. His unique knowledge, special status, and value as a hereditary ceremonial leader and traditional Native healer suddenly became of value to Indians and non-Indians, who began to search him out because they were fed up with the artificial approach and dehumanization of Western medicine and technological corruption, and of Christianity. Wahsek couldn't handle all the new popularity and workload so he began to place more and more demands upon Tela and me to help him. To become more qualified we had to do more training, so there was a time during the late 1970s and early 1980s when our lives were becoming very stressed.

Eventually we started going to higher and more powerful mountains because of certain dreams and the calling of special spirits who inhabited such places. There were times we went without supervision and experimented on our own, encountering failures and successes, and there were times we went under direct supervision of the older shamans, including Wahsek and Gina. On a number of occasions we had to fast, make medicine, and visit sacred sites to obtain stronger power and spirits to help heal a patient.

I suppose the situation was similar to what Jesus had to do, as related in Matthew 17 in the Bible. According to that story Jesus had to go to the mountain to get stronger healing powers in order to doctor a few of his more difficult cases.

Gradually we began to realize that for our generation, with all of its fast-paced changes, life was much more complicated than it had been for our predecessors. We were confronted not only with what our patients had inherited from their forefathers, but also with an incredible accumulation of transgressions that the patients themselves had committed.

In addition, more and more of our sacred sites and healing centers were becoming desecrated and contaminated by the public, the government, and industries. It was becoming more difficult for us to find the plants and herbs we needed in healing, it was becoming more difficult for us to seek visions and guidance from the Great Creator and spirits, and it was becoming more difficult for us to doctor new and increasing illnesses.

Western society, including all the races of humankind who were subscribing to the Western lifestyle and value system, was now being held accountable by Nature for its violations. The spirits of the Earth and Nature were enacting penalty and fighting back against the modern people. And for some strange reason, contemporary human beings, with all of their education, science, and technology, just couldn't seem to understand that Nature and God—or the Great Spirit, if you will—were one and the same.

Thus, Tela and I came to the conclusion that in order to help doctor the new generation we would now also have to teach them what was causing their diseases and illnesses. This is another reason that we decided to begin lecturing and writing. We felt an obligation to tell people that while they were destroying the Earth, they were also destroying themselves; even innocent bystanders got punished and hurt from the negative actions of others.

As part of a new generation of traditional Native healers we began to see that the new diseases and problems—such as cancer, leukemia, Hodgkin's disease, multiple sclerosis, pancreatitis, different kinds of arthritis, prostate gland diseases, vaginitis, severe yeast infections, diabetes, gallbladder stones, kidney stones, ulcers, colitis, hemorrhoids, psoriasis, eczema, ovarian cysts, tumors, thyroid gland disorders and diseases, hepatitis, liver disorders and diseases, acute diarrhea, chronic indigestion, bronchitis, asthma, emphysema, stronger venereal diseases, a new strain of tuberculosis, and HIV—were often a direct result of modern-day human violations against Nature and the Natural Laws. Western society was becoming very sick, and a sick society creates sick people; a healthy society creates healthy people.

Occasionally we found ourselves working on bug bites, Snakebites, sprains, torn ligaments, fractures, accident-related injuries and infections, and Lyme disease, in addition to dealing with increasing new diseases and illnesses that we didn't know anything about. In some cases our treatment was primary, but in most cases the Native shamanic application was supplementary, or provided in addition to Western medicine.

Many serious problems, and related physical and mental illnesses, were a result of alcohol and drug addiction, domestic violence, child abuse, molestation, pregnancy, abortions, divorce, increased auto accidents, death and dying, suicide attempts, and violent crimes. Some diseases were caused from natural and artificial chemical poisons, such as pesticides, insecticides, dyes, and other chemicals found in modern foods, water, clothing, housing, and industry. Electrical contamination, noise pollution, new bacteria and viruses, and the side effects of Western drugs created problems as well.

It was also becoming apparent that a considerable number of the modern illnesses resulted from stress, improper diet, exposure to chemical poisoning, and immoral lifestyles. Many were spiritual punishments for violating Nature, the Natural Laws, and the Great Creator's Laws. In addition, however, we began to encounter a substantial increase in illnesses involving demons, ghosts, and sorcery. The increased need and demand for our traditional Native healing services were a consequence of modern people's fascination with and involvement in shamanism and the occult, and their misguided quest for spirituality.

In this context we found ourselves assuming the roles and responsibilities that are more commonly associated with parapsychologists, psychiatrists, physicians, professors, priests, environmentalists, mythologists, and mystics, all in addition to carrying out the typical duties of traditional Native healers, ceremonial leaders, and spiritual teachers. And ironic as it may seem, we also found ourselves occasionally doctoring Western professionals in the above roles. The following short, diverse, and random list of examples will demonstrate the new kinds of modern illnesses we dealt with, what we discovered or believed was the cause of the illnesses, and how we tried to effect a cure for each different problem. Although our remedies had a very high success rate for the majority of the patients we doctored, we were not successful in all our cases. Perhaps the following Native myth can provide insight on the dilemma.

The Sick Buzzard

A long, long time ago, Buzzard was flying around the world. He went all over, eating anything he wanted, and because of who and what he was, he could basically do anything he wanted.

He ate dead animals, birds, reptiles, Snakes, fish, decayed human bodies, and even trashed fetuses. He ate any kind of garbage, anything dead, and he was constantly looking for something that was sick and dying. He was always eating and he wouldn't share his food with anyone else. He thought he was the biggest, strongest, and best-looking of bird. "After all," he bragged, "I must be special and have a special power to do all this."

One day he ate too much and started getting sick and weak. He started flopping around while he was flying, and he began to fall. He almost crashed into the river while trying to land on a big log. He decided to rest and recuperate. He had garbage and dead food all over his head. Some of it was dripping off his beak, neck, and chest. Blowflies came and landed on him, cashing in on the feast. Maggots began to cluster on the top of his head but he was too weak to wash himself in the water. So there he sat in the hot, dry sun and fell asleep.

Just before sunset he woke up and noticed the top of his head was burning. He was burnt so bad that it made him bald-headed, and yet he was still too sick to fly over to the river, wash up, and find a nice cool place to roost. So he started crying and moaning from the pain, the stench, the sickness, and his demise. He knew he was dying because of his greed and selfishness.

Otter came swimming by but she wouldn't help him. Deer came by, got scared, and left. She didn't want any of the sickness. Bear saw Buzzard and threw him a root to eat, but Buzzard didn't eat roots, only dead and decayed meat. Coyote came by and saw Buzzard as an easy catch. He thought for a minute about eating the big bird but he couldn't stand the smell, so he laughed at Buzzard and left. Crane, Fish Hawk, Eagle, and Redtail flew around and looked at the situation, but they wouldn't help Buzzard because they never liked his arrogant attitude.

Raven, Crow, and Magpie also heard the crying and cracking noise Buzzard was making but they wouldn't help either because Buzzard was stingy and never shared his food with them. Flickerbird and Humming-bird felt sorry for Buzzard so they sang over him, but they wouldn't touch him in doctoring because Buzzard was too dirty and filthy. While they sang Buzzard dreamed.

He thought he heard someone say, "Hey, you up there." He looked around but he was all alone. Once again he heard, "Hey, you up there, I can help you." Then Buzzard looked down and saw a bunch of green plants dancing back and forth in the breeze. He tried to bend over to see if they were the ones who were hollering at him, and he fell on the ground, rolling around in the plants. Some of the plants got into his mouth.

They smelled good, tasted good, and made him feel good. So he ate a bunch of them. He stayed all night long in the patch of green, mint-flavored plants. By morning he felt great, so he walked over to the river, puked, bathed, drank, and cleansed himself. He left behind some of his feathers as payment to the plants for sharing their medicine with him. It was the only thing he had to give. Then he took off flying in search of food but now he had a bald head. As he left the herbs he sang, "Round and around the Buzzard goes, where he will land nobody knows, so beware."

Case 1

A forty-five-year-old Indian-Hispanic male had arthritis in his back, legs, feet, arms, and hands, along with severe migraine headaches. He was prone to drinking and violence. Several domestic violence incidents had occurred in his marriage. He experienced tormenting dreams and constant pain, and he reverted to drinking alcohol, hoping to allay the problem. The fear, anger, and pain were therefore often displaced on his wife. He was educated and had a good, high-paying job in a college, but he had a habit of changing jobs frequently.

The Native doctoring diagnosis and ceremony revealed that the patient, as a Vietnam vet, was being tormented by the ghosts of dead people and flashbacks of the war and killing. He confessed for his violations against the Great Creator's Laws. We did a mock burial ceremony and made apology and restitution, and offered redemption to the dead by offering food and tobacco in a sacred fire. The patient was purged with herbs and doctored in the sacred sweat lodge for purification. We sang and danced over him with spiritual hand-healing. He was also placed on a follow-up program that required a four-day fast. He was directed to drink mugwort tea three times a day for four days and bathe in mugwort herbs and tea every night for one week; he continued fasting on fruit juices and fruit for two weeks, then gradually moved into a regular diet of rice, vegetables, and fruit, but not fruit and vegetables together.

He was completely healed of his problems, encouraged to seek marriage and family counseling and repair his marriage. He is now healthy and fine.

Case 2

A thirty-two-year-old half-Native American woman was completing her education and apprenticeship for becoming a chiropractor. She was constantly sick with stomach cramps, chronic diarrhea, colitis, rheumatism, allergies, sinus infections, and migraine headaches. She also said she couldn't sleep well at night and kept having bad dreams, but she could not see the dreams clearly. She felt someone was attacking her in the dreams but she could not see who it was. She was also pestered by a variety of different bugs in her house and at work, such as spiders, centipedes, roaches, beetles, flies, hornets, wasps, and scorpions. The insects had bit her on a number of occasions and made her sick, and the bites became infected.

Diagnosis of the case via a traditional Native healing ceremony revealed that the woman was being attacked by a Mexican *bruja,* or sorceress. Evidently the young woman had lived with an older woman some years previously who was a lesbian, although the younger woman didn't know it at first. The young Indian woman was very interested in psychic development and was eventually enticed into a number of seductive witchcraft rituals with the older woman.

The older woman had drugged and seduced her against her wishes. She felt uncomfortable in the relationship because she said the older woman was constantly flirting with her and sexually harassing her. She was financially trapped and couldn't get out of the living arrangement until she won a scholarship.

When she tried to leave, the older woman became angry and fought with her, beat her up, and threatened to do whatever was necessary to get her back. She said, "If I can't have you, nobody will." In a state of fear and desperation the patient sought out the services of an alleged Hispanic shamaness who requested five thousand dollars to "break the curse, hold, and torment." Evidently the young Indian woman got caught in a serious cross fire of ongoing witchcraft, and she withdrew from the clutches of the Mexican *bruja* prior to finalizing her payment.

At the time my wife Tela and I doctored the patient we began to experience similar symptoms. We were constantly under attack by bad dreams and insects. I was stung seven times by scorpions and my children were stung by bees and a hornet. Tela was bitten by several spiders, and almost bitten by a Copperhead Snake. Owls hooted at night around the woman's house, which was located in a rural part of Kentucky. She was involved in three different car accidents before we flew out to doctor her, and we had unexpected complications and delays with our prearranged flight.

The patient was advised to confess for her involvement in homosexual activity and certain immoral types of sex acts, and she had to clearly state to the Great Creator and good spirits that she did not love the older woman who was a lesbian, and that it wasn't her fault she had been molested and abused. She also had to confess for hiring a sorceress to get even and perform witchcraft on her behalf against the older woman. Two wrongs don't make a right.

In addition, the patient was instructed to seek out, find, and destroy any pictures, gifts, power objects, plants, herbs, or artifacts that either woman had given her in the past or present. Once all the items had been burned up and destroyed, all contact and connecting energies would be terminated; and this was done with positive results.

The woman was purified and spiritually strengthened in the sacred sweat lodge during the day, given a variety of different herbs to drink, and then prayed and sung upon at night. She was also given special herbs to douche with as a means of removing all contamination and negative energies, or intruding bad spirits, from her vagina and womb. Her home and office were spiritually sterilized with smudge and prayed upon to expel all bad things, seen or unseen; and protective medicine was made upon her home and office. In fact, on the third night of doctoring, Lightning and Thunder raged and it rained constantly. A lightning bolt hit her office and did minor damage.

Before the end of the week the woman's symptoms, illnesses, and problems all cleared up and she went back to work healthy and well. We taught her how to use cultural methods and rituals to protect herself in the event the problems might start again in the future. We then had to doctor ourselves and our children from the poisonous stings and bites and eventually got healed from the backlash.

Case 3

A fifty-two-year-old White male friend of ours came to be doctored. He was well built and led an athletic life. He was well educated, an active member in his church, and a longtime school principal. He got worried and scared one day because he suddenly urinated blood and kidney stones. His physician wanted to put him on a special kind of medicine but advised there could be side effects and a need for surgery.

We doctored him with a traditional Native ceremony for one night. He had to confess for having sex with women on their menses, for committing sodomy, and for eating Pheasant, Shark meat, and Turtle that was cooked, shared, and prepared by women on their menses. We had him drink dandelion root tea for several days, followed by sage tea for several days, then echinacea tea for a week; three cups a day was the recipe. He got completely well and didn't need to take Western drugs or go through surgery.

He wanted to know why his minister had not told him about the spiritual laws. I told him I didn't know what the White people did or didn't teach in their churches, so I suggested that he go ask his minister and church leaders the same question. I asked him if he believed in the Bible, had faith in God, and believed in his church teachings. He said, "Yes, I believe the Bible is the word of God." I responded by scolding him, "Then why don't you read, study, and follow the chapter in Leviticus? God's Law, the Great Spirit's Laws, are universal."

Case 4

A thirty-year-old woman was living on Social Security because she had been diagnosed with schizophrenia. She had spent one year in a mental hospital undergoing therapy; the treatment was primarily drug oriented. She lived in and had grown up in a southern state. She appeared to be African-American to a small degree, but she made no mention of it, and her behavior and household did not reflect that cultural background.

Since her release from the hospital she had met a White man, was in love, and wanted to get married. She wanted to be doctored and get well so she could lead a normal life, go back to college, and embark upon a career. She demonstrated unusual behavior while I was talking to her about the ceremony. She frantically and periodically pulled on her hair, shook her head violently, and screamed at voices that she said were tormenting her.

When I asked her what she was doing she said, "It's those goddamn Black people, little pigmy-type Black people who keep pestering me. They're always talking at the same time and they won't get out of my hair. They leave sometimes when I chase them away but then they sneak back. I hate them. They're driving me nuts with their arguing, trying to tell me what to do!"

I asked her if there was a history of schizophrenic illness in her family and her response was negative; she didn't know any relatives who had ever demonstrated similar symptoms or who had been diagnosed with the illness. I inquired about her diet and eating habits as a child growing up and it appeared to be impoverished; there were times when they didn't have enough food for several days or they lived on mainly rice, beans, and homemade bread and sometimes Possum, Carp, Swamp Rats, and Raccoon. She said they didn't have much in the way of fruits, vegetables, or dairy sources.

I also asked if there was a history of alcoholism in her family and she said no, because they couldn't afford it. She did say, however, that her mother had problems in pregnancy with her and had lost two previous fetuses. She also said that her mother and father were constantly arguing and fighting and had been abusive toward her. She claimed she ran away from home at age seventeen.

I diagnosed her illness and confirmed it as *ker-pey-it,* or insanity, comparable to what Western physicians and psychiatrists would consider schizophrenia. To the best of my knowledge Western doctors do not really know what causes the illness, nor do they have a cure for it; and evidently there are different stages and degrees of the illness.

I smoked my pipe, prayed to the Great Creator and my good doctor spirits, went into a trance, and "looked into her" in a psychic-spiritual way. I could see the little Black spirits all over her head, and when they saw me and realized I could "see" them, in a clairvoyant way, they tried to run. But my spirits captured them and held them until I could find out why they had made a claim on this woman.

It was at that point that I discovered the woman had been raped by a half-crazed older African-American male while attending a southern Christian type of revival conference, and evidently the Black man had been on drugs. The rape occurred at the same time the young girl was experiencing her first menses—and it was a late onset because she was about sixteen at the time.

The rapist beat her viciously upon the head, while forcing her into submission, and eventually she became unconscious. He had held her by the hair and supposedly said mumbo jumbo words while raping her. When she awoke she had an African shrunken head hanging from her neck, and it was a real one, not a fake. She threw it into the swamps and never told anyone about the incident.

The patient went into a rage when I recounted what I had seen and been told by my spirits. She screamed, ranted, raved, paced back and forth, started cussing at the voices she was hearing, and she pulled violently at her hair, ripping patches of it out and throwing it at me. Her boyfriend helped to hold her and calm her down. Then I made up a special batch of herbs to help relax and protect her.

I had her bathe in mugwort, asking her to understand that the magic and spirit of the sacred herb would purify her from the horrible incident; it would clean her mind, body, and soul from the contamination of the act and its related side effects. I assured her that she would be able to sense all the negative energy and injuries being taken away completely, absorbed by the herbs, and discharged into the sewage where they belonged.

Later on that evening I continued with the diagnosis and doctoring ceremony. She admitted to the incident, shamefully crying. I had to convince her that it wasn't her fault, that she wasn't guilty of doing anything wrong, and that she was simply an unfortunate victim. I also assured her that the Great Creator loved and would forgive her if she would forgive herself. I captured the tormenting spirits and had them destroyed. I also had her husband-to-be state loudly that he forgave her for the incident, and that he truly loved her, and that he did not consider her "dirty" or "spoiled."

I also had her purge her system with herbal laxatives, had her douche with a special herb as part of the vaginal purification and healing, and I had her cut her hair short and perform a ceremony outside in a fire pit. My intent was to symbolically and spiritually get rid of all bad little spirits and voices. She was then instructed to wash her hair every day for a week in a sage-based shampoo with the understanding that herbal sage is an ancient medicine with the power, spirit, and function of warding off bad spirits and negative energy. That is its purpose and function on this Earth.

I also placed her on a regular daily intake of strong vitamins and minerals and warned her not to use the Western drugs anymore; I wanted my own herbs to flush the narcotics out of her system.

I then used a series of herbs, such as ginkgo, lobelia, blue cohosh, purple sage, angelica root, and ginseng, to facilitate the mental healing and repair of any potential physical damage that had been done to the brain cells from her constant negative thinking and related mental energy. The herbal remedies were continued separately and on an intermittent basis for several months while I periodically prayed on her and sent spirits long-distance to check up on and continue doctoring her. I received a letter from her a year later that she had been diagnosed as healed by the Western doctors and her life and marriage were doing just fine.

Case 5

An older Indian male relative was experiencing heart disease and failure. He was scheduled for open-heart bypass surgery and was very scared. He didn't drink or smoke but he was a little overweight. He asked if I could doctor him to save his heart, or at least pray and make protective medicine on him while he was in surgery, and after he came out of surgery for a recuperation period.

I performed a traditional Native healing ceremony on him, diagnosed his sickness, and told him what I saw. He had violated Indian custom and laws, and the Great Creator's Laws against the Deer people. He had developed a bad habit of hunting without making ceremony, he never asked for permission to take the Deer's life, he never offered tobacco or *keeshwoof* root as payment, and he disrespected the Deer by letting women on their moontime cook, share, and eat the Deer meat.

In addition, he had a habit of letting his wife eat the Deer heart, which is men's medicine; there were times he took only the large legs and wasted the remaining parts of the Deer; and he let the dogs eat and drag the Deer parts all over the yard. A number of bucks and does suddenly showed up in my front yard at the exact moment I was trying to explain the cause of his sickness. I pointed and said, "See, we human beings can try to hide things, we can lie to each other, but you can't hide nothing from the Great Spirit; there is your omen and proof."

He confessed for his violations and promised to never insult the animal people again. He offered payment and made restitution via tobacco and pleas for forgiveness, and by promising to put a salt lick block out in the woods for the Deer as payment for insult and injury.

I sang and danced on him, used herbal laxatives for a period of three days while I had him fast moderately, and I gave him a prescription that required drinking different kinds of herbal teas. Some of the herbs—chickweed, for instance—were used to flush the cholesterol, fatty deposits, and toxins out of his heart valves. The other herbs, such as angelica root, ginseng, and wormwood, were used to heal, strengthen, and improve the effective functioning of his vital organs. I also had him go on a strict diet low in meats with a focus on eating a lot of brown rice, beans, green leafy vegetables, and fruits, while avoiding dairy products, such as ice cream, milk, yogurt, and cheese, and other foods high in fat and oil.

He didn't need the heart bypass surgery and got well, stayed well for another ten years, and then relapsed with age. Evidently he couldn't break an old habit and addiction. He lived through the surgery but was constantly weak and sick, and he died approximately five years later.

Case 6

A twenty-eight-year-old Asian-American woman came to see me for an illness involving problems with her menstrual cycle. She was sporadic on her cycles and experienced severe cramping and bloating and constant yeast infections. She said the ob/gyn was threatening to perform a D and C. She also thought she had a cyst on her ovary because of the pain around that area, and she was making plans to have an ultrasound scan done. She also had a history of urinary tract and bladder infections.

Sex was very painful for her. She was tired a lot and losing weight from lack of sleep and worry. She was also developing conflicts in her relationship with her boyfriend. He just didn't seem to understand her pain and predicament. Apparently he felt that she was rejecting him by denying him love and sex. She was therefore afraid she was going to lose him.

I made arrangements to doctor her at a time when she wasn't bleeding on her menses and explained the reasons for not being able to use my healing powers and spirits at that particular time. I started doctoring her during the day, after giving her an orientation to the healing ceremony, and upon giving her time to rest from the long trip.

As usual, I smudged the patient and the room. I then lit my pipe and made an invocation to the Great Creator and the good doctor spirits, asking for permission to doctor the woman; I asked that they lend me their power and help me. I saw a bleeding Snake all twisted up in the woman. It was strange what I saw in a psychic way: the Snake entered up through her vagina, then into the stomach, and it was trying to chase a Frog and eat it.

I was just about ready to tell the patient what I had seen in a supernatural way when all of a sudden I saw a Frog jump into the house, followed immediately by a large Bullsnake. The woman jumped and screamed, then I talked to the Frog and Snake, thanked them for reporting as omens and messengers, and asked them to leave while I escorted them out with an Eagle wing fan.

I proceeded to explain the Natural Laws, and how it was against the Natural Laws and the Great Creator's Laws for humans to torment, torture, experiment on, and harm certain creatures in Nature. I also explained why it was against the spiritual laws to cook and eat things such as Frogs and Snakes while a woman was menstruating. I encouraged her to search for this truth and possible custom in her own culture and traditional religion.

I asked her if she ever did these things, and she confessed. She said that she had experimented upon both Frogs and Snakes in a science class at college; she admitted that she had eaten Frogs and Snakes. So I had her *pegasoy,* and then I blew the sins and violations off her mind, soul, and body, all the while pleading for her penance.

I then had to use the Eagle feathers and the spirit of the Eagle to go inside her body and capture the Snake and the Frog and remove them from her. I also had to suck the negative energy out of her ovaries and spit the potential cyst and tumor into the fire to be destroyed. I worked on her for three days and nights while singing, dancing, and praying.

I used herbs such as yarrow to purge the toxins and infections out of her body, and I had her douche several times a day in juniper berry tea. I also had her do an enema on herself twice a day for several days using catnip tea. This was followed by drinking blue cohosh, raspberry, and blueberry leaf teas.

I had one more perplexing diagnosis to reveal to her: the spirits said she had a low-grade venereal disease. I said I saw a very strange-looking microscopic parasite inside her vagina that was causing a bad rash and infection. For a second I thought I saw a black-headed bird regurgitating in her vagina, but I didn't understand the symbolic message.

I told her the spirits said the name of her disease started with the letter *T,* but I didn't know what it was or how to pronounce the sickness. I suggested that she get a blood test from her physician. I later found out she had been diagnosed with trichomoniasis.

I finalized the healing by telling her how to do a special ceremony while using the spiritual powers of yarrow on a full Moon. She was to drink a tea made from yarrow, bathe in a hot bathtub full of yarrow tea, and then afterward sleep in the light of the full Moon. She learned how to pray during this time as a means to get her menses back in harmony. Evidently she got completely well and began to have her period with ease and harmony during the full-Moon phase on a regular basis. My grandmother spirit guides taught me how to do all this. I just followed their instructions while they worked through me.

Case 7

A young Indian male, age sixteen, kept staying out late at night. He was getting in trouble with the authorities, had been busted for smoking marijuana, and had been accused of trespassing upon a cemetery. His parents said he was incorrigible; they had no control over him. He had attempted suicide on several occasions. They were full-blooded Indians from a Montana tribe but they were second-generation urban Indians and Catholics.

They had placed the boy in professional therapy with the Indian Health Service Clinic and a local priest. They claimed he was experiencing nightmares, and so were his younger brothers.

The parents came to visit one day because my children played with their children. I knew they were concerned about the oldest boy's behavior, and I was worried about my children getting involved with him under the circumstances. At dinner the parents asked in passing what we thought about the situation. I said to the boy, "I see your friend is following you."

He got scared and ran but I stopped him at the door and asked him to sit down. I told him I saw a ghost following him. My spirits reported that the ghost was his cousin, who apparently had committed suicide. On that note the whole family started crying. They said their boy did have a cousin the same age, and the two boys had been like brothers. They did everything together. The traumatic ending of this relationship occurred a couple of months before we met the family, and consequently we had no knowledge of the situation. The parents went on to state that, when the cousin suddenly and mysteriously committed suicide, their son just freaked out and had been difficult to communicate with ever since. He hated to stay at home at night and left.

After further discussion I agreed to perform a healing ceremony for the entire family. During the ceremony the oldest son and the other brothers confessed that they had been seeing the ghost of their cousin at nighttime while they tried to sleep. They said their older brother kept having dreams that his dead cousin was calling him to the cemetery. The older brother was afraid to tell his parents or anyone else except his younger brothers. He didn't think they would believe him. So he just surrendered to the situation. He went almost every night to the grave and cried and visited with his dead cousin. He claimed he could see and hear the ghost. His cousin made him depressed and frustrated because he said he was lonely. The ghost pleaded with the living boy to come and join him, via suicide, or else he would find a way to kill the living cousin and his brothers.

I performed a mock burial ceremony, a sort of Native American séance. I had my spirits summon the deceased boy's ghost and gave him a lecture in front of the entire family. I stated how it was against the Great Creator's Laws for the dead to torment and pester the living. I then assured him that my spirit guides would be kind to him, and that they would escort him over to the land of the dead where he belonged. I had the family make an offering of gifts to the ghost and say their farewells. They offered tobacco, food, a cassette tape of Indian songs, and a cassette tape of rap music songs.

The gifts were obviously offered to the deceased by way of the fire and left with him in a spiritual way. I also had the oldest boy in the family *pegasoy* for attempting suicide himself and explained why it was against the Great Creator's Laws. I then took them all to a sacred sweat lodge ceremony, purified them with herbs, and doctored them with natural forces and ancient spirits. We also purified and cleansed their home with funeral-type herbs and medicines.

The oldest son readjusted and improved his behavior. He did well at home and at school for a couple of years. The bad dreams, poltergeist-type activity, parents' drinking, and other domestic problems in the family also cleared up for a long time. It was hard for the parents to work full-time, on rotating shifts, on low salaries, and still try to raise seven young boys.

I guess the social stress eventually got the best of them all, because a number of years after we left, we heard the oldest son had killed a local police officer, supposedly while trying to rob a store, and under the influence of heavy drugs. Apparently he and his brothers had joined a gang, perhaps hoping to find a way to get attention, recognition, and build self-esteem.

Torn between two conflicting cultures and accepted by neither, they were forced to find another way out of their demise. The city they lived in did not have any Native American social-cultural programs. Without a support system they became victims of their predicament.

Case 8

A middle-aged Hispanic couple with health complaints came to get doctored. They said they were jaundiced, they were tired all the time, their livers hurt, and they had aches and pains in their bones. They also complained of periodic nausea, diarrhea, occasional loss of memory, and the male was becoming impotent. They also explained that they had been to the Western physicians for all kinds of tests but a diagnosis was not provided for their illness.

I smoked and prayed to the Great Creator and good spirits. I used the spirits and my own psychic powers to scan them completely. They were fairly pure people in terms of not having sins or violations against Nature.

I sang, danced, and prayed on them several hours and still did not get an answer as to the possible cause of their illness. That night I had a dream. I dreamt I saw them both down in a remote Mexican village. They had bought different kinds of pottery; some were cups, some were flower vases, and other pieces were large bowls. I saw them in their house drinking from two cups that they apparently considered a matching set, and something special to them.

I told them about the dream the next day. They admitted that they had bought the artifacts approximately a year ago, in celebration of their anniversary and as a reflection of their culture. They also said the cups were special to them. I asked them if anyone else in their household had similar symptoms or ailments. They said no, only them. I asked if anyone else ever drank from their cups and they said no.

One of my spirits said they had been getting poisoned from the paint designs on the cups and bowls. I didn't know what kind of poison at first but upon further investigation with the spirits, I told the patients I thought they had lead poisoning. They went back to their clinic and asked to see an internist. At first the physician laughed but then had a blood and urine test conducted specifically for that kind of poisoning.

My diagnosis was correct. I told the patients to break up and get rid of all the pottery, and throw it in the garbage. To purify their systems, they used burdock, sage, chickweed, and then red clover tea for more than a month. I also had them stay on a special diet of brown rice, soybeans, no meats, plenty of fruits and fruit juices, and green leafy and yellow vegetables. They were completely healed.

Case 9

A young, wealthy White couple came to see me for special doctoring. I had doctored the woman's mother a number of years previously for spinal meningitis and the woman had gotten completely well. This couple had spent a fortune going to the best Western physicians in the nation with hopes of getting pregnant. They had tried everything imaginable, with numerous tests done to check the husband's sperm count and the woman's hormones and ovaries; both had been tested for potential low-grade infections. In addition to being unable to conceive, the woman had also been experiencing erratic menstrual cycles.

I doctored them in my usual manner and discovered a number of violations which they in turn admitted and had to confess about. Some of the violations involved desecration of the dead whereby the woman had attended funerals and had visited cemeteries while she was on her moontime. Such an act is against the Creator's Law. Some of the violations could be attributed to experimenting on Frogs in school.

I told them I had to make special medicine that would require a long trip, fasting, and visitation of a sacred site. I was living in Spokane, Washington, at the time so I had to travel all the way down to Humboldt County in California in order to do a ceremony at Coyote's Rock. According to ancient Native myth, this was the place where barren women could go and pray, and become pregnant. I was taught how to make the special medicine by one of my elderly female mentors. I also had both the man and woman change their diet, quit drinking coffee, and abstain from sex for three months.

I used a number of herbs on them both, including blue cohosh, yarrow, and angelica root for the wife, and sage, ginseng, and yohimbine for the husband. They drank the herbal teas in a sequence, in that order, three cups a day for a week on each different herb. I also had the man eat walnuts to help build up his virility; and I made a special medicinal tea from Deer antler for him to drink. She became pregnant and had a healthy and beautiful baby.

Case 10

An Indian woman came to see me concerning the birth deformity of her newborn. The infant had rickets and infantile arthritis as well. He had unusually small and crooked fingers and hands, and he was very hairy. The baby cried all the time in pain, and would not take breast milk or Western-style infant's milk. The Western doctors also said the baby was jaundiced and threatened to put him in the hospital for dialysis treatment.

I doctored the mother and the baby in the usual manner and told her that the baby was born that way because she had committed violations. For example, she had touched, handled, and eaten Bear meat, and she had handled a freshly killed Bear carcass. She had also been on a very poor diet while she was pregnant, with the bad habits of smoking tobacco, drinking alcohol, and smoking marijuana.

She *pegasoyed* for her violations and I sang and danced on them both for several nights. I made medicine by having the infant breathe the steam from boiling stinging nettle herbs, having him drink a mild concoction of the tea, and then massaging him with Bear fat while singing special Bear songs. On the second week the baby was placed on a diet of hazelnut milk, followed by pine nut milk, and soybean milk.

The infant gradually went back to a standard diet, the hair patches disappeared, and the jaundice cleared up. Several months later the deformity also cleared up. The mother also gave up drinking alcohol and smoking cigarettes, and I think she reduced her habit of using marijuana. I had her go on a diet of natural foods, plants, herbal teas, and brown rice, and she learned the Indian custom and laws and tried to follow the laws as a new code for living. I learned in later years that she had two more children who were born healthy.

Case 11

A middle-aged full-blooded woman married to an Indian male had cancer. She was my wife's cousin and an educated woman. Her husband had a Ph.D. He was a successful educational administrator and she was a college counselor. They were prosperous, happily married, and maintained some identification with their Native heritage and culture but subscribed to a Western religion and way of life.

They didn't know what caused the cancer and she had just started chemotherapy when I was first contacted. This was a very difficult case for a number of reasons: first of all, because I had known them both personally for a long time; second, because their belief system was not compatible with traditional Native shamanism, beliefs, and practices; and third, because the disease was advanced and terminal, and the use of chemotherapy was just making it worse.

I tried doctoring the Indian woman in the traditional Indian way and I wanted her to stop chemotherapy. I needed to flush that poison out of her organism so I could get down to the basics of Native healing. She was too scared and wouldn't follow instructions. I explained the cause of her disease, but she and her husband were reluctant to accept the diagnosis.

There were a number of violations and transgressions involved that they were unwilling to accept and reconcile. In addition, my spirits told me the woman was being poisoned by natural chemicals and electrical currents in the expensive house they had bought. They refused to give up the house and move. I prayed and used spiritual healing and herbal healing on the woman, and the cancer went into remission for a while.

Unfortunately, it resurfaced about a year later because she refused to cooperate with the traditional healing approach, instructions, and suggestions. She died, leaving behind two young children and a husband who grieved for many years.

A few years later it was discovered that a considerable number of children at a school in their neighborhood were getting cancer and leukemia. The research claimed that the children were getting sick from radon poisoning in the houses, school, and local church; there was also a possibility of electrical poisoning from the high intensity/high voltage transformers located near the neighborhood and school.

Why do such things affect some people and not others? I don't know. Maybe some people are more susceptible than others. People's immune systems are different, but I also believe spiritual violations can weaken a person's immune system.

<center>~~~~~~~~~~</center>

Case 12

This was a very interesting case but I did not want any part of it at first. It involved a young, attractive Black woman who was part Indian. She had chronic osteoarthritis, she was borderline diabetic, and she had candidiasis with chronic yeast problems. In addition, I later discovered that she had a venereal disease, skin rashes, and an ovarian cyst. She also claimed she had cancerous breast tumors.

I had strange and scary dreams for a period of two weeks before the woman contacted me. In the dreams I saw a very beautiful, sensuous, seductive, and psychic woman who was doing a ceremony with Snakes, dead people, and creatures from the swamp. I sensed, felt, and later found myself in a war with very evil people and spirits.

When the woman first approached me for a doctoring I knew that she was the woman I had dreamt about. Even when I first met her she had a necklace made from human bones, Snakeskin hair ties, and African-type artifacts and power objects that weren't familiar to me. Three times I told her I did not want to get involved. Each time she pleaded with me, she cried, she was very flirtatious and made strong sexual overtures to me; then she even got to the point that she offered sex and slavery as payment for doctoring and in exchange for an apprenticeship she was seeking. She wanted to be a medicine woman.

I strongly sensed that she was a temptress and had natural psychic power, which also made her dangerous. I prayed on the case after her third entreaty. The Great Creator and good spirits said that the woman was basically a very good spirit who had been misguided and abused. They said that she had been guided to me, and that I should help her, and further, that it would be to my benefit and learning to help the woman. She had nowhere else to turn.

I took the woman out in Nature, to a very sacred place, intending to protect my family from any potential backlash. I made her fast on herbs and fruit juices while I prayed, sang, and danced on her. She had to fast for a whole month and constantly bathe in a sacred waterfall while the spirits of Nature actually purified, healed, and strengthened her.

I discovered while doctoring that her grandparents had chosen her to be a voodoo priestess, but she had never felt comfortable with that calling. She had been sexually abused in certain ceremonies, taught how to perform acts of sorcery involving the dead, and taught how to use specific kinds of herbs, narcotic medicines, and rituals as a way to develop her clairvoyant abilities. She had also been taught how to use the sorcery knowledge against others as a means to make a living.

She had inherited powers that were both good and bad, from both racial sides. She was a gifted seer and had the potential to be a strong healer, and she had a number of ancestor spirits (ghosts) working with her. I had to doctor her off and on for more than a month while performing a number of exorcisms, and I had to make stronger protection on her so the evil spirits couldn't return and claim her. She did a lot of sincere confessing for her sins and violations.

I had her burn and destroy all inherited and acquired power objects related to sorcery, and I gave her new power objects to learn how to use for protection, spiritual development, and spiritual work in a good way. It was a very challenging affair because I was highly attracted to her and constantly fought both my innate sexual desires and her sexual overtures. But I kept it all clean, professional, very sacred, and got her completely well and on the right path. The White doctors had to handle some of the healing as it related to the venereal disease.

The last I saw of her she was healthy, happy, radiant, and in search of an older Indian medicine woman who would be willing to teach and train her in becoming a good shamaness in both cultures.

Case 13

A White male married to an Indian woman came to get doctored for chronic sinus infections, allergies, severe migraine headaches, an alleged brain tumor, and vertigo. He was a commercial fisherman. He was scared because he was becoming accident prone, and had fallen and injured his head, neck, and arms a number of times. Strangely, his wife was developing similar symptoms but she did not have a brain tumor. He was also upset by the fact that he had experienced bad fishing seasons for three years in a row and was losing a lot of money.

I doctored them both and discovered that he had made serious violations against the Sharks. They were mad at him because he never offered payment in exchange for the bountiful fish harvests he had been reaping from the Pacific Ocean. I also discovered that he hated Sharks, for whatever reason, and had a habit of beating them unconscious. For example, sometimes he found a live Shark in his fishing net. He would pull it out, cuss at it, and then beat it half to death with a hard, wooden mallet. Then he would throw it back into the Ocean.

I prayed, sang, danced, and doctored the patient and his wife. I pleaded on their behalf, asking for their penance to be redeemed. I had them confess for their violations and make restitution to the Shark people, fish people, spirits of the Ocean, and other creatures who lived in the Ocean. I taught him how to use a prayer offering to the Great Creator and the Ocean every time he went fishing, which is a way of following the Law of Reciprocity. I also taught him to learn how to be conservative and not waste anything, and to look upon any future Sharks as a fortunate gift, which he did. They both became well, healthy, and prosperous.

Case 14

A full-blooded Indian male relative was in the hospital with a broken leg. This was the third time the leg had been broken in the same place. Blood poisoning and gangrene had set into the damaged knee and leg, although the leg was in a cast and the patient had been taking antibiotics. The Western doctors were planning to amputate. The Indian patient was scared, intoxicated, and incorrigible. He wouldn't let the physicians or nurses touch him. He got so hostile that security officers were summoned to help the doctors subdue and sedate the patient.

His wife called me from the hospital pleading for help. I told her I couldn't interfere with the hospital and doctors or they might have me arrested. She was hysterical and kept crying and pleading for me to help her husband. Feeling sympathetic, I finally consented but told her she would need to remove the patient from the hospital to my house, with the understanding that the case was extremely critical. They would have to come on their own volition. I didn't want to be held accountable or blamed for removing the patient.

I told them both that I would try to help but I wasn't a miracle worker. The Western doctors made them sign a legal release form indicating that they would not be held responsible for the patient's leaving against their professional advice. They also advised the patient that they would not be held responsible for any kind of alternative healing arrangement that he was pursuing.

Quite frankly I was worried and scared. I didn't want to jeopardize the patient's health and possible recovery. I didn't know if I had enough power and knowledge to effect a cure; and I was worried about the potential legal repercussions. As a result, I also had the patient and his wife sign a disclaimer and agreement form that basically stated that they were taking a chance in this case, fully realizing that the Native doctoring was a form of indigenous religious healing, and if the approach didn't work, they would not hold me legally responsible.

I had my wife assist with the healing preparation and ceremony while I went to a special site to build a prayer altar, seek a vision, and plead with the Great Creator and higher doctor spirits to support me in my attempt. We had the patient soak his leg in the bathtub to remove the cast. I asked Tela to make a concoction of herbs that would immediately purge the patient of the poisons; I wanted him to vomit and defecate the toxins out of his body.

By the time I got back from praying at the power center, the cast had been removed and the patient was soaking in a tub full of mugwort leaves and juice. I used yarrow tea to reduce the patient's fever, and goldenseal herbal tea to flush the infectious toxins out of his veins and damaged knee and leg.

My wife and I both prayed, sang, and danced on the patient. We had him *pegasoy* for committing a number of violations against the Natural Laws as they pertained to hunting, fishing, and ceremony involving the negative influence and effects of women's moontime energy and power. He also had to confess and ask forgiveness because he had participated in local sacred dances and ceremonies while under the influence of alcohol and sex contamination.

We asked him about his dreams and about any unusual things happening around his home or in his daily life. He said that he had tormenting dreams about deceased relatives. He reported that he'd seen an Owl in broad daylight each time just before he fell and broke his leg upon the rocks near the river.

He said a strange bird landed on his boat while he and his brother were fishing with gill nets; the bird screamed at them both just before the boat flipped over and they almost drowned. He also said he had been in three strange auto accidents during the past year, and each time a bird had hit the car just before the accident occurred.

We could see, in a clairvoyant and shamanic way, that the patient was being witched up via sorcery. We used our doctor spirits to remove the curses, bad spirits, and negative forces that had been used against the patient by a local sorcerer. We doctored the patient day and night for four days straight. We doctored him in the sacred sweat lodge, and we used a variety of different kinds of tree barks and herbs to make a new cast on his leg and knee. By the end of the week he was well enough to go with me to a sacred site where he could pray for himself, and I could use a special set of spirits from Nature to finish the healing he needed. Within two weeks he was well enough to walk on crutches; one month beyond his initial healing session, he was completely well.

I recently saw this man during a family reunion. I asked him if he'd had any more problems with his leg or knee since the doctoring that had been done more than a decade ago. He said no, that he was very impressed and pleased. He also said the White doctors couldn't believe the results. I told him we couldn't take credit for the healing. It wasn't us who did it, it was the Great Creator and the good doctor spirits, such as the Grizzly Bear, who actually did the healing.

Case 15

A middle-aged Indian woman was diagnosed with diabetes. She was in the second phase of development with the disease, and on the verge of taking shots. She complained of having urinary, bladder, and vaginal infections, and that sometimes her liver hurt and caused her to be jaundiced.

I doctored her for several nights in a row. She had to confess for violating the Natural Laws, admitting that she had cooked, shared, and eaten Deer meat, Elk meat, Buffalo meat, and Pheasant while she was on her menses. She also had to *pegasoy* for swimming in local creeks, lakes, and the river while she was on her moontime because that is considered a violation.

The spirits from those places were punishing her and making her sick for contaminating their abode. The woman also had a history of alcohol addiction. I pleaded for her forgiveness, had her make penance to redeem the transgressions, and I doctored her with a variety of herbs that were stretched over a four-week period. For example, I used purple sage tea, followed by wormwood, then prince's pine and Oregon grape.

She was doctored and steamed in the sacred sweat lodge four different times, and I placed her on a strict diet of greens, brown rice, soybeans, and lemon juice. She was gradually allowed to start eating meats in moderation but she pledged to avoid all alcohol and soda pop drinks. She is healthy, happy, and no longer a diabetic.

Case 16

A full-blooded Plains Indian male, age fifty-five, was diagnosed with prostate cancer. The cancer was in the earlier stages of development. Arrangements were made to perform a traditional Native healing ceremony on him but with an orientation explaining that our way of doctoring and ceremony were considerably different from what he was accustomed to in his own tribal culture.

Upon smoking, praying, and talking to my spirits I discovered the cause of his illness: he had violated a number of Natural Laws, which in turn required a confession. For example, he admitted that he had been having sex with different women for a long number of years while they were on their menses. He had also sodomized women and had made love medicine on women.

Instead of singing, dancing, and using my hands, I turned the doctoring over to a special set of spirits that I work with, and had them do the actual doctoring. In the meantime, I had the patient purge his system with natural laxatives such as chitum (or cascara) bark tea. I also made an herbal concoction for him to use as an enema to flush, clean, and generate healing on the prostate gland. He used catnip tea, juniper berry tea, then comfrey root tea as herbal enemas once a day for seven days each.

This approach was then followed by having the patient pack his crotch with a poultice of hot comfrey leaves three times a day for seven days. In the meantime he also had to drink comfrey root tea and eat pumpkin seeds, and I told him to periodically eat walnuts and almonds. I also wanted him to quit drinking coffee, stay on herbal teas such as raspberry leaf, peppermint, or blueberry leaf tea, and avoid all red meats and all dairy products for a period of four months.

I placed him on a diet of vegetables, fruits, and poultry for a year until his cancer got completed healed; then he gradually got back to eating red meats but in moderation. Lastly, I suggested that he avoid all alcohol, soda pops, chocolate candy, and candy in general and get in the habit of eating fruits and drinking fruit juices. He got completely well in two months, with no further problems of the prostate gland.

Case 17

A White woman talked to us about her husband, who was in his midfifties, athletic, and a well-known physician in the local community. He was also a devoted Catholic. Apparently he had been experiencing migraine head-aches for a number of years but simply dismissed them as a symptom of stress. His wife had periodic migraine headaches but she believed they were sympathetic. At work one day he had a sharp pain on the side of his head. He was rushed to the local hospital, given a CAT scan, and diagnosed as having a tumor on the brain.

His wife asked whether we would be willing to doctor him if he was willing to cooperate. She claimed Western medicine couldn't do anything for him. Surgery would be too dangerous, and drugs and chemotherapy were not working.

I told her I would think about her request before giving an answer be-cause I intuitively felt that he would not accept our diagnosis and approach to healing. That night I had a dream. I dreamed I saw a skull hitting the man in the head, and on occasion the skull also banged into the woman's head. But more significantly, a skeleton belonging to the head was very angry at the physician and kept tormenting him in a ghostly and supernatural way.

We met with the woman a couple of days later and explained to her we would be willing to doctor the doctor, but he would have to follow our ceremony and instructions to the letter, otherwise we would not be able to help him. We told her about the dream involving the skull and the headless skeleton. We asked her if she had any idea what it meant. At this point she revealed that her husband kept a human skull on his office desk at home, and the skeleton part to it was in a basement trunk.

We told her that both she and her husband were being penalized for violating a Natural Law. We explained to her that it was against the Great Creator's Law to desecrate the dead, and that her husband was committing a sacrilege. We said that he would have to bury the skull and the skeleton to get it out of his house and out of his life, and that he would be required to confess for this sin/violation. In other words, he would need to make redemption in a ceremonial way.

We also told her that he was being tormented by other ghosts for experimenting on cadavers. As a follow-up to the *pegasoy* part of the ceremony, her husband would be expected to participate in a sacred sweat lodge ceremony, allow us to use natural plants and herbs to dissolve and eliminate the brain tumor, and he would be doctored by our traditional approach of praying, singing, dancing, and hand healing. We thought it would take approximately a week to work continually on the patient.

Well, the woman presented the opportunity and entire explanation to her husband. He laughed at it and dismissed the Native form of healing, the shamanic approach, as nothing more than faith healing, magic, and Satan worship. He refused to even talk about it. He died two weeks later. Afterward the doctor's wife came to my wife and asked for a healing.

She didn't want to end up like her husband, although she too was Catholic, and she wanted a ceremony to help her handle the grieving process and transition. Tela accommodated her and the woman has been healthy, happy, and well adjusted since.

Case 18

I tried doctoring this White, middle-aged male on several occasions for the same illness. I really didn't have much time to work on him when he first approached me, back in Pennsylvania, because I was in the middle of providing a series of lectures. I only had two days and a lot of travel in between different cities. He said he had chronic diarrhea, constant indigestion, and a lot of allergies. He further complained that he was tired and just didn't have much energy. He was becoming impotent as well.

I asked him what the Western doctors said was wrong with him. He responded that they didn't know. They had tested him for everything, including giardia and other kinds of parasites, bacteria, viruses, funguses, and allergies to certain foods. They had done blood tests, urine tests, and fecal analysis. Everything came out negative.

I told the patient I would need to arrange long-distance doctoring on him. This approach requires a mutual time frame during which both of us can stay clean, fast for a few days, and perform a synchronized ceremony in privacy. On a certain night, at a specific time, I wanted him to sit down in a quiet house, smudge the house with cedar, and burn the Grizzly Bear root as part of the prayer offering and invocation.

The house needed to be purified of negative spirits, forces, and energies; that's why I asked him to use cedar. I didn't want any of his friends or family to come around because they could interfere with the séance type of arrangement; it was especially important that women on their moontime or people under the influence of alcohol, drugs, or sex not be permitted in the house during the time of the ceremony.

At the same time, I would be under the same spiritual restriction. I told him I would build a sacred fire and altar in my prayer pit or visit a certain sacred place in Nature to use for the ceremony. At that time I would also make a prayer invocation to the Great Creator and the good spirits, and I would use an ancient myth to help me go into meditation and a trance state. In the trance state I would attempt to soul travel, or use out-of-body experience to travel three thousand miles back east and visit him in spirit form. I would travel with my spirit guides and protectors.

Sometimes people sense or feel my presence during this special kind of ceremony, while others do not. Some people claim they have seen me in an ethereal or ghostlike form and heard singing. Each patient is different and all people are different, so they may or may not have similar types of encounters and experiences. Other patients claim they had dreams about me during this time and saw me singing and dancing over them while waving feathers, and they further claim that they saw certain animals and birds with me in the dream while I was trying to doctor them in spirit form.

Anyway, at that time I did go back and visit him via soul travel. I saw that he was getting sick from bad water. I also saw dead people tormenting him. So I asked the dead people to leave and quit pestering him, and I had my spirits doctor him. The next day I called and told him what I'd seen, and I asked him if he had ever drunk water from an old well, creek, stream, or spring and felt himself get sick shortly thereafter.

He said in recollection, yes, that he had gotten sick after a hiking trip. I asked him if he knew any reason why dead people would be tormenting him and he said no. We discussed all the different reasons that could cause dead people to torment a person and could not seem to come up with an answer. So I had him use herbs over a period of time to remedy his problem. His health improved considerably but the symptoms reappeared about a year later.

In the meantime he started searching out other kinds of healers, such as an acupuncturist, Chinese herbalist, homeopathic practitioner, and a naturopath; he even tried an internist. Nothing seemed to work. Once again I tried to doctor him long-distance and I asked him about the dead people. I told him I kept seeing a dead person in a well or spring where he had drunk water. In this sense he was spiritually poisoned.

One day his younger brother came to see my wife, Tela, to get doctored for similar symptoms. She tried her approach but doctored him directly, not long-distance, and came up with a similar diagnosis. It wasn't until after quite a lot of discussion and on the second day that her patient remembered that his father had had a skeleton. His father had died and one of his other brothers now kept the skeleton.

Evidently the patient's father had found the skeleton while digging out an old spring to make a well. After that discussion we called the other patient and told him what we'd learned, and his memory also came back about the incident. It happened so long ago, when they were just kids, that they had forgotten.

So now a ceremony had to be enacted in such a way as to bury the skeleton in a safe place, remove its ghost and contamination off both patients, and purify them both for the transgression and related sicknesses. But once again I kept asking the other patient who lived back east, who was the older brother of the patient now being doctored by Tela, about his water system. I asked him where he got his water. It was at that point that I discovered he got it from an old spring and well.

Upon further investigation we learned that the water system was next to, and downhill from, an old cemetery. Thus, we told both patients that they would probably never get completely healed until they either moved from the existing house, or developed a different water system far away from the influence and effect of the cemetery. We still don't know if they ever got completely healed because we haven't heard from them since the last doctoring.

Case 19

An Indian man and woman came to see me to get doctored because they said they had hepatitis A and B, and the Indian Health Clinic physician told them there was no cure for the diseases. They also said that they were occasionally jaundiced, felt tired and listless at times, and they claimed their livers hurt. They also said that they were very susceptible to bronchitis, flu, common colds, allergies, and as a consequence felt their immune systems were very low; and they bled too much even from minor cuts.

I made an arrangement to doctor them in the sacred sweat lodge. During that time I talked to the Great Creator and the good spirits about their illnesses. I was shown a vision in response. I saw them both in a sacred Sun Dance, the kind used by the Plains Indians, although this couple were not Lakota Sioux, Crow, or from a Plains-type tribe. They were also mixed breeds, being part White, Hispanic, and Indian.

I saw in the vision that they were both cut with a metal scalpel, the kind used by Western physicians in surgery. I also saw other people being cut by the same instrument for what was considered a piercing preparation as part of this ancient ceremony. I heard a song and saw spirits coming in from that dance in the form of Buffaloes, Eagles, and Indian ghosts dressed in Sun Dance regalia; they had sage wreaths around their heads, wrists, and ankles. The spirits from that part of Indian Country talked to me.

They told me they were upset with the way this particular ceremony had been conducted. They said the ceremonial leader was not following traditional custom and law while supervising the ceremony. The spirits said the medicine man for this ceremony was supposed to fast and abstain from sex, was not allowed to drink water, and that he should have purified himself daily by use of the sacred sweat lodge. The spirits claimed that none of the religious laws had been adhered to and as a consequence everyone who had participated was being penalized for violating the laws.

In addition, these same spirits also told me that the woman had been dancing while she was on her moontime, which is a violation of the ancient custom and law. And last, the spirits also told me that the dancers should have been cut for piercing in the old way, which required using a ceremonial flint knife, a bone knife, or a quartz rock. Evidently it was against the spiritual law in that area to use any form of Whiteman's metal in the ceremony, either in knife form or as utensils, such as a water bucket and scupper for the sweat lodge, or eating instruments for the dancers and singers.

I told the patients what the spirits had reported to me, and I asked them if what I had been shown was true. They said yes, and they were willing to confess for their violations, and they pleaded for forgiveness. In return, I purified them in the sweat lodge using Douglas fir and mugwort. I had to use a series of herbs for more than a month in order to purify them from the hepatitis, and as a remedy for healing the liver, the cut wounds, and related illnesses. I used dried yarrow and goldenseal on the open cuts and infected wounds. They drank herbal teas made from burdock, followed by nettle, followed by wormwood, and then teas made from Oregon grape and Grizzly Bear root. They were completely healed.

Case 20

A young White male asked me to doctor him for arthritis in his hands. He also said he had occasional aches and pains in his spine, legs, and head. I did not need to conduct a complete healing ceremony on him because I already saw the cause of his illness while discussing the case. I asked him if he did massage work for a living, and he replied affirmatively.

I told him he was getting hurt via psychic transference. In other words, he was a very loving, caring, and sympathetic person who was ethical and took pride in his profession. But he did not know how to protect himself from the negative energies, forces, thoughts, feelings, and aches and pains of his clients.

I explained the problem by using an analogy of lint on clothing. I said, "Suppose you just bought new clothes and you sit down on a couch at a friend's house, and the friend has cats. The clothes pick up hair and lint that is visible to the human eye, and yet difficult to remove, right?" He said that he had experienced that before.

"You might not be able to see the negative energies on the patients you're working on but after a while you begin to absorb their energy into your aura, which in turn can be absorbed into your body. That's why whenever we, as medicine people (Native shamans), do doctoring we always use a ritual and certain herbs to protect ourselves, or to clean ourselves afterward." I told him that massage is a form of healing and doctoring, and it needs a ritual, too.

I explained that we shamans smudge ourselves and the patient with cedar, sage, or pepperwood. We drink a tea or bathe in mugwort, sage, or angelica root; or we wash our hands in mugwort tea before and after using them in the doctoring ceremony. For the more difficult cases we use the sacred sweat lodge as a means to make stronger protective medicine, or as a way to purify ourselves afterward.

I then proceeded to smudge him completely while using my Eagle wing fan to remove the negative energies out of his aura and off his body. I had him fast for four days and purge his organism with herbal laxatives. I then placed him on a variety of herbal teas designed to clean his body, strengthen his spirit, and protect his aura. I also encouraged him to bathe in mugwort tea or sage tea on a regular basis, and at least twice a month use the Whiteman's type of sauna to cleanse himself. His health problems cleared up.

A number of patients from different racial or mixed racial and cultural backgrounds who were professional nurses, physicians, psychologists, and therapists experienced similar symptoms and illnesses as the patient in Case 20. They were all serving in the role of healer and getting sick from their work. Some of their illnesses could be attributed to stress, but what kind of stress? Sometimes the stress was a result of psychic-spiritual transference; that is, they weren't taught how to protect themselves, and hence they were absorbing the illnesses and negative energies of their patients. Healers should be forewarned that the constant accumulation of negative energies can eventually cripple a person.

11

Living a Spiritual Life

When Water Snake Tried to Outsmart the Great Spirit

There is an old story our Elders teach us about a Water Snake who lived in a pond up high at the base of a sacred mountain. He was a very healthy, wealthy, strong, and handsome man. He was on top of the world, you might say. He had the whole pond to himself and he had everything a person could ask for in life: plenty of natural resources, open space, lots of food, good weather, ample shelter, protection, a number of wives whenever he needed a woman, and a lot of free time to reflect on the meaning of life. Yes, the Great Creator had been very good to him.

But for some strange reason it just wasn't enough for him. He didn't know what to do with all that free time. Instead of using it for prayer, ritual, ceremony, and spirituality, he began to use it for mischief. Instead of using the free time to give thanks for his prosperity and as a way to help and share with others in his community, he began to use it in trying to impress others with how important he was. In his search for meaning in life, he forgot how to make life more meaningful. After all, he reasoned, he already had everything a person could ask for but it still just wasn't enough.

One day he began to notice that he was starting to age. He wasn't as strong and fast as he used to be. He had gotten too fat from overeating and from being lazy, and he had eaten all the food within his immediate range without practicing some form of conservation. So on this one morning he got up, surveyed his surroundings, and tried to figure out a way to find some food. There was no food in sight and he started to panic. "Now what am I going to do?" he said to himself.

213

He crawled from his house into the water and started a search. At first he looked close by, and then with a weaving pattern he went back and forth until he found that he was farther out, almost into the middle of the pond. He felt his strength leaving and got scared, so he headed straight back to shore, just barely making it before landing. For four days he tried this, all the time getting weaker from lack of food, age, and fear. Sometimes during the day he would cry and holler out to his neighbors for help but nobody would come. He had not been good to his neighbors all these years. He had not cared about them, so now the circle was going back; they did not care for him.

On the fifth day he devised a plan. He would find somebody stupid enough to help him. After all, he thought to himself, I am a very wise and important man here. He noticed a small group of Frogs sitting out on a large lily pad in the very middle of the pond. He knew they were probably the last of their bunch but he didn't care; he was awful hungry. Thus, with the last bit of his strength he silently swam out to them.

Just as he was about to sneak up and grab one, the village headman of the Frog people saw the Snake and started to send out a warning, but the Water Snake had power; he managed to charm the Frog. Then he said, "My brother, the Great Creator has sent me to help you. But in helping you I will also be helping myself."

"No!" the Frog reacted, "I don't trust you. Nobody can trust you. You lie too much and you are a very greedy person. Just look at what you have done to this sacred pond. There is nothing left anymore."

The Water Snake pleaded with the Frog. "Look at me, brother, I am an old man now. I am weak and tired. I have nothing left. I must redeem myself. That is why I have come out here to help you. I realize that I have been eating your people all my life and I never gave anything back. I realize now, after all these years that I have been greedy and I did wrong. So I had a vision. The Great Creator told me that in order to make my record straight I would have to come out here and use the last of my wisdom and strength to help you, to give something back."

The Frog was just about ready to leap into the water and run off but he saw the tears in the old Snake's eyes and hesitated. The Snake said, "I know where the biggest and best bugs are. There are still some left on the other side of the pond, hidden in a secret place. So if you and your family will hop onto my back I will carry you all there with the last of my strength."

The Frog people had a big discussion and argument. Some wanted to go but others were apprehensive. They didn't trust their enemy. But finally it was decided. The older and bigger Frog said, "Look at that pitiful old Snake. He can't really hurt anyone anymore. Besides, we need food to live and survive and to continue our work here in the water for the pond and the rest of the community."

So reluctantly they all climbed on the Snake's long back. One by one they filed on in a row. They were so heavy that they caused the Snake to sink somewhat Into the water, which in turn made it look like he was indeed weak. Then toward the other side of the pond they went. Slowly the Water Snake went, weaving in and out of the tules and marsh reeds. Slowly he sang his song, telling the Frogs that it was his death song. But as his long body weaved through the reeds he would sneak his head around to the back, and one by one he would snatch up and eat another Frog. Finally there was only one left, the large village headman Frog who had been so busy eating all kinds of the new bugs that he hadn't really noticed what was happening to his family. Then before he knew it, the Snake opened up his large mouth and grabbed the last Frog, all the while laughing to himself.

But the Frog fought back. Around they thrashed, causing the currents to move them farther away from shore. They made such a ruckus that the Wind came up, and it too pushed against the water, moving them both farther from shore. In time the Snake had devoured the very last Frog in the pond, and feeling proud of himself decided to swim back home.

Laughing and bragging to himself he swam, but slower and slower he swam, and then he noticed that he was beginning to sink. His strength was running out. He had gotten too fat from eating too many Frogs, and panic overcame him. He cried, begged, and pleaded with someone to help him. He cried and pleaded with the Great Creator to help him. He didn't want to die this way, by drowning. After all, he was a Water Snake, and drowning would not be an honorable way to die. He told the Great Creator he would do anything to redeem himself, he made all kinds of promises, pleading for his life. He could hardly keep his nose above water while the rest of his body was sinking and beginning to pull him down.

It seemed as though it took forever for him to reach the other side of the pond. He was constantly fighting fear and impending death. With his last bit of breath and strength he finally made it, barely pulling himself up out of the water onto the mud and plants. "Whew, I did it, I actually did it!" he hollered and bragged to himself. "I knew I really had more power than anyone. I don't have to follow the spiritual laws. Those laws are archaic. I can live by my own laws. See, I really didn't need the Great Creator or anyone because I am so powerful and wise that I can do anything. Now I will just lie here for a while, eat my herbs, rest, and renew myself."

Just when he thought he was safe, lying there in the warm sun, gloating, thinking that he could live a long time not needing anyone, or anything, and that he was even beyond the laws of Nature, he heard the most terrifying scream. His body froze in fear as the shadow of wings crossed over him. He knew what it was and wanted to hide as fast as he could but it was too late. He was just too stuffed, too tired, too weak, and too old, and before he knew it the Hawk swooped down and carried him off to his death, into her nest and into the mouths of newborn babes. Nobody can escape the Natural Laws of the Universe, no matter how important they think they are.

Years of ongoing shamanic and spiritual training have taught me many lessons. Such lessons can only be learned through suffering and sacrifice, commitment, and faith. Whether it be the shaman's path or anyone's, the quest for spirituality always involves trials, tests, and tribulations; there is no easy way no matter what society would have us believe. We have all been put here on the Earth for a reason, as has everything else in Creation. But for human beings it is a little different because we have also been put here on the Earth to learn, to improve ourselves from the mistakes we have made in this life and in many past lives, and to learn how to evolve as higher spiritual beings so we can become what we were in the beginning: spirit.

Perhaps the main lesson is that life is a never-ending learning process. Although we reach a certain level in our growth and development, there is always something new to learn, to experience, and to help us evolve to a higher level of spirituality—even if it means failing, backsliding, and hitting rock bottom, and having to start all over again. This includes medicine men and women or spiritual teachers and tribal leaders. We are all also human and therefore will make mistakes in life. Thus, we should not be so quick to judge and criticize those who are trying, or those who assume higher roles.

The secret to discovering this reality can be found in what my Elders have taught me to know as the Natural Laws and the Great Creator's Laws. There are many laws that, if learned and practiced, will promote peace, balance, harmony, good health, and prosperity. The Natural Laws and the Great Creator's love for us all provide us with an opportunity to learn, redeem ourselves, and move forward in a positive spiritual way. This reality is the same in all traditional cultures and for all races; if you search deep enough, you can find it hidden behind all good religions, especially the religions that are based on Nature, not artificiality.

There have been times in my life when I worked hard, suffered and sacrificed tremendously, and made every concerted effort to get all the way to the top, not only to the highest mountain in our aboriginal territory as part of my shamanic training and ordainment, but symbolically and in terms of lifestyle by setting goals and achieving a good career, status, and recognition in Western society.

The world as we know it has drastically changed since primitive times and the days of my mentors and their spiritual mentors. In the olden days an Indian doctor, or medicine man or woman, was highly respected by the people. Indian doctors, ceremonial leaders, and village headmen were all given high status because they were so valuable to the tribe, community, and people. These spiritual leaders took care of the people by sharing their unique knowledge, powers, psychic abilities, and special relationship to the Great Creator, spirits, and Nature. The Indian doctor had a difficult and full life, and suffered a lot of worry and stress in caring for the people.

It takes a lot of time to continue one's development, acquire and tame power(s), and do all the necessary work involved in the responsibilities of diagnosis, healing, teaching, ceremony, and ritual. It takes time to prepare for such things, study new bodies of knowledge, meditate, and seek visions as a means to solve new problems and cure new illnesses. As a consequence, the Indian doctor and spiritual leaders did not have the time to work and perform duties that are required of the common people, who are continually faced with the obligation to work at some kind of trade or career in order to support themselves and their families.

In the past, the people understood this situation, and according to the Law of Reciprocity, they took good care of the shaman; it was a natural arrangement according to spiritual and Natural Laws. It was an exchange for privileges. So the local people, community, and sometimes even neighboring tribes made sure that all the basic needs were met for the shaman and his or her family. They probably did not know about Maslow's hierarchy of needs and how it all relates to self-actualization, but they certainly understood and applied the same basic principles, perhaps intuitively realizing that a sick society makes a sick person, and a healthy society makes a healthy and balanced person. Hence the community made sure that the shaman's family had the best house to live in, the best canoe(s) or horse(s) to use in transportation, the best clothes, plenty of utensils, ample food, and protection by the warriors in the event of conflict and danger.

But as I said earlier, such is not the case today, because a lot of Indians and non-Indians have lost their values system, or they don't really know about the true shamanic part of their heritage and culture. So I have always had to work for a living plus carry out the duties and responsibilities of my sacred profession, a profession that, for the most part, is no longer supported and appreciated by the people, tribe, or community. In order to support my family and take care of our own basic needs, I had to become educated in the Whiteman's world. I had to get a job, pursue a career, and make money in order for us to survive. I studied hard, worked full-time while attending college, kept trying to get more degrees, achieve higher status, and learn how to compete in a modern system for recognition and reward. I learned to use my spiritual strengths and ongoing shamanic training and techniques in this endeavor, while pursuing higher goals and being tested for higher knowledge, experience, and powers. Eventually I went as high as I probably could in both worlds and cultures: I became a full-fledged and bona fide Native healer via evaluation, confirmation, and ordainment by my tribal Elders, the spirits, and the Great Creator; and I became a full professor, department chair, acting assistant dean, and acting associate dean after many tests, evaluations, and confirmations. I therefore tried to blend the best of both worlds, and to synthesize the spiritual with the physical, the Native with the Western, in order to survive and live.

But life sometimes takes a strange turn. Just when we think we have made it to the top of the world, that we "own the pond," so to speak, and that we are now safe, secure, and prosperous, we get a strange kind of reality check and lose everything we have. Granted, it doesn't happen to everyone in the world who has achieved status and recognition, but it does happen quite often to spiritual people. So there came times in my life when I ended up flat broke with no job, no money, no domestic or worldly possessions, and separated from my family. I became deserted by everyone and totally stripped of everything except my basic doctor regalia, spiritual tools, and power objects. I had no place to turn except to the Great Spirit, the ancestors, and Nature for help. And it was during severe hardships like this that Tela, the children, and I packed up what little we had left and went into the sacred High Country to seek a vision, to heal ourselves, to find the spiritual support and strength to start over.

Fortunately there are a few pristine, unspoiled, and holy places still left in the country where we, as Indians and Indian doctors, can go to pray in privacy. But these few remaining places are hidden in the wilderness areas and very difficult to access. Sacred places within our aboriginal territory provide some sanctuary for us to fast, pray, seek visions, and talk to the Great Creator and all of Creation in privacy. In those ancient and holy places known to us as the sacred High Country can be found old prayer altars that date back thousands of years—the same altars that our forefathers used when they needed help, or when they needed to call upon higher powers as a means to help the people. So on this particular occasion, once again we went back home to the source of our Creation, to the center of the world for our people.

We sat there by the prayer altar at the base of Turtle Rock, constantly praying, occasionally singing, but mostly meditating and staying still to let the natural powers, energy, and spirits of the Earth in this holy place work a healing on us and the children. This was an opportunity for the children to also be quiet, listen, and learn; it was an opportunity for them to follow in the footsteps of their ancestors. We taught them how to pray, where to bathe, what to learn, and how to conduct themselves in a respectful and religious way while being bonded with Nature. It is important that children learn how to bond with the Earth matrix at a young age because they can draw upon vital life energies needed to establish a solid spiritual foundation for their lives; but it is also important that this process be continued periodically as they become adults.

It is important that we teach our children, all children, how to pray, and teach them that the ancient rituals and ceremonies with the Earth, for Nature, and to the Great Spirit are essential to our survival as human beings. We must teach our children, all children, and we must remind the adults that Nature is not our enemy, nor simply a resource to be exploited for our own needs and greeds. We must all take time in our lives to reconnect and bond with the Earth and Nature in order to maintain the sacredness in our lives. Without some form of sacredness we are not living a full life. Without spirituality we will never know the meaning of life. As adults, we have the responsibility to let our children learn that Nature is a teacher and a healer, and that it is always there for us when we need help.

So as I sat there by the sacred fire, I had plenty of time to fast, pray, meditate, and think. Tela and the children also had plenty of time to think, listen, and learn. By the use of an ancient and sacred fire, by the offering of tobacco and angelica root, we sent our prayers up to the Great Creator and all of Creation. Then we waited for a return communication that would come physically and spiritually. During the day Flickerbirds came around and sang to us. A few Pileated Woodpeckers visited, and they hammered away on old cedar trees, an ancient form of communication similar to drumbeats. The constant rhythm and sound serve to put one into a hypnotic state, into a higher level of consciousness, hence enabling one to become more receptive to spiritual contact and to receive visions. Nature is full of many different songs, and with the songs come knowledge and a healing. If a person listens carefully, he or she might receive a song from Nature as a gift. I have many such songs that I have learned to use in healing. When I was young, my grandfather told me, "As long as you have even one song, you will never be poor." It took me more than twenty years to finally realize what he meant by that teaching.

Every once in a while a Hummingbird would come and fly around our heads. In a circular motion it gathered the negativity and illness from our minds, and the illness in our bodies caused by stress and the contamination of living in a modern world. With its tiny but colorful and vibrant power, it took the negativity straight up to the Grandfather Sun.

There were other forms of healing we received in this sacred place. The tiny fish and salamanders in the small stream, springs, and alpine lakes also did their job; they nibbled away at our sicknesses while the spirit of the holy water purified and regenerated us body and soul. Occasionally the Redtail Hawks and Falcons came in for protection and as messengers, swooping down on the currents of Wind, and the ancient purifiers (Wind gusts) came and blew away our worries, problems, and bad luck. Before we left from the ten days of fasting and vision seeking we were fortunate to be visited by the ancient ones who manifested in the form of Ravens, and who came to teach and let us know our prayers were being answered. At least once a day the other doctor spirits would come into the camp and visit; they took the form of the old Black Bear, rare White Deer, Golden Eagle, or even Coyote. Grizzly Bear, Wolf, Bigfoot, and the Little People are thought to be extinct, but they too will let themselves be seen if it is meant to be, and if one is truly connected, in this sacred and holy place. One thing we have surely learned after all these years of shamanic training is the fact that the Great Creator can take the form of anything at anytime, if He so chooses, including the Lightning and Thunder that came to visit us on the last day as we prepared to leave. Such natural forces and powers of Nature serve to regenerate the soul.

It became apparent to Tela and me before we left that the bad luck, hardship, and difficulty we had been experiencing were of our own making. We couldn't blame anyone else; sometimes people, even shamans, get out of balance in life. As spiritual people we needed to reconnect. We had become weak and sick from living in the city and from the constant influences of Western society.

Although we didn't like what we had been experiencing, we needed a new lesson. We needed a reminder of who and what we were, and where our knowledge, power, and spirituality came from. We had to be reminded that in order to carry out the Great Spirit's work and teachings we had to come back and reconnect with Him; we had to be recharged and strengthened in order to go forward in a positive way.

Thus, herein lies another teaching we can share with others as a result of our own learning: All human beings do, indeed, have a soul, and that soul is encased with spirit. That soul needs a spiritual healing, a spiritual recreation, and a spiritual connection with the Great Spirit every so often; otherwise it will get out of balance. It will become weak. It will begin to attract problems and bad luck if it is not kept clean and vibrant. A lost soul, or a soul that has become weak and does not receive spiritual cleansing and regeneration, can eventually become sick and die. A polluted soul can become a dead soul, and it is of no use to the Great Creator or Creation. So the questions here become, what do you know about your own soul? What kind of soul do you want to be in this life? What can you do to spiritually protect and strengthen your own spirit and soul? To find the answer to such questions a person must go out into Nature and seek a vision.

I honestly don't believe that the Great Creator wants any human being, race, culture, group, nationality, or country to be poor, sick, miserable, ignorant, and spiritless. He has given us everything we as humans need to live and survive, but we must learn to live life in peace, balance, and harmony. We must learn to live a spiritual way of life, which means to have respect for the Great Creator, for Nature, and for all that He has created—including all those who walk, crawl, fly, swim, seen and unseen—and this includes human beings of different racial and cultural backgrounds.

This means living a life with good spiritual principles and practices that are consistent with the Natural Laws and the Great Creator's Laws. Human laws or religious laws cannot replace or suppress the Great Creator's Laws on the pretense that such laws are ancient, therefore archaic and obsolete. Humans can't change the laws whenever it is convenient to do so, or make the laws fit changing social ideas or popular concepts. The spiritual laws and the physical laws are very similar, and sometimes one and the same, as in the law of physics: for every action, there is a reaction.

Some of the Natural Laws might seem dogmatic, or be considered sexist, or appear to be unfair, but once again I caution human perception as it relates to Truth. It is not my intention to force my personal or cultural beliefs and practices upon other people. Truth is universal, and can be found in the teachings of other cultures by great spiritual leaders of the past, including Mohammed, Buddha, and Jesus. It can also be found in the teachings of our past and great Native American spiritual leaders, such as Handsome Lake, Ben Black Elk, Sword, Chief Seatl, and Chief Joseph; the Hopi spiritual leaders; other Native spiritual teachers from the past few decades; and even contemporary leaders such as the hereditary Six Nations *sachems* (Iroquois term for religious leaders) and chiefs, or Wallace Black Elk, Charlie Red Hawk Thom, and Corbin Harney. Respect these special people, learn from them while you can, and help support them, because they are becoming an endangered species. In fact, the role, function, status, knowledge, and the much needed spiritual healing practices of the traditional Native healers (that is, Indian doctors, medicine men, and medicine women) are on the verge of extinction because they are all dying off.

A lot of people have asked me what the Natural Laws are, and how a person can use this knowledge as a form of preventive medicine, or as a guide for spiritual development, or as a code for living a spiritual life. What I am about to share here should not be considered comprehensive or as representing all Native tribes and people; it is simply a listing of the spiritual principles that I have been taught by my Elders, that I have learned through communication with the Great Spirit and through my years of spiritual quests and training, and that I acquired while performing Native healing.

1. The worst sin of all is not murder; it is having sexual intercourse with animals. Just for the record, the majority of venereal diseases and a number of other diseases originated from having sex with animals. Such diseases are a spiritual form of punishment. Venereal diseases and many other diseases, including small pox, measles, chicken pox, tuberculosis, and so forth, were brought over from the European countries where they had sheep, goats, pigs, and cows. The Native people did not have these diseases because they considered the animals sacred, and they would have considered such an act repulsive and sacrilegious.

2. It is an offense to harm, hurt, torment, experiment upon, or destroy any living thing, human or otherwise, without just cause and fair compensation. Every living thing was put here on the Earth for a reason, purpose, and function; all aspects of Creation have power. Power should be respected and not played with. Remember the law of physics: for every action, there is a reaction. (Today we see a lot of modern diseases and viruses coming from birds, animals, bugs, reptiles, and fish, and in the air, soil, and water as a result of experimentation, desecration, and pollution of the life forces. It will get worse if we do not start correcting our malicious actions.)

3. It is against the Natural Law for women on their menses to cook, prepare, eat, or share certain foods, especially meats that come from four-legged wild animals. It is against the law for women on their menses to participate in sacred dances, rituals, sweat lodge ceremonies, or funeral rites, or to trespass upon cemeteries, burial grounds, ceremonial grounds, sacred sites, and certain places in Nature. The Great Creator has given women a universal ritual to use during this time in a sacred and spiritual way to release negative energy and replenish themselves with positive energy from the Mother Earth and Grandmother Moon. Menstrual power and energy do not mix with other kinds of natural energies and forces,

and different spirits in Nature find it offensive. The ancient, Natural, and Universal Law has nothing to do with sexism. It is a realistic understanding of the spiritual power, both positive and negative, inherently connected to the process of menstruation and the potentials of blood. If you want to learn more about this in a positive and meaningful context, then please refer to Tela Starhawk Lake, *Hawk Woman Dancing with the Moon* (New York: M. Evans, 1996).

4. It is against the Natural Law for men to hunt, fish, and gather natural resources while intoxicated from alcohol, while under the immediate influence and smell of sex, or while under the influence of drugs. It is considered an offense to hunt, fish, and gather without making proper ritual and payment according to the Law of Reciprocity. Remember, everything that is in Nature has a spirit in it, and we should therefore learn to respect these spirits and their codes for living, and not try to impose negative energy upon positive energies; they don't mix.

5. It is against the Creator's Law for all human beings to participate in sacred dances, rituals, ceremonies, or healings, such as healing ceremonies performed in the sweat lodges, while under the influence of drugs, alcohol, sex, or while unclean physically and spiritually. This also includes funeral rites and childbirth rituals. By the same token, all "offerings" made to the Great Creator and the good spirits, such as food, tobacco, herbs, and teas, should be "clean" and not contaminated with alcohol or toxins.

6. It is an offense for human beings to have sexual intercourse with each other during the woman's last two weeks of pregnancy, during childbirth, and for one full moon cycle after childbirth. Such an act can be injurious and contaminating to the mother and baby. Women's blood, afterbirth, dead cells, and "negative" discharge can have a negative and unhealthy effect on the male's energy, spirit, and body; for that reason men did not traditionally participate in childbirth ceremonies and activity.

7. It is against the Great Creator's Law and Natural Laws for any human to rape, molest, sodomize, or abuse another human being, or to commit incest. It is a violation for men to have sexual intercourse with women during menses because it is a form of molestation and disrespect; it is unhealthy, and it robs a woman of her power and spirit needed to regenerate herself during this phase of her cycle.

8. It is against the Great Creator's Law to deliberately commit abortion without just cause and ceremony. Life is considered sacred. Thus, it is also against the Great Creator's Law to experiment upon deceased people, including fetuses, or to desecrate the dead or "sell" dead people's body parts for profit.

9. It is against the Great Creator's Law to steal or covet another person's material possessions or personal religious regalia, or to kidnap family members.

10. It is against the Natural Laws and the Great Creator's Laws to harm, desecrate, or destroy Nature or any part of Creation without just cause, spiritual request, or payment according to the Law of Reciprocity. Natural resources are in reality also natural spirits, powers, and forces put here on the Earth for a reason and purpose. As humans, we must "relearn" to respect such gifts, and to live in harmony with the natural resources according to Natural Laws—not according to humans' laws, avarice, and exploitation. If we respect the Earth, love the Earth, pray for the Earth, and care for it in a right and proper way, then it will share with us, take care of us, and help us survive as it survives.

As a spiritual teacher and healer I recognize the value of various beliefs, teachings, and practices. There are many laws that exist and operate in the Universe, and some of these laws may differ from culture to culture, place to place, and religion to religion. Identifying the spiritual laws that appear to be held in common could reduce possible confusion and provide a basis for greater understanding among people from a variety of belief systems.

As seen in the examples from the case studies provided in chapter 10, a number of different things can make a person sick. I don't want to give the impressionthat every sickness, injury, accident, disease, streak of misfortune, or ailment is a direct result of violating a Natural Law or the Great Creator's Laws. Some sicknesses and problems, however, can indeed be attributed to spiritual transgression. As a consequence, many potential illnesses, diseases, accidents, and ailments might be prevented, averted, or allayed by knowing the spiritual laws and trying not to violate them. A clean, strong, and healthy spirit is in better condition to fight off the sicknesses and diseases caused by the pollutants, viruses, and industrial mistakes and ignorance of in modern society.

Becoming spiritual and living a spiritual life also sometimes require common sense. For example, the moontime laws that are universal have a practical side worth understanding. A woman at that time is weaker and more vulnerable, hence more receptive to attack by wild animals, domestic animals, bugs, germs, diseases, viruses, psychic forces, negative energies, and bad spirits.

That is why in most traditional cultures and religions women isolated themselves, fasted, prayed, worked on developing their dreams and creative faculties, and utilized the menses as a blessing. They knew it was a source of power, both positive and negative, and anything that powerful required a ceremony.

Intuitively women know this. Nature has favored women with a stronger instinct and greater psychic powers than men. Re-creating female rituals, ceremonies, and spiritual activities would allow women to develop these innate gifts, abilities, and natural powers. Western society has devastated the female psyche to the point that women often have a worse identity crisis than a lot of our Indian people. Without strong, healthy, and spiritual women, we cannot have a strong, healthy, and spiritual family, tribe, or society. That is a reality.

When women violate the Natural Laws and the Creator's Laws, they violate themselves and cause sickness and problems for others. I don't say this to insult women; I state it with compassion, special knowledge, and higher expectations. I have doctored many women and helped get them well when Western physicians failed. In the majority of the cases the female patient was sick because she had made a spiritual offense related to her menses.

It takes time to transform a society, but Western society needs to support the spiritual development of both men and women. Women need to insist upon salaried time off from work to handle pregnancy and childbirth in a spiritual way, as well as paid time off to use the menses as a time for re-creation, healing, and creativity. Women are worth the investment; and in the long run it would probably save companies a lot of money that is now being paid out for health-related problems and loss of work time.

Men should respect women more and leave them alone while they are on their menses, while they are pregnant, and when they are recuperating from childbirth. A long time ago women had their mothers, aunts, sisters, and other women to help them with domestic duties and work, but today they don't have this natural type of support system. Therefore husbands, male mates, or the children should assume more responsibility and take the stress off women during these times. Men should spiritually cooperate with their women and learn how to pray for their women.

By the same token, men need to learn that they too can be held accountable for their violations of the Natural Laws and the Great Creator's Laws. For example, when men try to be macho, get drunk, and go out hunting for trophy catches rather than for subsistence and survival, or when they abuse and offend a sacred animal such as a Deer, it will hurt the entire family. (Refer to my teachings about this subject in *Native Healer* and *Spirits of the Earth*. I once doctored a mother and her baby who became sick simply because the woman picked up and moved her husband's rifle and knives. Now, that might seem superstitious to some, but the cause of sickness can be attributed to symbols, power objects, and negative influences. In another situation I doctored a woman who had been diagnosed for a mental illness and yet the Western physicians couldn't cure it. They simply pacified her with drug therapy. I found out while doctoring that the woman was being tormented by stuffed Rattlesnakes, birds, and animals in her house, all trophies that belonged to her husband.

Furthermore, a lot of the sicknesses and diseases we have today are caused by ignorance, avarice, irresponsibility, and apathy. We are poisoning ourselves by using bug sprays around the house, strong detergents in our laundry, herbicides on our lawns, insulation in our homes, harsh chemicals in the carpeting, and from carelessness in cleaning the mold from the bathroom or changing the filters in the forced air heating system. Obviously the chemicals we let society dump into the air, water, and ground have a profound effect upon our health.

We also poison ourselves when we make restaurants out of funeral parlors and don't tell anyone, when we build stores and apartment houses on top of old cemeteries and Indian burial grounds, when we buy artifacts that were robbed from ancient tombs and burial grounds or used in sorcery, when we build churches and cemeteries side by side, when we allow schools to be built next to gigantic transformers, and when we build houses on top of radon deposits. We are causing sickness when we allow hospitals, nursing homes, convalescent homes, and clinics to become contaminated from dead people. (In the olden days housing structures were burnt down and purified whenever somebody died in the building, and that approach was consistent with the Natural Laws.) The medical establishment might try to disinfect the premises physically but they never disinfect it spiritually, as in the case of purifying the premises with cedar, sage, or some other herbal medicine designed for that purpose. Hence, the contamination from the dead people and the negativity from the ghosts serves to create sickness, disease, and more death.

A former patient, whom I doctored for breast cancer and cured, brought me an interesting book that in turn helped her understand the cause of her disease. Spiritually she was a fairly clean person; she had very few offenses. The book, entitled *Diet for a Poisoned Planet*, by David Steinman, offers more concrete information and evidence about the ways chemicals contaminate our foods.

For example, the author states how one grape can have more than 15 different poisonous chemicals in it, or an apple might carry more than 25; milk has more than 20 chemicals, collard greens and spinach can contain as many as 87, and peanuts alone might have as many as 183 different chemicals in them. And he gives many more examples in his research, reporting that the worst foods to eat include hot dogs, salami, pizza, bacon, and so forth. Cigarettes and alcohol can contain as many as 150 different chemicals. In addition, we are also making ourselves sick with poor eating habits and the fast-food syndrome of modern living. We are all guilty of eating foods saturated with fats, high in cholesterol, and low in natural vitamins. But even worse, less than 1 percent of the total population ever takes the time to clean out their colons or purify their organisms via fasting and herbs; Western society pays more attention to changing the oil and filters of the automobile than it does to caring for the human body. And yet we wonder why the human vehicle breaks down so much.

In conclusion, there are a number of spiritual techniques you can use in your life as forms of preventive medicine without offending the Native religions. Some of these techniques are universal and were used in all cultures at one time; for example, all cultures once had a women's moontime ceremony. All cultures had some form of a sacred sweat lodge or purification system, such as a sauna, steam bath, hot springs, or hot tub. Air, fire, earth, and water are the four natural elements and powers from the Earth. We can use them for protection, purification, and healing; and they are found in the sweat lodges, saunas, steam baths, and women's moontime huts or ceremonial lodges.

All cultures once used sacred herbs for healing, in the form of teas or soaps, as prayer offerings and for invocation, or for bathing and cleansing. All cultures and most religions used herbs and medicines from the trees to smudge with (to *smudge* means to purify with smoke made from burning cedar, sage, mugwort, or other herbs); for purification of themselves, their homes, and their religious sites; to ward off bad spirits, ghosts, and negative energies; and as a tea for disinfectant.

In traditional Native healing we are taught by our Elders to purify and protect ourselves before going to a funeral and to smudge our clothes, home, and family after we return. *Some* of us still use a purification ritual in the sweat lodge with herbs to finalize the process and as a means to eliminate death contamination.

We are taught to pray and offer tobacco, herbs, or food to anything in Nature, under the Law of Reciprocity, as a means to ask permission and give thanks before we hunt, fish, or gather food, herbs, and natural resources. Everything has a spirit and power in it; we don't have the right to take it and use it without permission and just cause. Our relationship to Nature is an ancient agreement, and if people violate that spiritual contract they will get punished—for every action, there is a reaction.

We don't have the right to desecrate the dead, experiment upon deceased people, and abuse skeletons, even if we try to justify it under the concept of education and science. I have seen a lot of physicians, nurses, medical practitioners, chiropractors, college professors, and even students get hurt and sick because they didn't know the Natural Law or because they refused to accept it, treating it as superstition. Hence, if you find yourself in that predicament, learn to smudge yourself before and after the contact; bathe in a hot tub full of salt, mugwort tea, or sage tea for a cleansing.

Learn to pray to the Great Spirit and Nature on a daily basis, at least once a day, preferably at Sunrise or at Sunset. Give thanks to the Sun, Moon, Stars, Wind, Rain, Fog, Snow for their gifts; pray and give thanks to the spirit of the water every time you drink it, bathe in it, and use it, because otherwise we might lose it. Talk to the natural things around you— the trees, plants, birds, animals, bugs, reptiles, Snakes, rocks, and all of Nature; thank them for their gifts and ask them to protect and watch over you. Put tobacco in your hand if you don't smoke, or use cornmeal or oatmeal and blow the offering to Nature in a gesture of gratitude.

Learn to take time in your life to perform a smudging ceremony on your home. Make sure you open the doors and windows and let out all the negativity, and pray with your mate or family; pray for one another. I have even prayed to the Great Spirit and Nature right downtown in New York City or Los Angeles, because something from Nature is always around us to hear and witness the prayer.

There is no excuse for people to pollute their mind, body, and soul with alcohol and drugs. Try to stay off that kind of poison, and if you are addicted get professional therapy. Even coffee is a drug. I have been fighting it for years, so I have tried switching over to decaf and herbal substitutes. Coffee is a real killer to men's prostate glands. And any form of sugar, except certain natural sweeteners, is a real poison to the human organism. White flour, candy, cakes, pies, milk, soda pop, and numerous other kinds of Western starchy foods are destroying our Native American people, generation after generation. Historically, genetically, and physically, we have been primarily meat and fish eaters; our diets were high in protein and very low in carbohydrates. We need to get back to that "natural" type of diet if we want to become healthy and survive in the future! In this sense our tribal and traditional foods are, indeed, medicine.

It is always best if you can grow or gather your own foods, but if not, then try using health food stores or co-ops where the food doesn't have chemicals. Be sure not to eat fruits and vegetables together at the same meal: their natural chemicals and energies don't agree with each other and can cause sickness. Another way to maintain spirituality is to always pray over your food, put good thoughts in it, and give thanks to the Creator and Nature for the food. Don't cook food or eat it when you are angry and upset. The negativity will cause sickness.

I eat meats, although I know all the valid arguments against it. I have learned from all these years of doctoring that the human organism needs some kind of meat, at least on a periodic basis. I try to eat the natural meats from animals in Nature when I get the opportunity. Otherwise I have learned to cleanse my intestines and organism by fasting for three to four days, a few times a year, or at least once a year. I use natural laxatives to purge my system. Chickweed, sage, red clover, and burdock teas are good herbs to use for purifying and strengthening the organism along with the laxatives and fasting. I also try to use my sacred sweat lodge as much as possible to remove stress, mental negative energies, and body toxins. Good common sense and instinct should tell us: the more the world around us becomes polluted, the more ways we will have to find to deal with it, and clean ourselves.

In conclusion, if you would like to become more spiritual and clean up your mind, body, and soul, you can do the following. Review the section on Natural Laws and make a list of any offenses you may have committed. Use vacation time or make free time to perform a healing ceremony on yourself. Take along a friend or family members. All cultures at one time used confession as a form of healing, and all cultures used Nature and the natural elements for purification. Our Native tribes were using confession as a part of the healing ritual long before Christianity came to North America.*

You can go out into the wilderness and build a small sacred fire to pray with, or use the privacy of your home, beginning with a smudging ceremony. Fast at least one day, and abstain from drugs, alcohol, and sex for a few days to prepare for the prayer ceremony. Make an invocation to the Great Creator, the four sacred powers and directions of the Universe, and to all of Nature; offer clean tobacco, herbs, or food to the fire and spirits, and to the Great Creator. State your name, race, and why you are praying, and what you are asking assistance for.

Tell the Great Spirit and the good spirits of the Earth that you want to purify yourself of your sins and violations. Read each offense separately, confess that you made the violation, state that you didn't know any better, plead for forgiveness, and promise that you won't commit the same violation again.

Then have one of the other participants blow and smudge you three times; a cedar or sage smudge stick is a good spiritual tool to use for this purpose, or blow tobacco from a pipe. You can finalize the healing ceremony by bathing in a hot tub full of cedar, juniper, sage, or mugwort tea. (Boil a big batch of it in a two-to-three-gallon pot for fifteen minutes, strain, and pour the herbal tea in the tub full of water. Soak, relax, meditate, and feel the essence of the herbs while healing.) Better yet, use a sweat lodge, if you can, to finalize the cleansing.

---

*Refer to Ari Kiev, "Confession as a Catharsis" in *Magic, Faith, and Healing: Studies in Primitive Psychiatry Today*, (Free Press, 1974).

Appendix I

Shamanic System of Knowledge and Cosmology
for Northwestern California Tribal Cultures and Neighboring Tribes

1. Prior to European contact, the indigenous people of what is now northwestern California not only believed in a Great Creator (Great Spirit), they also worshipped and believed in Creation and all things that were part of Creation and Nature. This religious system was also based on a hierarchy of rank and status according to powers. In other words, indigenous people honored a World and Universe full of natural beings that were all part of the Great Spirit, but these beings, including human beings, also had spirits of their own.

2. Everything in the Universe (on the Earth, in the Earth, around the Earth, and in outer space) is a source of power. Such "powers," also known as natural forces, are placed in the Universe for a reason and purpose; they can be positive, negative, or neutral. In the indigenous religious system, the powers were considered to be "spirits," but only humans were considered to have a soul in addition to a spirit.

3. Religious doctrines (known as ancient myths), along with rituals and ceremonies, attest to this spiritual reality and were historically used as a means to teach, perpetuate, and preserve the knowledge.

4. Creation and the Universe were held together in a system of Natural Laws. Adherence to Natural Laws created balance and harmony, health, wealth, and happiness. Violation of the Natural Laws caused an imbalance in the microcosm or, if serious enough, could even affect the balance of the macrocosm. Hence, an imbalance caused by a violation of the Spiritual Laws could cause sickness (mental, physical, or spiritual), bad luck, accidents, injury,

disease, near death, or death itself. These consequences taught the people to be accountable for their actions toward the Earth, all living things, and one another. Ignorance was no excuse for violating the Laws; even innocent bystanders could be punished by the Great Creator, Nature, or spirits and powers. Family members could inherit the violations of other family members, even violations committed by their parents and forebears before they were born. Hence, the need for "confession" arose as part of the process of redemption and healing. Confession of violations helped to put things back into perspective and balance.

5. Not just anyone could become an Indian doctor, or Native healer. Such people were born with special psychic gifts, traits, abilities, and powers. They could inherit the powers physically (genetically), mentally, or spiritually. But they would not take on the role, function, and purpose of a healer unless they had "the calling," which could come in a variety of forms. Such unique individuals were called by the Great Creator or by the Universal spirits, powers, and forces via dreams, psychic and mystical experiences, sickness, disease, accidents, injuries, near death, or actual death experiences. The phenomena they encountered and had to overcome served as a form of initiation that in turn placed them on the path to becoming shamans. They were often spiritually guided to an older shaman, or sometimes to a number of different shamans, who in turn verified their calling, doctored them, served as mentors to the neophytes, and placed them into special training to be tested and evaluated within the tribal-cultural context. Dependent upon passing very strict tests and evaluations, the neophytes then often entered into an apprenticeship, which could last ten years or more. Certification as a healer required confirmation and ordination at an ancient "power center," or sacred place that had been used for that purpose since time immemorial. Apprenticeships were usually kept secret from society in order to protect the mentors, the neophytes, and their family members from negative and jealous people, spirits,

powers, and forces. After European contact, shamanic training became even more secretive because Western society tried to impose its own religion, beliefs, customs, and laws upon the Native people, and eventually outlawed Native religion. History has proven that Western society always tried to exterminate the Native healers, religious leaders, medicine men and women, chiefs and village headmen in their efforts to break down, suppress, control, and assimilate the indigenous tribes.

6. For northwestern California tribal systems and their neighbors, the definition of the terms *medicine man* and *medicine woman* is different from the definition of *Indian doctor* or *Native healer*. The medicine man or medicine woman, as we understand that role, has more of a religious function; this includes such roles as ceremonial leader, ritual performer, mystic, or formulist. His or her position is defined by status, psychic abilities, power(s), and training. Examples include the Deerskin Dance medicine man, Jump Dance medicine man, War Dance medicine man; or the Brush Dance medicine woman, Moontime (First menses at puberty) medicine woman, Acorn Festival medicine woman; or, in neighboring tribes, the Bear Dance medicine man, Big House medicine woman, or Salmon Rite medicine man.

7. An Indian doctor, or what I have termed *Native healer*, often takes on the combined roles of physician, psychologist, priest, and psychic. There are different levels and degrees of Indian doctors and they are ranked according to their powers, training, skills, and abilities. For example, some are herbalists, some are dreamers, some are seers or trance doctors, and some are sucking doctors; the highest doctors have all these abilities and are more holistic in their approach. So just like Western doctors and mental health practitioners, the Native healer can specialize in handling mental illness, certain diseases, wounds and injuries, childbirth and female problems, or other medical specialties.

8. The "highest" doctors and ceremonial leaders have always been "called" to the highest and most powerful mountains and sacred places. As an analogy, their call to higher powers parallels the call to the wilderness of Jesus, Moses, Mohammed, and Buddha. In order to qualify for the higher powers, status, and recognition, they have to fast, suffer, and sacrifice and be tested and ordained by the Great Creator, spirits, powers, forces, and sociocultural mentors. Whereas most tribes across the continent traditionally required a "vision quest" for this purpose, which involved four days of fasting, dreaming, and purification, the northwestern California tribes required a "power quest." This shamanic journey into the wilderness usually lasted five to ten days and nights; the highest doctors had to endure thirty days and nights.

9. Some medicine men and women and Indian doctors could be considered sorcerers, meaning they could have both good and bad powers, intentions, actions, and behavior. However, such "shamans," as Western society has called them, were usually lower-level doctors and religious leaders. Their lower status was often defined by the kind of powers they inherited, acquired, and used. Anyone whose power and spirit-allies included the Owl, Blue Jay, Snakes (except King Snake), Two-headed Snake, Black Panther, Black Wolf, poisonous Spiders, poisonous herbs, or any number of evil spirits, forces, and ghosts was considered to be a sorcerer. Lower-level sorcerers, what we call "Indian devils" or "demons" (*umaa* in the Yurok language, *uputawon* in the Karuk language), quested and trained for their powers in bad places in Nature where evil spirits, powers, and forces resided. In some cases a person could purchase the required evil objects and powers from a practicing sorcerer. Such people were therefore considered evil; they had no respect for the Natural Laws and made lots of money by inflicting fear, pain, harm, suffering, sickness, injury, and death upon others.

10. Not all the Native people knew about the concept of reincarnation or "repossession." This was considered "high" knowledge among the Indian doctors and medicine men and women. To the best of my knowledge it was not even revealed to earlier anthropologists who came to our region for research and documentation of our people's heritage, cultures, beliefs, practices, religion, and shamanistic phenomena. The term *repossession,* as I have come to understand it, refers to a particularly intense type of spiritual calling. Most Indian doctors and certain medicine men and women were Native healers or spiritual leaders in a former lifetime. Now their souls have come back into the earthly plane, and according to destiny they have spiritual contracts to fulfill. In this case, the Great Spirit (Great Creator), along with His spirit allies and the ancestral spirits of the souls in question, will call to the souls in an effort to draw them back onto a spiritual path in their current lifetime—sometimes going so far as to reclaim the souls via "good possession." If the reincarnated souls refuse to recognize the call, for whatever reason, they will keep encountering more accidents and sicknesses and injuries, or even termination of their current life and body (death), until they succumb and fulfill their destiny, purpose, and function on this Earth. Unfortunately, those who are "repossessed" in this way encounter more suffering, sacrifice, spiritual testing, and extraordinary experiences than those with a lower spiritual calling.

11. Every kind of sickness, injury, accident, or life crisis needs a ceremony for healing, and it should be holistic in approach.

12. Traditional Native healing is holistic in approach because the patient is not treated simply as an object to be cured. The patient should be considered a whole human being who has a mind, body, soul, and spirit. All parts are related to the whole and need to be put back into balance and harmony with one another.

13. A Native healer, or Indian doctor (or what some other tribes across the continent call a medicine man or woman), is a "culturally and spiritually" trained healer who uses Nature to doctor a patient in a

"natural" and holistic way. The Native healer uses natural powers, symbols, spirits, forces, and medicine from Nature. Such healers are therefore the original naturopathic and holistic doctors and practitioners, in addition to being experts on the soul.

14. Traditional Native healers, or Indian doctors (or authentic medicine men or women), do not charge a fee for their services because they believe it is against the Great Creator's Law. But according to the Law of Reciprocity they should be given a generous donation for their time, knowledge, expertise, skills, abilities, and use of special healing powers and as compensation for conducting a ceremony.

In the olden days they were supported by the tribe and by individual people. They were highly respected (though also sometimes feared) and were considered of high value to the community. Today the Native healers, Indian doctors, and medicine men and women are on the verge of extinction; they are, in fact, an endangered species. They are not financially supported by their tribe(s), they are not supported by the Bureau of Indian Affairs, and they are not supported by the Indian Health Service. They are not supported by a religious organization as are priests, ministers, rabbis, gurus, or lamas. Religious leaders with a church or temple affiliation are respected both by Western society and by Indian people who are Christianized or followers of nontraditional Indian religion. Native healers and spiritual leaders are not afforded the same respect. Perhaps this is the reason they are becoming extinct.

In closing, I would like to ask why Western society and Indian tribes can't band together and try to preserve, protect, perpetuate, and support the few remaining Native healers, Indian doctors, or medicine men and women in the same way that environmental groups have banded together to help the endangered species of the Eagle, Grizzly Bear, and Wolf. Why don't Indian Health Clinics employ the Native cultural shamans as part of their medical staffs with the same respect, recognition, support, and salary that is currently being given to non-Indian physicians, physician's assistants, or nurses?

Appendix 2

The Story of Grizzly Bear and Mt. Shasta

by Charles Red Hawk Thom

There is a real old legend amongst our tribes in northwestern California that tells a story and teaching about Grizzly Bear and a very sacred mountain known as Mt. Shasta. The real name of this mountain from the Shasta and Karuk tribes is Wyreka, and by translation it means "Holy One That Is Covered with Snow (Purity)." It is the highest and most powerful of all mountains on Turtle Island, the North American continent.

The power, energy, and spirit of this mountain is what helps keep all the other mountains across the land alive and vibrant. As an analogy, Mt. Shasta is like a gigantic natural generator: she transfers and transmits strength, healing, and a very high spiritual energy to all the other mountains. It is so sacred and holy that our Native people are taught not to climb to the very top of it because the Great Creator has His sweat lodge up there, and we as humans are not qualified to visit Him in person, in His personal abode. If the Great Creator wants us there then He will take us to His lodge in spirit form, or what you might call via soul travel, perhaps in the form of a dream or vision. He doesn't live there all the time; He simply comes down to Earth every once in a while to visit, to check up on things going on in the world, or to sometimes share His teachings, power, and healing with the people.

One of the most powerful Indian doctors that I heard about back in the days when I was just a little boy was Charlie Klutchie; he was Wintun and Pit River, I think. He trained up on Mt. Shasta for thirty days and nights fasting; the Great Creator felt sorry for him, heard his crying and felt his suffering, and gave him the Grizzly Bear doctor power; and this of course is considered the highest. According to our Elders, Indian custom and law, and rights of inheritance and evaluation, the only person that has earned that right, to train up there and become a doctor since the olden days, and since Charlie Klutchie, is one of my sons, Bobby. He too has the Grizzly Bear doctor power, songs, regalia, power objects, and knowledge that he has been given to use as his spiritual tools for healing, and this regalia came in a clean and spiritual way by his efforts in earning it.

How Grizzly Bear Gathered the Righteous on Mt. Shasta

One time, many thousands of years ago, the Great Spirit came and visited Mt. Shasta. He sat in His sacred sweat lodge, prayed, and meditated about Creation and how things were going in the World. He was sad because the World was getting out of balance; people were no longer following His original instructions and laws, and hence they were creating an imbalance.

Grizzly Bear lived up there and had been assigned to protect the Great Creator's lodge. He was the only one who had enough strength, power, and spirituality to actually live and survive up so high on the mountain. On this one particular day, the Great Creator called Grizzly Bear to His lodge and spoke to him. He told Grizzly Bear that He was upset and angry about the way things were going on the Earth, that people had put it out of balance by their malicious actions and disrespect. So He instructed Grizzly Bear to go down off the mountain, and to gather all the people (animal people, bird people, fish people, reptile people, and human people), and bring them to the holy mountain.

He wanted Grizzly Bear to tell the people that He, the Great Creator, was going to send in the Purifiers; and as a result the world would be flooded. He wanted Grizzly Bear to gather up the righteous and to lead them to safety. So Grizzly Bear did as he was instructed. At first the people did not believe him and many of them did not want to come. They were afraid of Grizzly Bear and felt they could not trust him. But eventually the righteous ones knew that the Grizzly Bear was close to the Great Creator, so they started to come from every direction and gather at the base of the holy mountain.

Eagle, White Deer, Wolf, Raven, Hummingbird, Flickerbird, and

Woodpecker also went out to help Grizzly Bear spread the word; and Lightning and Thunder Grandfathers also went behind Grizzly Bear just in case the people needed a little more warning and encouragement. Then everyone gathered and built a ceremonial fire, they made prayers to the Great Creator, and they purified themselves with Douglas fir boughs. After making medicine this way, they then followed Grizzly Bear up the steep mountain trail. But Owl and Snake did not want to go; they didn't like Grizzly Bear, and they didn't believe him. (The old people say that this is probably why, even to this day, there are no Owls or Snakes up high on Mt. Shasta, and if a person sees one, it is a very bad sign or omen.)

As everyone continued to hike up the trail, the Rain and big Winds became stronger, while the very top of the mountain became covered with deeper Snow. Grizzly Bear took them all up to a safe place, on the side of the mountain, to his cave, and there they waited. But because there was not much food they all had to fast, have faith, and just keep praying for protection, strength, long life, all the while giving thanks and praising the Great Creator. It continued to rain for one full Moon, until the whole world was flooded.

After a while they began to wonder how long they would have to stay up there. They had a meeting and it was decided that Raven would fly off the mountain and go around the world to find out if it was safe for everyone to come down. He was gone for five days, and upon his return he brought back dried pieces of willow root; Frog helped him find them. This served as evidence that the Flood had left, that the land was now dry and safe, and they could all come back down. (And willow root is what the people have used ever since to make fires with; it is used to start the sacred fires for all our ceremonies, rituals, and ancient dances; and the women learned how to use the new gift of willow roots in making the baskets.)

After-story comment: I have heard that the very last Grizzly Bear in California was killed at Mt. Shasta around 1924. Ironically, this was about the same time the U.S. government made us Indians officially "citizens" of the United States. Just like they wiped out the Grizzly Bear, I guess they wanted to wipe us out, too, as sovereign people and independent

Native Nations. Mt. Shasta is an ancient and holy place and symbol for our people; it needs to be preserved and protected. No ski slopes, resorts, and recreational businesses and buildings should be put up there. People are violating the Natural Laws when they climb all the way to the top and trespass up there, and people should not be camping up there while having sex, or during menses, or when taking drugs or drinking alcohol. They are committing a sacrilege. We heard rumbling in the mountain a few years ago, a bad avalanche occurred, and some scientists now say that they see signs of earthquake and deep inner volcanic activity going on. That is a bad sign; it is a warning. The good people of the Earth should all band together to try to respect, protect, and preserve this holy place; otherwise the Great Spirit will become angry and send in the Purifiers again. But whom will He send to warn us this time? Grizzly Bear is gone. Or is he really?

Epilogue

I had a vision a long number of years ago and I need help to make it become a reality. I would like to create, develop, implement, and administer a Native American Natural Healing Institute and Center, located somewhere close to our ancient and holy Mt. Shasta, in northwestern California. I want to bring together the last of the Native healers—medicine men and women—to use their traditional indigenous knowledge as a form of holistic healing and alternative medicine to help those in need, both Indians and non-Indians. Native healers will doctor patients on a donation basis only, and they will share their unique knowledge and expertise with Indian tribes, Indian health clinics, and natural resources agencies. If you would like to help with this vision, in some small or great way, please visit or e-mail me at my new Web site: www.nativehealer-medicinegrizzlybear.com. I have a complete proposal ready for grant submission, or to use as a means to solicit a much needed and very large donation; I can send you a copy of this proposal if you are sincere and want to help. You can also send small or large donations via check or money order, which will be fully tax deductible. Please make checks out to:

> Robert Lake-Thom
> c/o Wakan
> P.O. Box 154
> Woodacre, CA 94973